DEFENSE, SECURITY AND STRATEGIES

OPTIONS FOR DEPLOYING MISSILE DEFENSES IN EUROPE

DEFENSE, SECURITY AND STRATEGIES

Additional books in this series can be found on Nova's website
under the Series tab.

Additional E-books in this series can be found on Nova's website
under the E-book tab.

DEFENSE, SECURITY AND STRATEGIES

OPTIONS FOR DEPLOYING MISSILE DEFENSES IN EUROPE

MELISSA V. JORDAN
EDITOR

Nova Science Publishers, Inc.
New York

NOTICE TO THE READER

The Publisher has taken reasonable care in the preparation of this book, but makes no expressed or implied warranty of any kind and assumes no responsibility for any errors or omissions. No liability is assumed for incidental or consequential damages in connection with or arising out of information contained in this book. The Publisher shall not be liable for any special, consequential, or exemplary damages resulting, in whole or in part, from the readers' use of, or reliance upon, this material. Any parts of this book based on government reports are so indicated and copyright is claimed for those parts to the extent applicable to compilations of such works.

Independent verification should be sought for any data, advice or recommendations contained in this book. In addition, no responsibility is assumed by the publisher for any injury and/or damage to persons or property arising from any methods, products, instructions, ideas or otherwise contained in this publication.

This publication is designed to provide accurate and authoritative information with regard to the subject matter covered herein. It is sold with the clear understanding that the Publisher is not engaged in rendering legal or any other professional services. If legal or any other expert assistance is required, the services of a competent person should be sought. FROM A DECLARATION OF PARTICIPANTS JOINTLY ADOPTED BY A COMMITTEE OF THE AMERICAN BAR ASSOCIATION AND A COMMITTEE OF PUBLISHERS.

LIBRARY OF CONGRESS CATALOGING-IN-PUBLICATION DATA

Options for deploying missile defenses in Europe / Editor, Melissa V. Jordan.
        x, 174 pages : illustrations, maps ; 26 cm.
Includes bibliographical references and index.
ISBN 978-1-60741-889-4 (hard cover)
1. Ballistic missile defenses --Europe. I. Jordan, Melissa V.
UG745.E85 O69 2010
358.1/74094

2010513266

Published by Nova Science Publishers, Inc. ✦ *New York*

CONTENTS

PREFACE

One of the greatest threats facing the world today is the increasing proliferation of ballistic missiles and weapons of mass destruction. Non-proliferation activities, to include diplomacy and arms control agreements with Russia, have been successful in reducing this threat. Despite reductions in the number of weapons deployed by the United States and the former Soviet Union, ballistic missile proliferation continues on a wide scale today and could increase as technology is transferred. This new book proposes the creation of anti-missile systems to serve as protection against long-range ballistic missile threats facing the United States and European nations.

Chapter 1 - For some time now, ballistic missile defense (BMD) has been a key national security priority, even though such interest has been ongoing since the end of World War II. Many current BMD technologies date their start to the 1980s, and even earlier. This effort has been challenging technically[1] and politically controversial. More than $120 billion has been spent on a range of BMD programs since the mid-1980s; Congress appropriated $9.4 billion for FY2007 and $9.9 billion for FY2008. This chapter provides a brief overview of U.S. BMD efforts to date.

Chapter 2 - One of the greatest threats facing the world today is the increasing proliferation of ballistic missiles and weapons of mass destruction. Non-proliferation activities, to include diplomacy and arms control agreements with Russia, have been successful in reducing this threat. Despite reductions in the number of weapons deployed by the United States and the former Soviet Union, ballistic missile proliferation continues on a wide scale today and could increase as the technology is transferred. Countries make these investments because ballistic missiles provide them with the means to project power both in a regional and strategic context and a capability to launch an attack from a distance. A country with no ballistic missiles today may acquire them in a very short period of time, and these missiles could become available to non-state terrorist groups.

Chapter 3 features testimony before the U. S. House of Representatives.

Chapter 4 - For some time, U.S. ballistic missile defense (BMD) programs have focused primarily on developing kinetic energy interceptors to destroy attacking ballistic missiles. These efforts have evolved over 30 years and have produced a significant amount of test data from which much can be learned. This chapter provides a broad overview of the U.S. investment in this approach to BMD.

The data on the U.S. flight test effort to develop a national missile defense (NMD) system remains mixed and ambiguous. There is no recognizable pattern to explain this record nor is there conclusive evidence of a learning curve over more than two decades of developmental testing. In addition, the test scenarios are considered by some not to be operational tests and could be more realistic in nature; they see these tests as more of a laboratory or developmental effort. Success and failure rates (and their technical causes) have shown relative consistency through this period.

The U.S. flight test effort to develop theater missile defense (TMD) systems appears more promising. In relative terms, developmental and operational testing of TMD systems has been more successful than the NMD effort. Nonetheless, TMD systems that evolved from mature, existing ground and sea-based air-defense systems have demonstrated greater test success than other TMD programs.

How effective has the U.S. investment been in developing kinetic energy BMD systems? Observers could make any number of arguments as to what the record means and what could be done to improve the effectiveness of systems under development and of those deployed. Some observers have suggested that the 110th Congress might review the U.S. investment in the kinetic energy concept to date to determine how best to proceed with the U.S. BMD effort in the coming years.

Chapter 5 - Successive U.S. governments have urged the creation of an anti-missile system to protect against long-range ballistic missile threats from adversary states. The Bush Administration believed that North Korea and Iran represent strategic threats, and questioned whether they could be deterred by conventional means. The Bush Administration's position on this issue remained unchanged, even after the intelligence community assessed that the Iranian nuclear weapons program halted in 2003. The Bush Administration built long-range missile defense bases in Alaska and California to protect against adversary missile threats, especially North Korea. Although the system has been tested, most agree that further testing is necessary. The Bush Administration proposed deploying a ground-based mid-course defense (GMD) element of the larger Ballistic Missile Defense System (BMDS) in Europe to defend against an Iranian missile threat. The system would include 10 interceptors in Poland, a radar in the Czech Republic, and another radar deployed in a country closer to Iran, all to be completed by 2013 at a reported cost of at least $4 billion.

The proposed U.S. system has encountered resistance in some European countries and beyond. Critics in Poland and the Czech Republic assert that neither country currently faces a notable threat from Iran, but that if American GMD facilities were installed, both countries might be targeted by missiles from rogue states—and possibly from Russia. The Bush Administration signed agreements with both countries permitting GMD facilities to be stationed on their territory; however, the two countries' parliaments decided to wait to ratify the accords until after the Obama Administration clarified its intentions on missile defense policy. NATO has deliberated long-range missile defense, and has taken actions that many interpreted as an endorsement of the U.S. GMD system.

The GMD plan has also affected U.S.-Russia relations. Former President Putin and his successor, Vladimir Medvedev, have argued that the proposal would reignite the arms race and upset U.S.- Russian-European security relations. U.S. officials dispute Russia's objections, noting that the interceptors are intended to take out Iranian missiles aimed at Europe or the United States and could not possibly act as a deterrent against Russia. Some argue that Russia has been attempting to foment discord among NATO allies. In mid-2007, Russia offered to cooperate on missile defense, proposing the use of a Russian-leased radar in Azerbaijan, but urging that U.S. facilities not be built in Eastern Europe. President Bush welcomed the idea in principle, but insisted upon the need for the European sites. Despite ongoing discussions over the issue, sharp Russian criticism of the program has continued. Medvedev has said that Russia might deploy Iskander tactical missiles to Kaliningrad, but later stated that Moscow would not do so if the United States reversed its plan to emplace GMD facilities in Poland and the Czech Republic.

For FY2008, Congress examined the European GMD proposal and eliminated proposed funding for initial site construction pending formal agreement with Poland and the Czech Republic, independent studies on missile defense options for Europe, and DOD certification of the proposed interceptor. The FY2009 request for the European site was $712 million, which Congress largely supported with funding for site construction available only after Czech and Polish ratification.

Chapter 6 - As part of ongoing efforts to protect the United States and its allies from attack by ballistic missiles, the U.S. Missile Defense Agency (MDA) is working to deploy a missile defense system in Europe. As proposed, the system would be fielded by 2013 and would include interceptor missiles in silos to be built in Poland, a tracking radar in the Czech Republic, and another radar at an unspecified location near Iran. The goal of the system, according to MDA, is to "defend [U.S.] allies and deployed forces in Europe from limited Iranian long- range threats and expand protection of [the] U.S. homeland."[1]

MDA's proposed system is controversial. Some critics argue that testing of the system to date has been insufficient to verify that it will function as intended. Other critics argue that even if the system performs according to expectations, it is unnecessary given the current status of Iranian missile development and the likelihood of an Iranian missile attack on Europe or the United States. The United States has signed agreements with Poland and the Czech Republic to host the missile defense system, but those agreements have been the subject of debate in the host nations and have not yet been fully ratified by their parliaments. The system as proposed would not be able to defend some areas—including parts of North Atlantic Treaty Organization (NATO) member Turkey—that are within striking distance of missiles that Iran has tested or claims to have developed. The Russian government has also sharply protested the deployment by the United States of missile defenses in eastern Europe.

Chapter 7 - Some of the world's most dangerous and unpredictable regimes either have already acquired, or are attempting to acquire, weapons of mass destruction. These regimes are also developing and/or acquiring ballistic missiles of increasing ranges, payloads, lethality, and sophistication as a means of delivery. In the future, these regimes could use these asymmetric weapons to pursue their objectives through force, coercion, and/or intimidation as they have done in the past.

Today's ballistic missile threat from potentially hostile states is fundamentally different from Cold War era threats and risks. In response, the United States is fielding limited and purely defensive capabilities. In our comprehensive strategy to combat weapons of mass destruction, missile defense is just one element of a multi-faceted approach, which includes diplomacy, export controls, threat reduction assistance, nonproliferation regimes, and counter-proliferation programs. At the same time, missile defense is our ultimate insurance policy if these other elements of our strategy fail. History has taught us that, despite our best efforts, the free world will be challenged by military surprises as well as failures in diplomacy, intelligence, and deterrence. Given this reality, missile defenses have become highly desirable because they both reinforce deterrence and hedge against its failure.

Because of the expanding ballistic missile threat, it is essential that we develop and deploy missile defenses capable of protecting not only the United States and our deployed forces, but also our friends and allies. Trans-atlantic security is indivisible. We have learned from experience that decoupling our defenses from Europe is very much against the interests of the United States and our European allies. If Europe is not secure, the United States is not secure. To ensure our common security, we need defenses stationed and operational in Europe **before** a threat fully emerges. For this reason, negotiations are currently underway to locate up to ten silo-based long-range missile defense interceptors in Poland and a midcourse tracking and discrimination radar in the Czech Republic. These defensive interceptors contain no explosives, and destroy attacking reentry vehicles by kinetic energy, that is, a body-on-body collision outside of the atmosphere between the kinetic kill interceptor and the reentry vehicle.

In: Options for Deploying Missile Defenses in Europe
Editor: Melissa V. Jordan pp.1-7

ISBN: 978-1-60741-889-4
© 2010 Nova Science Publishers, Inc.

Chapter 1

BALLISTIC MISSILE DEFENSE: HISTORICAL OVERVIEW[*]

Steven A. Hildreth

SUMMARY

For some time now, ballistic missile defense (BMD) has been a key national security priority, even though such interest has been ongoing since the end of World War II. Many current BMD technologies date their start to the 1980s, and even earlier. This effort has been challenging technically[1] and politically controversial. More than $120 billion has been spent on a range of BMD programs since the mid-1980s; Congress appropriated $9.4 billion for FY2007 and $9.9 billion for FY2008. This chapter provides a brief overview of U.S. BMD efforts to date.

INTRODUCTION

Since the mid-1980s, many decision makers and others have demonstrated serious interest in deploying ballistic missile defense (BMD) systems capable of defending the United States from ballistic missile attack. Events over the past two decades contributed to strengthen these views. The collapse of the Soviet Union in the early 1990s heightened concerns about the possibility of an accidental or unauthorized launch of ballistic missiles from the remnants of that nation. The Persian Gulf War in 1991, with Iraq's use of Scud missiles, proved to many that the growing threat posed by ballistic missiles had to be addressed. The proliferation of ballistic missile technologies, including sales from nations such as China, Russia, and North Korea to nations such as Iran, Syria, and Pakistan became more worrisome to many. Finally, many also argue that some U.S. adversaries, such as North Korea and Iran, are

---

[*] This is an edited, reformatted and augmented version of a CRS Report for Congress publication dated January 2008.

developing longer-range missiles that might reach the United States, or threaten U.S. military forces deployed abroad, as well as U.S. friends and allies.

But interest in missile defense stretches back much further than the 1980s. In fact, efforts to counter ballistic missiles have been underway since the dawn of the missile age at the close of World War II. Numerous programs were begun, and only a very few saw completion to deployment. Technical obstacles have proven to be tenacious, and systems integration challenges have been more the norm, rather than the exception. Since 1985, the United States has spent more than $120 billion on a range of BMD efforts. In 2004, the United States deployed a small-scale national-level missile defense, which is still being tested but considered by most military leaders to be operationally effective.

This short report provides a brief overview of the history of the BMD efforts undertaken to defend the United States. It begins with a brief summary of the provisions of the 1972 ABM Treaty, which shaped most of the history of the U.S. BMD effort, and includes a short review of U.S. programs leading to the current program.

THE 1972 ANTI-BALLISTIC MISSILE (ABM) TREATY

Negotiations with the Soviet Union on the Anti-ballistic Missile (ABM) Treaty began in November 1969. Early on the United States proposed that the treaty limit Russia to one deployment site around Moscow (which it was building) and permit the United States to deploy four sites around ICBM fields, which was the U.S. program at the time (construction had begun on a site near Grand Forks, ND). The Soviets rejected this proposal, insisting any agreement include equal limits on each nation. They had the same reaction when the United States proposed that the treaty permit either nation to deploy one site at its capital or two sites at ICBM fields. Eventually, the Nixon Administration agreed to accept parity in ABM deployments; each nation could deploy two sites, one around its capital and one around an ICBM field. This permitted the continued construction of each nation's existing ABM site.

Signed in May 1972, the Anti-Ballistic Missile (ABM) Treaty prohibited the deployment of ABM systems for the defense of the nations' entire territory. It permitted each side to deploy limited ABM systems at two locations, one centered on the nation's capital and one at a location around ICBM silo launchers. When it became clear that neither nation would complete a second site, the two sides agreed in a 1974 Protocol that each would have only one ABM site, located either at the nation's capital *or* around an ICBM deployment area. Each ABM site could contain no more than 100 ABM launchers and 100 ABM interceptor missiles. The Treaty also specified that in the future any radars that provided early warning of strategic ballistic missile attack had to be located on the periphery of the national territory and oriented outward. The Treaty banned the development, testing, and deployment of sea-based, air-based, space-based, or mobile land-based ABM systems and ABM system components (these included interceptor missiles, launchers, and radars or other sensors that can substitute for radars). The Treaty placed no restrictions on the development, testing, or deployment of defenses against shorter range missiles. Although the United States withdrew from the ABM Treaty in 2002, the treaty profoundly shaped U.S. BMD efforts up to that point.

HISTORY OF NMD IN THE UNITED STATES

Sentinel and Safeguard Programs

The United States has pursued research and development in anti-ballistic missile (ABM) systems since the late 1940s. In the mid-1960s it developed the Nike-X system, which would have used ground-based, nuclear-armed interceptor missiles deployed around a number of major urban areas to protect against Soviet missile attack. Many analysts recognized that such protection would be limited, in part because the Soviet Union could probably saturate the system with offensive warheads and just a few warheads could achieve massive damage against a "soft" target like a city. In response, supporters argued that the system could provide a "thin" defense of U.S. cities against an attack by an anticipated Chinese intercontinental ballistic missile (ICBM) force. Consequently, in 1967 Defense Secretary McNamara announced the deployment of the Sentinel ABM system, based on the Nike-X system, as a defense against a future Chinese ICBM threat.

In 1969, the Nixon Administration renamed the system "Safeguard," and changed its focus to defend strategic offensive (i.e., nuclear-tipped ICBMs) missile fields, rather than cities, to ensure that these missiles could survive a first strike and ensure retaliation against the Soviet Union. Many in Congress objected to the program, citing its costs, technical uncertainties, and the risk of accelerating the arms race. Congress almost stopped the program's deployment in 1969, when the Senate voted 50-50 to approve an amendment halting construction. Safeguard continued, however, when Vice President Agnew broke the tie with a vote for the program. Nevertheless, sentiment against ABM deployments and in favor of negotiated limits on ABM systems was growing.

The United States completed its nuclear interceptor ABM site near Grand Forks, North Dakota. It operated from October 1975 to February 1976, then was shut down at the direction of Congress because it was viewed to be not cost-effective and had major technical problems. The facilities at that location, however, continued to count under the ABM Treaty because it had not been dismantled according to a classified post-Treaty agreement reached with the Soviet Union. Russia continues to this day to operate its ABM site around Moscow.

U.S. research and development into ABM systems, especially for ICBM protection, continued, albeit at lower budget levels through the late 1970s. By the time of the Carter Administration, however, spending on BMD programs had began to rise again, primarily as a means to defend the newest generation of U.S. ICBMs — the MX missile system.

The Strategic Defense Initiative (SDI)

The Reagan Administration continued to increase funding for defenses against ICBMs begun under the Carter Administration. But, in March 1983, President Reagan announced an expansive, new effort to develop non-nuclear BMD to protect the United States against a full-scale attack from the Soviet Union. Although the Strategic Defense Initiative (SDI) remained a research and development effort, with little testing and no immediate deployments, President Reagan and the program's supporters envisioned a global defensive system with thousands of land-, sea-, air-, and space-based sensors and interceptors. This defensive "shield" would employ both non-nuclear interceptor missiles and more exotic laser or x-ray devices in space designed to destroy incoming missiles. With these technologies, the United States would replace deterrence with defense in its effort to protect itself from Soviet attack. However, as cost estimates and technical challenges increased, the Reagan Administration scaled back its objectives for SDI. It announced that it would begin with a "Phase I" deployment of land-based and space-based sensors and interceptors. This system would not provide complete protection from Soviet attack, but would, instead, seek to disrupt the attack enough to call into question the attack's effectiveness. Phase I of SDI would, therefore, according to their arguments, enhance deterrence, while the United States continued to seek a way to replace deterrence with defense. Although Congress largely supported BMD research and development, it generally opposed plans for significant BMD deployments at that time.

The Reagan Administration and the program's supporters recognized that many of the technologies pursued under SDI would not be allowed by the ABM Treaty when they entered the testing or deployment phases. Therefore, the Reagan Administration outlined a new interpretation of the ABM Treaty that it hoped would allow for the testing of space- based and exotic missile defense technologies. Many in Congress at that time objected to this re-interpretation of the ABM Treaty, with Senator Sam Nunn mounting a particularly comprehensive defense of the traditional interpretation of the Treaty. Throughout this period, Congress tendered strong support for the ABM Treaty. The Reagan Administration also opened new negotiations with the Russians, known as the Defense and Space talks, in an effort to reach agreement on modifications to or a replacement for the ABM Treaty.

Global Protection against Limited Strikes (GPALS)

The first Bush Administration responded to the costs and technical challenges of Phase I and the changing international political environment with a further contraction of the goals for SDI. Instead of seeking to protect the United States against a large-scale attack, the United States would seek to deploy a defensive system that could provide Global Protection Against Limited Strikes (GPALS); a more modest version of the original SDI vision. This new focus recognized that the demise of the Soviet Union had reduced the likelihood of a large-scale attack, but also the increased likelihood of a small accidental or unauthorized attack. In addition, this type of ballistic missile defense would have sought to protect the United States, its forces, and allies against an attack by other nations who had acquired relatively small numbers of ballistic missiles.

The Bush Administration envisioned a GPALS system that would have included up to 1,000 land-based interceptors and perhaps another 1,000 space-based interceptors, along with space-based sensors. The Administration recognized that this system would have exceeded the limits in the ABM Treaty. It therefore held negotiations with the Russian government in 1992 in an effort to identify a more cooperative and flexible regime to replace the ABM Treaty. The Clinton Administration suspended these negotiations in 1993, when it also scaled back U.S. objectives for a national missile defense program. Meanwhile, some in Congress, notably Senator Nunn, had argued since the late 1 980s for the deployment of a more limited NMD system, that would comply with the ABM Treaty, to protect against limited or accidental attacks.

National Missile Defense Technology Development

The Clinton Administration restructured BMD programs to reflect the results of the 1993 Bottom Up Review, a major DOD-wide review of U.S. military plans and programs. At the time, it decided to emphasize missile defense deployment geared toward short-range missile threats, and focus national level efforts on technology development. Secretary of Defense Aspin noted at the time that these program changes reflected an assessment that the regional ballistic missile threat already existed, while a ballistic missile threat to the United States *per se* might emerge only in the future. This raised questions about the need for an NMD system in the near- to mid-term, particularly as compared with the need for robust theater missile defense efforts. The Department of Defense also determined that these programs would still be conducted in compliance with the 1972 ABM Treaty.

Key legislation was passed during this time. The Missile Defense Act of 1995 (in P.L. 104-106 — National Defense Authorization Act for Fiscal Year 1996) declared it the policy of the United States to: (1) develop as soon as possible affordable and operationally effective theater missile defenses; (2) develop for deployment a multiple-site national missile defense system that is affordable and operationally effective against limited, accidental, and unauthorized ballistic missile attacks on the United States, and which can be augmented over time as the threat changes to provide a layered defense against limited, accidental, or unauthorized ballistic missile threats; (3) initiate negotiations with Russia as necessary to provide for the national defense systems envisioned by the act; and (4) consider, if those negotiations fail, the option of withdrawing from the ABM Treaty.

The Clinton Administration adjusted its efforts and adopted a new NMD strategy. In 1996, the Clinton Administration adopted a 3+3 strategy, to guide development and potential deployment. Under this strategy, the United States would develop a national missile defense system to defend the United States against attacks from small numbers of long-range ballistic missiles launched by hostile nations, or, perhaps, from an accidental or unauthorized launch of Russian or Chinese missiles. The strategy envisioned continued development of NMD technologies during the first three years (1997-2000), followed by a deployment decision (in 2000) if the system were technologically feasible and warranted by prospective threats. If a decision to deploy an NMD system were made, the plan then was to deploy it within the second three year period (2000-2003). Development and deployment was to be conducted within the limits of the ABM Treaty. This approach was later modified to allow a longer lead time for possible deployment (possibly 2005), and according to the Pentagon at that time, to reduce the amount of program risk. Ultimately, in September 2000, President Clinton decided not to authorize deployment of an NMD system at that time. He stated that he could not conclude "that we have enough confidence in the technology, and the operational effectiveness of the entire NMD system, to move forward to deployment."

National Missile Defense Acquisition

President George W. Bush entered office prepared to advance long-range BMD deployment as a key national security objective. The Bush Administration substantially increased funding for BMD programs and laid the foundation for withdrawal from the 1972

ABM Treaty, which was announced in June 2002. Much of the Bush Administration's argument centered around a different strategic environment from 1972: Soviet forces no longer threatened the United States and the greater threat came from the proliferation of ballistic missiles and weapons of mass destruction from other countries, especially rogue states, and terrorists. The Russian government gave little opposition to the Administration's decision to withdraw from the treaty, and potential allied criticism in Europe was notably muted.

Also in 2002, the President announced his decision to deploy a limited BMD capability against long-range missiles by the fall of 2004. A handful of ground-based interceptors was deployed in Alaska by this date. To most observers, on-going testing is demonstrating the capabilities of that deployed system. More than 20 interceptors are now deployed in Alaska and California. The Bush Administration wants to expand this capability to a third site in Europe to defend against Iranian ballistic missile threats, but Congress has put this effort on hold pending further testing of the interceptors and final agreement on deployment with Poland and the Czech Republic.[2] Russian opposition has been strong, and European support is mixed.

HISTORY OF TMD IN THE UNITED STATES

U.S. efforts to develop effective defenses against shorter range ballistic missile threats to U.S. forces deployed overseas grew out of the Army's formal requirement for a theater ABM system in 1949 and produced a succession of systems, including the development and maturity of the Patriot air defense system from the 1960s to the present. As Patriot developed further in the 1980s, some argued for its potential also as a theater missile defense (TMD) capability. Although the Pentagon, Army, and the SDI Organization initially were not supportive of the effort at first, Congress increasingly argued successfully for Patriot's development of an anti-tactical missile (ATM) defense. By the time of the 1991 Persian Gulf War, the Patriot ATM had experienced a remarkably successful test record.[3] Acquisition of Patriot missiles for Desert Storm was accelerated after Iraq invaded Kuwait. On the battlefield, however, Patriot's success, or lack of it in Desert Storm, remains a subject of controversy despite most public perceptions of unequivocal success.[4]

Nonetheless, Congress and the Department of Defense determined subsequently that the Patriot concept to defend against shorter range ballistic missile threats to U.S. forces overseas warranted further support. The Patriot system had been upgraded several times by the time of the recent war against Iraq. On the battlefield, Patriot was considered more successful than in 1991, but with mixed results.[5] Congress and the Pentagon continue to support development of other highly effective TMD systems, especially a maritime capability built around existing naval systems and infrastructure that have been deployed or in development for decades.[6] In terms of program and testing success, most observers agree that the U.S. effort to develop and deploy effective BMD against short-range missiles has been more successful relative to the U.S. effort to develop and deploy effective BMD against long-range or strategic ballistic missiles.

End Notes

[1] For a 25-year review of the major BMD technology thrust, see CRS Report RL33240, *Kinetic Energy Kill for Ballistic Missile Defense: A Status Overview*, by Steven A. Hildreth.

[2] CRS Report RL3405 1, *Long-Range Ballistic Missile Defense in Europe*, by Steven A. Hildreth and Carl Ek, January 18, 2007.

[3] CRS Report 91-456F, *The Patriot Air Defense System and the Search for an Antitactical Ballistic Missile Defense*, by Steven A. Hildreth and Paul C. Zinsmeister (available from author upon request).

[4] Hearings before the House Government Operations Sub-committee on Legislation and National Security, April 7, 1992, on Patriot Performance in Desert Storm.

[5] CRS Report RL3 1946, *Iraq War: Defense Program Implications for Congress*, by Ronald O'Rourke (section on Ballistic Missile Defense).

[6] CRS Report RL33745, *Sea-based Ballistic Missile Defense — Background and Issues for Congress*, by Ronald O'Rourke.

In: Options for Deploying Missile Defenses in Europe
Editor: Melissa V. Jordan pp.9-12

ISBN: 978-1-60741-889-4
© 2010 Nova Science Publishers, Inc.

Chapter 2

THE BALLISTIC MISSILE DEFENSE SYSTEM: FACT SHEET*

Missile Defense Agency

One of the greatest threats facing the world today is the increasing proliferation of ballistic missiles and weapons of mass destruction. Non-proliferation activities, to include diplomacy and arms control agreements with Russia, have been successful in reducing this threat. Despite reductions in the number of weapons deployed by the United States and the former Soviet Union, ballistic missile proliferation continues on a wide scale today and could increase as the technology is transferred. Countries make these investments because ballistic missiles provide them with the means to project power both in a regional and strategic context and a capability to launch an attack from a distance. A country with no ballistic missiles today may acquire them in a very short period of time, and these missiles could become available to non-state terrorist groups.

---

* This is an edited, reformatted and augmented version of a Missile Defense Agency publication dated January 2009.

Through its capabilities for defending critical nodes, military assets, and seats of government, missile defense enhances non-proliferation activities. In other words, missile defenses can provide a permanent presence in a region and discourage adversaries from believing they can use ballistic missiles to coerce or intimidate the U.S. or its allies. In times of crisis, we can surge mobile missile defense capabilities (Aegis BMD, for example) into a region to enhance deterrence and, if a missile is launched, improve protection of critical assets and limit damage over a wide area. The ultimate goal of missile defense is to convince countries that ballistic missiles are not militarily useful or a worthy investment and place doubt in the minds of potential aggressors that a ballistic missile attack against the United States or its allies can succeed.

Missile defense technology being developed, tested and deployed by the United States is designed to counter ballistic missiles of all ranges—short, medium, intermediate and long. Since ballistic missiles have different ranges, speeds, size and performance characteristics, the Ballistic Missile Defense System is an integrated, 'layered" architecture that provides multiple opportunities to destroy missiles and their warheads before they can reach their targets. The system's architecture includes:

- networked sensors and ground- and sea-based radars for target detection and tracking
- ground- and sea-based interceptor missiles for destroying a ballistic missile using either the force of a direct collision, called "hit to kill" technology, or an explosive blast fragmentation warhead
- a command and control, battle management, and communications network providing the warfighter with the needed links among the sensors and interceptor missiles

Missile defense elements are operated by United States military personnel from U.S. Strategic Command, U.S. Northern Command, U.S. Pacific Command, U.S. Forces Japan, U.S. European Command and others. The United States has missile defense cooperative programs with a number of allies, including United Kingdom, Japan, Australia, Israel, Denmark, Germany, Netherlands, Czech Republic, Poland, Italy and many others. The Missile Defense Agency also actively participates in NATO activities to maximize opportunities to develop an integrated NATO ballistic missile defense capability.

BALLISTIC MISSILES FOLLOW A THREE-PHASED TRAJECTORY PATH: BOOST PHASE, MIDCOURSE PHASE, AND TERMINAL PHASE

Boost Phase

The boost phase defenses can defeat ballistic missiles of all ranges including Intercontinental Ballistic Missiles (ICBMs), but it is the most difficult phase in which to engage a missile, because the intercept "window" is only from one to five minutes. Although the missile is easiest to detect and track in the boost phase because its exhaust is bright and hot, missile defense interceptors and sensors must be in close proximity to the missile launch. Early detection in the boost phase allows for a rapid response and intercept early in its flight. Because the enemy missile is far away from its target and countermeasures have yet to be deployed, boost is the most desirable phase in which to engage. Currently, the Airborne Laser and the Kinetic Energy Interceptor technologies are in development to provide a defense in the boost phase. Both programs have critical development milestones in FY 2009 to prove technical feasibility.

Midcourse Phase

The midcourse phase begins when the enemy missile's booster burns out and it begins coasting in space towards its target. This phase can last as long as 20 minutes, allowing several opportunities to destroy the incoming ballistic missile outside the earth's atmosphere. Any debris remaining after the intercept will burn up as it enters the atmosphere. The Ground-based Midcourse Defense element is now deployed in Alaska and California to defend the U.S. homeland against a limited attack from countries like North Korea and Iran and is also being developed for deployment in Europe to defend against an attack from Iran. This system can only defend against intermediate and long-range ballistic missiles. The Aegis sea-based missile defense element utilizes existing Aegis cruisers and destroyers armed with interceptor missiles designed to defend against short- to medium-range ballistic missiles. A network of advanced sensors, radars and command, control and communication components provide target detection, tracking and discrimination of countermeasures to assist the interceptor missile in placing itself in the path of the hostile missile, destroying with hit-to-kill technology. These sensors and radars include transportable X-band radars capable of going to wherever they are needed, as well as advanced radars aboard Aegis cruisers and destroyers capable of operating in the world's oceans. We have also built the largest X-band radar in the world, the Sea-based X-band, which is mounted on a floating platform allowing it to traverse the world's oceans. This radar provides precise tracking of target missiles of all ranges and discriminates between actual missiles and countermeasures that could be deployed with a hostile missile.

Terminal Phase

The terminal phase is very short and begins once the missile reenters the atmosphere. It is the last opportunity to make an intercept before the warhead reaches its target. Intercepting a warhead during this phase is difficult and the least desirable of the three because there is little margin for error and the intercept will occur close to the intended target. Terminal phase interceptor elements include the Theater High Altitude Area Defense (THAAD) now undergoing advanced flight testing, the Aegis BMD near- term Sea-Based Terminal Defense capability using the SM-2 Block IV missile, and the U.S. Army's PATRIOT Advanced Capability 3 (PAC-3) now deployed worldwide. These mobile systems defend against short- to medium-range missiles.

Fielded Capabilities

From its establishment in early 2002 through the end of 2009, the Missile Defense Agency is fielding a Ballistic Missile Defense System consisting of:

- 28 Ground-Based Interceptors
- 21 Aegis warships capable of long-range surveillance and tracking and missile intercepts
- Standard Missile-3 interceptors for Aegis Ballistic Missile Defense warships
- An upgraded Cobra Dane radar in the Aleutian Islands
- Three upgraded early warning radars (Beale Air Force Base, California, Fylingdales, U.K., and Thule, Greenland)
- Four transportable X-band radars, with one currently deployed to Japan
- A sea-based X-band radar now operating in the Pacific Ocean to support flight testing and actual defensive operations

Testing

Testing must account for the ever-changing ballistic missile threat and the latest technological developments. Ground and flight tests provide data needed for highly advanced modeling and simulation activities that allow us to measure and predict the performance of all missile defense technologies. Successful flight tests in particular give the warfighter greater confidence in the system's capabilities. Since 2001, the Missile Defense Agency has conducted 47 hit-to-kill flight tests resulting in 37 intercepts.

In: Options for Deploying Missile Defenses in Europe
Editor: Melissa V. Jordan pp.13-43

ISBN: 978-1-60741-889-4
© 2010 Nova Science Publishers, Inc.

Chapter 3

DO THE UNITED STATES AND EUROPE NEED A MISSILE DEFENSE SYSTEM? JOINT HEARING BEFORE THE SUBCOMMITTEE ON EUROPE AND TERRORISM, NON-PROLIFERATION AND TRADE[*]

U.S. Government Printing Office

The subcommittees met, pursuant to notice, at 1:05 p.m. in room 2172, Rayburn House Office Building, Hon. Robert Wexler (chairman of the Subcommittee on Europe) presiding.

Mr. Wexler. Thanks for being here. I would like to call the joint subcommittee meeting of the Subcommittee on Europe and the Subcommittee on Terrorism and Nonproliferation to order.

Just as a matter of housekeeping; Mr. Gallegly and the chairman, Mr. Sherman, will be here shortly. There has been a bit of confusion regarding the vote schedule on the floor. We thought there were going to be votes about 5 minutes ago. It appears they will now start in about 15 minutes. Since Mr. Royce is here we have decided to start now, with the permission of the witnesses, and then take a break for what will probably be not more than 20 minutes, I hope.

I want to thank my distinguished colleague, Congressman Brad Sherman, who chairs as I said earlier, the Subcommittee on Terrorism, Nonproliferation, and Trade. I also want to thank Mr. Royce, the ranking member on that subcommittee, as well as Mr. Elton Gallegly, the ranking member on the Subcommittee on Europe, for cooperating and putting together what I think is a very timely hearing.

The hearing today is, I think, aptly titled: Does the United States and Europe need missile defense? This is a critical question for American and European officials, given the mounting and complex global threats from non-state actors, such as al-Qaeda and Hezbollah, and from rogue nations, such as North Korea and Iran. In this increasingly dangerous environment, it is

---

[*] This is an edited, reformatted and augmented version of a Committee on Foreign Affairs publication for the House of Representatives, dated May 3, 2007.

essential that America, along with our allies in Europe, be proactive and cooperate closely to ensure that both sides of the Atlantic are protected and secure.

To this end, I have deep reservations about the President's proposed Europe-based missile defense plan that would include placing ten interceptor missiles in Poland and a radar base in the Czech Republic. I am also deeply concerned about the administration's rush to put in place an unproven ballistic missile defense system, as well as its impact on our relations with our allies in Europe.

According to the *Washington Post*'s editorial page yesterday, this system has had "only one successful test," and that was "under controlled conditions that would not be present in a real attack." Frederick Lamb, who co-chaired a 2003 American Physical Society study on boost-phase intercept systems for missile defense noted that "not a single test of this system has ever been carried out under realistic combat conditions. To assume it is going to work under realistic conditions with only a few minutes warning is like assuming a gun that has only been fired against a single, carefully arranged target in a brightly lit firing range is going to be successful in a fast-moving night battle against many enemies."

Congress is correct to question whether U.S. resources are best spent on a questionable ballistic missile defense program or better spent securing our Nation's borders, ports and railways against another 9.11-type attack. Given the political, economic and security concerns being raised, it is unacceptable for the American people— who have footed hundreds of billions of dollars for the war in Iraq—to once again provide a blank check to the President to spend billions more on a questionable missile defense program—whose costs, at a minimum, are to be shared by our European allies.

I strongly support the bipartisan vote yesterday in the House Armed Forces Strategic Subcommittee that significantly cuts funding for the President's plan for a missile defense site in Europe. I believe the subcommittee acted in the best interest of America by halting construction of the system while at the same time providing funding for an independent, comprehensive study to be conducted to examine the technical feasibility of the system, its economic impact, as well as the effect on our NATO and European allies.

I would like to address to our witnesses—whom I am very grateful for being here— specifically to Secretary Fried, I stand in great admiration of both your efforts and the efforts of Under Secretary Burns. Particularly, in the last 2 years, I think you two gentlemen, along with others in the administration, have shown an extraordinary ability to engage with Europe and repair transatlantic relations, and my hat is off to you for doing so.

On the other hand, it would seem that one of the lessons we could learn about the beginning of the war in Iraq, whether one supports the President's plans now or whether one opposes it, is that there is a value to multinational cooperation. I believe this is a lesson that has been learned and incorporated by the administration in terms of the manner in which we now deal with Iran and the manner in which we now deal with North Korea.

I would respectfully ask that the witnesses address the issue: Why would we engage at the beginning of this process in a bilateral way with Poland and with the Czech Republic and not engage with NATO, not engage in a multilateral forum, which would seem to make the most sense?

The other question, which I think is self-evident, is: If this is a missile defense program that is designed to benefit our European allies in addition to benefiting America, then wouldn't it make sense that our European allies would be on the ground floor of the funding of the system?

To suggest that America would be funding a system that has joint benefits or disproportionate benefits for Europe suggests that we are acting in a unilateral way, which suggests we are footing a bill that we irrationally have taken on ourselves, or does that suggest that we are pursuing a program that has little or no public support in Europe and that funding would be impossible to procure from European Parliaments?

Then that raises the question: If European Parliaments and European leaders do not believe either that the missile defense program meets a legitimate threat, then how is it that we will be successful if we foist this upon them?

Having said that, I would like to turn over the time now to Mr. Royce and give him an opportunity to make whatever statements he wishes, and when we come back, I will properly introduce the witnesses.

[The prepared statement of Mr. Wexler follows:]

PREPARED STATEMENT OF THE HONORABLE ROBERT WEXLER, A REPRESENTATIVE IN CONGRESS FROM THE STATE OF FLORIDA, AND CHAIRMAN, SUBCOMMITTEE ON EUROPE

The joint subcommittee hearing will come to order. I would like to welcome my distinguished colleague, Congressman Brad Sherman, Chair of the Subcommittee on Terrorism, Non-proliferation and Trade, who is co-chairing this hearing. I also want to welcome the Ranking Member of the Europe Subcommittee Elton Gallegly and the Ranking Member of the Subcommittee on Terrorism, Non-proliferation and Trade Ed Royce.

Today's hearing is aptly titled "Does the United States and Europe Need Missile Defense?" This is a critical question for American and European officials given mounting and complex global threats from Non-State Actors, such as Al Qaeda and Hezbollah, and from rogue nations, such as North Korea and Iran. In this increasingly dangerous environment, it is essential that America, along with our allies in Europe, be proactive and cooperate closely to ensure that both sides of the Atlantic are protected and secure.

To this end, I have deep reservations about the President's proposed Europe-based missile defense plan that would include placing 10 interceptor missiles in Poland and a radar base in the Czech Republic. I am deeply concerned about the Administration's rush to put in place an unproven ballistic missile defense system as well as its impact on our relations with our allies in Europe.

According to the *Washington Post*'s Editorial page yesterday, this system has had "only one successful test" and that was "under controlled conditions that wouldn't be present in a real attack." Frederick K. Lamb, who co-chaired a 2003 American Physical Society study on boost-phase intercept systems for missile defense noted that, "not a single test of this system has ever been carried out under realistic combat conditions. To assume it is going to work under realistic conditions with only a few minutes warning is like assuming a gun that has only been fired against a single, carefully arranged target in a brightly lit firing range is going to be successful in a fast-moving night battle against many enemies"

Congress is right to question whether US resources are best spent on a questionable ballistic missile defense program or securing our nation's borders, ports and railways against another 9.11-type attack or on additional funding to beef up our counter intelligence agencies and military capabilities to combat global terrorist networks.

Given the political, economic and security concerns being raised, it is unacceptable for the American people—who have footed hundreds of billions of dollars for the debacle in Iraq—to once again provide a blank check to the President to spend billions more on a questionable missile defense program—whose costs at a minimum ought to be shared by our European allies.

I strongly support the vote taken in the House Armed Forces Strategic Forces Subcommittee yesterday that significantly cuts funding for the President's plan for a missile defense site in Europe. The subcommittee has acted in the best interest of America by halting construction of the system while at the same time providing funding for an independent comprehensive study to be conducted to examine the technical feasibility of the system, its economic impact as well as effect on our NATO and European allies.

It is clear there is no consensus of opinion in Congress whether this particular missile defense program is in the best interest of the United States, and it is painfully clear that many of our European allies are wary of placing this system in Europe and its impact on relations with an increasingly bellicose Russia. Europeans also question why—if this program is really intended to protect Europe—did the Administration choose to bilaterally negotiate with Poland and the Czech Republic rather than collectively decide this issue in NATO.

Mr. Fried, you along with Under Secretary Nick Burns have spent the last two years tirelessly working to reverse America's setbacks in Europe—I say this with the greatest amount of respect for your efforts. If that is the case, shouldn't the Administration be wary of cherry picking allies—a kind of coalition of the willing—instead of making certain that our missile defense policy is agreed to by our European allies in a Transatlantic organization such as NATO?

From an Al Qaeda terrorist carrying a suitcase bomb to ensuring energy security to addressing proliferation of missile technologies—the US along with European must determine collectively whether it makes strategic sense to deploy this missile program or to focus our collective resources on more immediate threats facing America and our allies.

Mr. Wexler. Mr. Royce.

Mr. Royce. Thank you, Mr. Chairman. Thanks for holding this hearing.

I think I will start my remarks here by saying that when we begin this discussion, we should start by gauging the threat. Today, we know that missile proliferation is a growing menace. Today, some 24 countries possess missiles of various ranges. The most troubling though are those countries seeking weapons of mass destruction. Primarily for us here today in this debate, I think it is North Korea and it is, certainly, Iran; the topic at hand is about Iran.

Given what we know about Iran's technical capabilities and what we suspect of its intentions, based upon the remarks by its head of state, enhancing our ability to counter its missiles is common sense. The proposed missile defense deployments in Poland and in the Czech Republic would help do that, better protecting the United States and Europe from any future threatening attack from Iran.

Russia's diplomatic attack on this proposal has certainly done some damage to our standing in Europe. The fact that this modest deployment of radars and non-lethal interceptors poses no threat to Russian security, is almost beside the point, I think, to the Russians. Of late, outreach to help Europe has helped change the debate some. It is beneficial that the President has engaged with European leaders, including on Monday of this week. It also helps that the United States has been exceptionally open to Russia; going the extra mile in offering its technology and offering the Russians site visits to see what we are doing here.

President Putin, though, has gone an extra 2 miles in the other direction; leading a public relations assault. This reflects, to some extent, Russia's trend away from democracy. This controversy, stripped to its essence, is about Russia's ambitions to diminish United States clout and expand its power eastward, not its national security. In attacking this deployment, Russia says Iran will pose no threat to Europe for a long time, if ever. Many Europeans respectfully disagree with that Russian assertion.

Russia, not coincidentally, has profited by arming Iran with a state-of-the-art air defense system and an increasing amount of weaponry. Some have suggested that Iran is using Russian technology for its missiles. Meanwhile, Russia is resisting meaningful international action against Iran's nuclear weapons ambitions. All of this makes Moscow, to my mind, no fair judge of the Iranian threat to Europe or to the United States, nor am I particularly interested in Moscow's view of the appropriateness of our responses, including missile defense deployments in Eastern Europe.

I differ with the point that throwing away this missile defense deployment would make Russia more cooperative in defaming Iran's nuclear program. It is unlikely that Russia would meaningfully compromise a deepening relationship with Iran over what its leadership surely understands is our relatively minor and unthreatening defensive deployment. Besides, the Russians are enjoying tweaking our tail over this. Some sensitivity to Russians is called for, but not here.

Missile defense will not address all of the threats we face, as its critics unrealistically demand, but it certainly is a valuable tool among others, including export controls, deterrents and the Proliferation Security Initiative that we need to counter missile proliferation which knows no borders, especially in a world awash in WMD material and technology. Given the threat we face, it is only prudent to press forward, overcoming the considerable technical challenges and working with our European allies to build the best protection possible against all classes of missiles.

The majority party has largely opposed missile defense over the years. A key subcommittee chair yesterday moved legislation to cut out the Polish interceptors. This opposition, I am afraid, is partly because missile defense is a legacy of President Reagan. It is my hope that this Congress does nothing to weaken our missile defense efforts which might encourage Iran, North Korea, and others to redouble their missile development efforts.

I look forward to the administration witnesses making their cases, and I would just close by mentioning that President Clinton said that we have enough confidence in the technology and in the operational effectiveness of the entire NMD system to move forward to deployment. That was the view of President Clinton. That is also my view.

I yield back the balance of my time.

Mr. Wexler. Thank you to Mr. Royce.

The votes have been called. I thank Mr. Wilson for joining us. I think what we will do at this point is break. We will come back. If Mr. Sherman and Mr. Gallegly at that point wish to say a few words, we will do that, and then I will introduce the witnesses.

Before I break I just want to associate myself with some of the remarks of Mr. Royce— which I think are very well stated—and simply suggest that I think most in the majority party understand there is a value to missile defense. I do not think there is any debate about that. I also do not think there is a debate in terms of the threat that Iran and North Korea face to the United States.

The question, from my mind, is does this proposal meet the threat, and if it does, are we going about its implementation in a way that would ensure the greatest likelihood of its success? That is, I hope, what we could engage in when we come back.

I thank Mr. Royce very much for his thoughtful remarks, and we will break for the two votes. Thank you very much.

[Recess.]

Mr. Wexler. The votes just ended a moment ago, so I am going to give my colleagues a couple of minutes to get here.

Mr. Royce having arrived, I think it is time to begin. I would like now to introduce our witnesses. I will first call the joint subcommittee hearing back into order.

Our first witness is Ambassador Daniel Fried, the Assistant Secretary for the Bureau of European and Eurasian Affairs for the Department of State. Prior to his current position, Ambassador Fried served as Special Assistant to the President and Senior Director for European and Eurasian Affairs at the National Security Council. His long and quite distinguished career has seen service in the former Soviet Union and as a Senior Advisor on European policy for several administrations. In addition, he served as U.S. Ambassador to Poland from November 1997 to May 2000.

Our second witness is Mr. John C. Rood, the Assistant Secretary for the Bureau of International Security and Nonproliferation at the Department of State. Previously, Mr. Rood served as the Special Assistant to the President and Senior Director for Counterproliferation Strategy at the National Security Council. He worked for over 5 years at the National Security Council, holding several positions. Additionally, Mr. Rood was a Senior Policy Analyst for Senator Kyl after holding a variety of positions at the Central Intelligence Agency.

I would also like to note that we are joined by Air Force Major General Chris Anzalone, the Deputy for Test Integration and Fielding, and Mr. Keith Englander, the Director of Engineering, both of the Missile Defense Agency, who will not be testifying but who will be able to answer questions related to the technical aspects of the missile defense system.

Before we go to our witnesses, as I mentioned earlier this is a joint subcommittee hearing, Congressman Brad Sherman has joined us, who chairs the Subcommittee on Terrorism, Nonproliferation, and Trade, and I would invite Mr. Sherman to make his opening statement.

Mr. Sherman. Thank you, Mr. Chairman.

I would have been here at the beginning of the festivities, but I had been informed that we were going to hold them after the votes. I then went into a place where my Blackberry would not work, and have reemerged.

Despite spending approximately $110 billion since the 1980s, our system of national missile defense does not inspire confidence in a rush to deploy this system, notwithstanding test failures; and I should point out that in the vast majority of those tests, the participants knew the missile was coming. There was only one missile to hit at a time, and the incoming missile offer had no countermeasures. But in spite of those test failures, in 2002 the Bush administration scrapped the 1972 Anti-Ballistic Missile Treaty so it could deploy the renamed Ground-Based Midcourse Defense System. The Pentagon installed missiles in Alaska and in Vandenberg, California. Two intercept flight test systems failed to launch. The Alaska site was flooded due to poor planning.

Now, the administration wants Congress to spend $4 billion on another ground-based system, this time in Europe. It will consist of—and I will not go into the details as to how many missiles will be in Europe—but of course, as we know, the system will be in Poland and the Czech Republic. Not only does the administration want to deploy a system that does not work, but it is willing to do so at the expense of cooperation with Russia and our NATO allies and a host of issues far more important to our defense.

Before I go on, I should also point out that the real threat to the United States is a nuclear weapon smuggled into the U.S., much like a bale of marijuana is smuggled into the U.S. You do not have to be a rocket scientist to smuggle a bale of marijuana into the United States, and that, of course, could come either from an Iranian nuclear weapon or as a result of the failure to fund the Nunn- Lugar program, a loose nuke from Russia.

The question, then, is not whether our newly reminted Star Wars system fails and whether it just costs us $110 billion to no avail, but whether it actually increases the likelihood that an American city will be destroyed by a smuggled nuclear weapon.

I will enter into the record a description of how the missile tests have been, if anything, rigged—or "slanted" is probably a better word than "rigged"—to show that missile defense was capable and, at the same time, demonstrate failure after failure. But again, even the best missile defense system is harmful to our national security if it increases the likelihood that a weapon will be smuggled across our borders.

Keep in mind, unlike the marijuana smugglers, a nuclear weapon only has to reach a mile offshore. It does not actually have to cross the border into the United States. An explosion in Juarez could destroy a big chunk of El Paso. So it is considerably harder to stop a nuclear weapon from entering the United States than a bail of marijuana, and I am told that marijuana has been successfully smuggled into the United States by entities far less sophisticated than a government capable of creating nuclear weapons.

So, other than the $110 billion, though, what has this system cost us?

Well, in my view, it has caused a severe irritant in our relationship with Russia at a time when Russia's cooperation is critical on the two real threats to us. We need Russian support on Nunn- Lugar implementation and the resulting control of loose nukes.

How can we turn to Russia and say, "We are deploying an antimissile system in the Czech Republic and Poland designed," you would think, "to eliminate your strategic capacities—although we will tell you it is not—and at the same time, we want to send our inspectors to 'help you' reduce your nuclear capacity"?

Needless to say, via the tearing up of the anti-ballistic missile treaty, followed by the creation of a Star Wars system and now, just to stick it to them, the deployment in the Czech Republic and Poland, it is virtually guaranteed to stop any real cooperation on Nunn-Lugar, although I am sure that they will still go through the motions for a diplomacy stake.

Another issue: We need Russia's cooperation with regard to Iran. The key to stopping Iran is U.N. sanctions. The key to those U.N. sanctions is to prevent the importation into Iran of refined oil products. We are nowhere near getting Russia's cooperation on that. Our plan to put pressure on the Iranian Government is a manifest failure. The centrifuges turn at Natanz, and I can think of no better way to assure that Russia will do very little—and they have done a little—but do very little to help us stop the Iranian program than to stick it to them by putting our missiles in what used to be their allies.

I yield back.

Mr. Wexler. Thank you, Mr. Sherman.

[The prepared statement of Mr. Sherman follows:]

PREPARED STATEMENT OF THE HONORABLE BRAD SHERMAN, A REPRESENTATIVE IN CONGRESS FROM THE STATE OF CALIFORNIA, AND CHAIRMAN, SUBCOMMITTEE ON TERRORISM, NONPROLIFERATION, AND TRADE

Despite spending approximately $110 billion since the 1980's, our system of national missile defense does not inspire great confidence. In a rush to deploy the system, notwithstanding test failures, the Bush Administration decided in 2002 that it would scrap the 1972 Anti-Ballistic Missile Treaty, so that it could deploy the newly reminted Ground-Based Midcourse Defense System (GMD).

In 2004, the Pentagon installed missiles at Fort Greely in Alaska and additional missiles at Vandenberg Air Force Base in California. Since then, two of the intercept flight tests of the system failed to even launch, and the Alaska site was recently flooded due to poor planning.

Without any acknowledgement of these failures, the Bush Administration now wants Congress to spend $4 billion on another ground-based ballistic missile system, this time in Europe. It will consist of ten Ground-based Midcourse Defense Interceptor missiles in Poland, a mid-course radar moved from the Marshal Islands to the Czech Republic, and an x-band radar positioned in a second area, one closer to the Middle East, potentially in the Caucasus.

Not only does the Administration want to deploy a system that does not work, it is willing to do it at the expense of cooperation with Russia and our NATO allies on a host of critical issues, including nuclear and missile proliferation, the very concerns missile defense is meant to counter.

Our Missile Defense System Will Likely Fail If We Ever Have to Call on It.

Even if we had the luxury of ignoring the political ramifications of moving forward on the President's proposal, the reality is that this system we have does not work. It makes no sense, therefore, to put it in other places.

The recent record of the GMD is not good. Out of the five tests conducted since 2002 in which an "intercept" of a target missile was planned, three failed. Curiously, the 6th and most recent test, and the one touted by missile defense supporters as proving the critics wrong, did not involve a planned intercept. The Missile Defense Agency and the contractors stated prior to that September 2006 test that their objective was just to see if certain components worked properly, not to hit an incoming missile. Lo and behold, the interceptor did hit the target. T

These tests are generally conducted under favorable conditions. The September 2006 test unlike previous tests, did not involve any countermeasures. It had to be put off for a day due to bad weather at Vandenberg. The tests are rigged in favor of the intercept vehicle—the flight paths of the target have often been plugged into the system. Even then, it still has a success rate of just 50 percent since 2002— but only 40 percent when the Missile Defense Agency is actually trying.

This leaves us with the same failure rate of 60 percent that we have witnessed since missile interception tests began in the early 80s. Both the GAO and the DOD Director of Operational Test & Evaluation recommended that the Missile Defense Agency conducts additional flight tests to validate its effectiveness *before* deployment. I know that the Pentagon often has to rush systems into the field due to the exigencies of war—but this is the only major system I am aware of that was deployed in the R and D phase *by design.*

We should not compound this error by placing the system in a provocative location overseas. I cannot fault the Bush Administration for trying to protect America from a nuclear Iran. I do feel, however, that pushing missile defense will fail to protect us. I am afraid it may actually make it more likely that we will actually have to face a nuclear Iran.

The Deployment will Further Fray U.S.-Russian Relations

While the threat of an Iranian ICBM capability is not yet upon us, and in my view is somewhat exaggerated anyway, the day that Iran can carry out a nuclear attack with a smuggled weapon or an attack through a terrorist proxy is coming much quicker than many in our government think. Rather than focusing on an aggressive strategy to diplomatically and economically isolate Iran, the Bush Administration is pushing the deployment of system that strains U.S. relations with Russia, a necessary and not always very willing partner in international efforts to stop Iran's nuclear weapons program.

Senior Russian officials have publicly and loudly raised concerns about the proposed deployment. President Putin went so far as to describe this system as the start of "an inevitable arms race." Now, instead of talking to the Russians about the problems in Tehran, we are involved is a tit-for-tat exchange with the Russians over missile defense program that may never work.

Russia has suspended, and may actually terminate, its adherence to the Conventional Forces in Europe Treaty (CFE). It has threatened to withdraw from the Intermediate Range Nuclear Forces Treaty (INF) which prohibits America and Russia from possessing ground based nuclear and conventional missiles with a range of 500–550 kilometers. Russia has also warned that it may cease cooperation on a joint missile launch warning center.

Not worried by those prospects? Think Russia is all bluster, no bite? You can add the European missile defense to list of Russian grievances—when it comes time to vote on the next round of Iran sanctions, or when we seek greater Russian cooperation on any of the issues where we *need* Russia, we pay a high price for antagonizing Moscow. We often do so for little or no gain.

Another Coalition of the Willing

These problems could be mitigated somewhat if the system were deployed within the framework of NATO. The Bush Administration has tried to sell this program as helping both America and European security. But because the Bush Administration has pursued agreements with the governments of Poland and the Czech Republic, it seems we are unwilling to sell it to the wider Europe that would benefit.

Because we are again "going it alone," we are again paying for it alone. Deployment of this missile system will drain an estimated $4 billion from our defense budget over the next six years.

The Real Threats From Iran

Again, this approach completely neglects the reality of the threats we face. This system is intended to protect against a nuclear ICBM strike from Iran. But a missile defense shield does nothing to protect us against a smuggled bomb or nuclear weapon hidden on a ship in one of our ports. Iran is far more likely to use terrorist proxies to carry out an attack on the United States (or Europe for that matter), than use missile technology it does not posses yet.

A missile defense shield simply will not deter a rouge government from providing a terrorist organization with nuclear materials, and it will not deter radical governments from using one by unconventional means. We have an obligation to increase international pressure on Iran to abandon these programs entirely, and we need to step up cooperation from Russia and our European allies. We do not need to deploy a system which is still, for all intents and purposes, still in the development phase.

Ineffective missile defense cannot substitute for an effective nonproliferation policy. Unfortunately, I think that substitute is exactly what we are being sold today.

Mr. Wexler. With that, we will go to Ambassador Fried. Thank you very much.

STATEMENT OF THE HONORABLE DANIEL FRIED, ASSISTANT SECRETARY, BUREAU OF EUROPEAN AND EURASIAN AFFAIRS, U.S. DEPARTMENT OF STATE

Ambassador Fried. Chairman Wexler, Chairman Sherman, Ranking Member Royce, thank you for this opportunity to appear before you again. It is a pleasure to be here. Thank you, Chairman Wexler, for your kind words earlier.

The short answer to the question of whether Europe and the United States need a missile defense system is, in my view and in the administration's view, an emphatic "yes." This answer is based on an assessment of the strategic context we face today, which is radically different than that prevailing during the Cold War.

We face the possibility that some of the world's most threatening and unstable regimes will develop and deploy lethal nuclear arsenals and the ballistic missiles to deliver them to Europe and to the United States. In the Cold War, classic deterrence theory held that near-absolute vulnerability and reliable retaliatory capability—the so-called "Mutual Assured Destruction" theory—provided security. During the debate over President Reagan's Strategic Defense Initiative, the so-called "Star Wars" 25 years ago, others argued that defenses were a better answer to strategic challenges. That debate was never settled, but it is not, at any rate, relevant today. Today, we face threats of a different kind and need different answers, unencumbered by heated arguments and positions of the past.

Iran already possesses many medium- to short-range missiles. The Shahab-3 missile is capable today of reaching targets in Southeast Europe, and Iran will not stay put. The Intelligence Community estimates that Iran could have long-range missiles capable of reaching all of Europe and the United States before 2015 if it chooses to develop them. Iran's development of threatening capability is matched by threatening rhetoric, including direct threats to Europe.

As an example, let me quote Iranian President Ahmedinejad from last October, and this is, let me recall, a leader who denies the Holocaust ever existed and who says the State of Israel should be wiped off the map. Referring to possible war between Israel and the Palestinians, this is what the Iranian President stated to our European friends:

> "We have advised the Europeans that the Americans are far away, but you are the neighbors of the nations in the region. We inform you that the nations are like an ocean that is welling up, and if a storm begins, the dimensions will not stay limited to Palestine, and you may get hurt."

Other threats may develop as well beyond Iran. As Defense Secretary Gates told European allies and the Russians last week, we must think 20 years ahead and consider all of the threats we may face. Diplomatic efforts may help reduce or even prevent these threats. Along with our European allies and Russia, we are engaged in intensive diplomacy intended to change Iran's current nuclear development plans. This is the best course, and we may succeed, but we may not; and we have, in any event, a responsibility to defend the American people and our allies.

In this context, our proposal for a limited missile defense system makes sense. It allows for a wider, more flexible range of options to respond to a potential attack should deterrence fail. Let me stress that the system we are contemplating is nowhere as ambitious as was the missile defense plans, the so-called "Star Wars" of the Cold War. It is limited, fitting the threats we face.

The importance of having multiple options was evident last summer when we activated our fledgling defense system for the first time in response to the North Korean missile launch preparations. A missile defense system does not mean that the United States is abandoning nonproliferation efforts or other efforts to prevent other sorts of nuclear threats.

On the contrary, a missile defense system can help our non-proliferation efforts. Effective defenses reduce incentives for states to acquire missiles in the first place. The missile defense system we are proposing to place in Europe, in cooperation with Poland and the Czech Republic, would provide an extra layer of protection against possible missile attacks to our NATO allies, other European friends, and the United States.

The threat is real, and the system we are proposing can work. It calls for fielding ten interceptor missiles in Poland and a radar facility in the Czech Republic. These assets would be for purely defensive purposes to counter missile threats from the Middle East, particularly Iran. They have no offensive capability. The interceptors carry no explosive warhead of any type, but rely on kinetic energy to collide with and destroy incoming warheads.

Poland and the Czech Republic have accepted our offer to negotiate with them. My colleague, Assistant Secretary Rood, will lead the first round of negotiations later this month. Basing missile defense assets there deepens our strategic relationships with Poland and the Czech Republic. Deploying this limited system on the territory of these two important NATO allies would extend defensive coverage to their territory and most of Europe as a whole. Secretary Gates was in Poland last week, and I accompanied him. The Poles and Czechs will have questions about the systems, and we will have answers. We have agreed that these systems must increase net security to Poland and to the Czech Republic. A great deal has been said and written about Russia's reaction to our plans.

The system poses no threat to Russian security. The interceptors cannot be used effectively against Russia's strategic forces, and the Russians know this. We have consulted with Russia on this issue on numerous occasions and at very high levels, starting last year. We have recently intensified our consultations with Russia, and President Bush offered President Putin cooperation on missile defense. Assistant Secretary Rood can explain this in more detail. In Moscow last week, Secretary Gates made clear to the Russian leadership that we were prepared to address their concerns.

Mr. Chairman, transatlantic security is indivisible. If Europe is not secure, the United States is not secure. We cannot have U.S. security decoupled from that of our NATO allies. We cannot take a unilateral or isolationist approach to security. Indeed, we have on multiple occasions, over some time, consulted and cooperated with our NATO allies and friends on missile defenses, both within the NATO Alliance and the NATO-Russia Council. President Bush made it a priority to offer extended coverage to our friends and allies and deployed forces. We have been working on theater missile defenses within NATO and the NATO-Russia Council for some time now, and we have made progress. Our most recent discussions were on April 19th in Brussels and last week in Oslo at the level of NATO Foreign Ministers, where I accompanied Secretary Rice.

We have made significant progress within NATO and the NRC, NATO-Russia Council, in explaining the security rationale for the system, its technical capabilities, what it can do against Iranian capability in particular, and what it cannot do against the Russian arsenal. After the April 19th NATO-Russia Council meeting, NATO Secretary General Jaap de Hoop Scheffer told reporters that "there is a shared threat perception and that allies agree that a threat from ballistic missiles exists." Last week's meeting of the NATO Foreign Ministers in Oslo showed near unanimity in support of the concept of missile defenses from our NATO allies. Security is indivisible, as I said.

The location of the proposed defense installations in Poland and in the Czech Republic is optimal for covering the most Alliance territory possible. We are currently working with NATO to explore how a U.S. long-range missile system could work with NATO missile defense systems. The U.S. proposed system is designed to counter long-range threats from the Middle East and would be able to protect all of those NATO countries facing such threats. However, some allies still could face threats from short- and medium- range missiles. For these countries to be protected, they would require short- and medium-range missile defense systems. These systems are more mobile than the systems we are proposing and can be deployed quickly if a need should arise.

As I mentioned, NATO has already launched a development effort focused on countering shorter-range threats specifically through its Active Layered Theatre Ballistic Missile Defense system, a NATO-funded, command-and-control system integrating sensors and interceptors which will be provided by member nations.

NATO is also exploring options to protect the Alliance against the full range of ballistic missile threats, including long-range missiles. At the 2006 Riga Summit, NATO heads of state in government noted the conclusions of the Missile Defense Feasibility Study, which agreed that missile defense for NATO territory is technically feasible within the assumptions of the study. U.S. and NATO efforts are complementary and could work together to form a more effective defense for Europe. We would be able to link NATO systems with the ones we plan to deploy. We have raised this idea of cooperation with NATO.

In sum, we have made progress with our European allies, with NATO, and potentially with Russia about our proposed missile defense system in Europe.

Thank you for your attention. I appreciate the opportunity to be here, and I look forward to your questions.

Mr. Wexler. Thank you, Ambassador Fried.

[The prepared statement of Mr. Fried follows:]

Prepared Statement of the Honorable Daniel Fried, Assistant Secretary, Bureau of European and Eurasian Affairs, U.S. Department of State

Chairman Wexler, Chairman Sherman, Ranking Member Gallegly, Ranking Member Royce, members of the Subcommittees, thank you for giving me the opportunity to appear before you again. Today, I will speak about our missile defense plans for Europe, focusing on the regional issues, while Assistant Secretary John Rood will focus on the more technical and performance issues related to missile defense.

I will start by asserting that the strategic context we face today is radically different than that prevailing during the Cold War. We face the possibility that some of the world's most threatening and unstable regimes can develop and deploy lethal nuclear arsenals and the ballistic missiles to deliver them to Europe and even the United States.

In the Cold War, classic deterrence theory held that near-absolute vulnerability and reliable retaliatory capability—so-called Mutual Assured Destruction—provided security stability. Others, especially in the 1980s during the debate over President Reagan's Strategic Defense Initiative, argued that defenses were in fact a better answer to the strategic nuclear challenge of the time. That debate was never settled; my point is that this debate is no longer relevant and should not be carried forward to the early 21st century. We face threats of a different kind and need different answers unencumbered by heated arguments of the past.

The missile and nuclear threat from Iran is developing. That country already possesses hundreds of medium range Shahab-3 and short-range ballistic missiles. Iran is developing follow-on medium range systems that will be capable of reaching targets in southeast Europe. Iran has expressed its intent to develop space launch vehicles (SLVs), which is cause for some concern given the similarities between SLV technology and that found in longer-range ballistic missiles. The Intelligence Community estimates that Iran could develop long-range missiles capable of reaching all of Europe and the United States by 2015 if it chooses to do so.

Iran's worrying development of a threatening capability is matched by threatening rhetoric, including direct threats to Europe. As an example, let me offer recent remarks by Iranian President Ahmadinejad made last October 20 in Tehran. Referring to possible war between Israel and the Palestinians, he stated, "We have advised the Europeans that the Americans are far away, but you are the neighbors of the nations in the region. We inform you that the nations are like an ocean that is welling up, and if a storm begins, the dimensions will not stay limited to Palestine, *and you may get hurt.*"

There may be other threats that develop in the region of the Middle East or else where. As Defense Secretary Gates told European Allies and the Russians last week, we must think twenty years ahead, and consider the threats we may face.

Diplomatic efforts may help reduce these threats and even prevent some of them from arising altogether. We hope for the best and indeed are engaged in intensive diplomacy with our European allies and Russia intended to change Iran's current nuclear development plans. We may succeed, and this is the best course. But we may not succeed.

We have in any event a responsibility to defend the American people and our allies. In this context, limited missile defense makes sense. It does not substitute for deterrence, but in a situation where we may face smaller threats from countries more radical and potentially more dangerous than was the Soviet Union, it allows for a wider, more flexible range of options to respond to a potential attack should deterrence fail.

Let me stress that the system we are contemplating is nowhere as ambitious as was the missile defense plans of the Cold War. It is limited, fitting the threats we may face. And the new strategic environment is not hypothetical, but emerging in our time. The importance of defenses and multiple options was evident last summer when we activated our fledgling defense system for the first time in response to the North Korean missile launch preparations.

Developing a missile defense system does not mean that the United States is abandoning an emphasis on non-proliferation. Indeed, putting a missile defense system in place could help our non-proliferation efforts as effective defenses reduce incentives for states to acquire missiles in the first place.

The missile defense system that we are proposing to place in Europe—in cooperation with Poland and the Czech Republic—would provide an extra layer of protection against possible missile attacks not only to the United States, but also to NATO allies and other European friends. The goal is to field a system that is capable of enhancing protection of the United States that also has the benefit of protecting Europe.

Transatlantic security is indivisible. As we learned the hard way in the 20th century, if Europe is not secure, the United States is not secure. We cannot have U.S. security decoupled from that of our NATO allies. We cannot take a unilateral or isolationist approach to security. We need a common level of protection from threats for the United States and for our European allies.

The threat is real, and the system we are proposing is practical. Testing has demonstrated that the limited missile defense system we are proposing works. Since 2001, the Missile Defense Agency (MDA) has had 27 successful hit-to-kill intercepts out of 35 attempts. And 15 of the last 16 flight tests have been successful.

The proposed system calls for fielding 10 interceptor missiles in Poland and a radar facility in the Czech Republic. These would be for purely defensive purposes— to counter missile threats from the Middle East, particularly Iran. They have no offensive capability. Indeed, the ballistic missile defense interceptors carry no explosive warheads of any type, but rely instead on their kinetic energy to collide with and destroy incoming warheads. Moreover, the silos constructed for the deployment of defensive interceptors are substantially smaller than those used for our offensive missiles. We have no plans to modify these silos in the future, and any conversion would require extensive modifications, thus precluding the possibility of covertly converting the interceptor silos for use by offensive missiles.

We have made a formal offer to begin negotiations with both Poland and the Czech Republic. They have accepted our offer; Assistant Secretary Rood will lead the first round of negotiations, which are scheduled to begin in late May. Basing these missile defense assets in Europe presents the United States with an opportunity to deepen our strategic relationships with Poland and the Czech Republic. Mutually agreeing to deploy a limited capability on the territory of two important NATO Allies would extend defensive coverage to their populations and territory, and to most of Europe as a whole.

We have consulted intensively with the Poles and Czechs on these issues; Secretary Gates was in Poland last week and I accompanied him. The Poles and Czechs will have questions about the system, and we will have answers. The Poles and Czechs will want to make sure that their national security is increased as a result of any deployment that takes place. We look forward to discussing with both these allies the nature of current and potential threats to their security from any quarter and how we can address them together.

I said earlier that we did not believe in unilateral security. Indeed, we have on multiple occasions over several years consulted and cooperated with our Allies and friends on missile defenses within both NATO and the NATO-Russia Council (NRC). President Bush made it a priority to offer to extend coverage to our friends and Allies and deployed forces. We have also been working on theater missile defenses within NATO and the NRC for some time now and have made progress.

NATO's work on missile defense has focused on three activities: the Active Layered Theatre Ballistic Missile Defense (ALTBMD) program, technical work to support decisions on possible missile defense for the protection of NATO territory and population centers, and cooperation with Russia on Theater Missile Defense (TMD).

In 2005, the North Atlantic Council (NAC) approved the ALTBMD program, a NATO-funded Command and Control structure integrating sensors and missile defense interceptors which will be provided by member nations. This system is focused on the protection of NATO deployed forces against ballistic missiles with a range of up to 3,000 km (shorter-to-medium range missile defense). NATO plans to an initial capability to defend its forces by 2010; a fully operational system capable of protecting areas against missiles up to 3,000 km is planned for the 2015-2016 time- frame.

NATO has also begun to explore options to protect the Alliance against the full range of ballistic missile threats, including long-range missiles. At the 2006 Riga Summit, NATO Heads of State and Government noted the conclusions of the Missile Defense Feasibility Study, which found that missile defense for NATO territory is technically feasible within the assumptions and limitations of the study. Now that the U.S. is proposing a long-range missile defense system in Europe, NATO is assessing how the U.S. plan could work with NATO missile defense.

We have had three senior-level NATO and NRC discussions on U.S. missile defense plans in Europe within the past six months. Our most recent discussions were on April 19 in Brussels and last week in Oslo at the level of Foreign Ministers, where I accompanied Secretary Rice.

A great deal has been said and written about Russia's reaction to our plans. As we have stated publicly and privately, the system poses no threat to Russian security. The interceptors do not have the capability to be used against Russia's strategic forces. Moreover, ten defensive missiles would be of no use against Russia's hundreds of missiles and thousands of nuclear warheads. The Russians know this.

We have consulted with Russia on this issue on numerous occasions and at very high levels, starting last year. We have recently intensified our consultations with Russia, and President Bush offered to President Putin U.S.-Russian cooperation on missile defense.

Two weeks ago my colleague Assistant Secretary of State John Rood and DoD Deputy Assistant Secretary Brian Green traveled to Moscow and offered Russia a detailed proposal for such cooperation. He can explain this to you in more detail. In Moscow last week, Secretary Gates expanded on this proposal, and made clear to the Russian leadership that we were prepared to address their concerns about our program and plans.

Although Russia remains wary of U.S. missile defense plans, I believe that we have made significant progress within NATO and the NRC in explaining the security rationale for the system, its technical capabilities, what it can do against Iranian capability in particular, and what it cannot do against the Russian arsenal.

Our most recent consultations have been well received. After the April 19 NRC meeting, NATO Secretary General Jaap de Hoop Scheffer told reporters that "there is a shared threat perception" and that "Allies agree that a threat from ballistic missiles exists." He also stated that, "There is a shared desire that any U.S. system should be complementary to any NATO missile defense system." The missile defense assets we propose to deploy in Europe have been designed to be complementary to any future NATO ballistic missile defense system. We welcome NATO cooperation in missile defense, particularly in addressing the short-range threats that Europe faces from the Middle East.

At last week's meeting of NATO Foreign Ministers in Oslo there was near unanimity in support of missile defense from our NATO allies. Minister after Minister acknowledged that a genuine problem exists, a genuine security threat that missile defense is designed to address. Allies support further NATO work on the subject and supported our offers to cooperate with the Russians. During his press statement on April 26, Secretary-General de Hoop Scheffer noted that U.S. missile defense plans do not upset the strategic balance of Europe. He stated, "It is clear that there is a full understanding between the allies that the plans in the framework of the third site cannot, and will not, and do not upset the strategic balance in Europe. There was a lot of support for the wide-ranging United States proposals vis-&-vis our Russia partners for closer cooperation on missile defence." De Hoop Scheffer also publicly stated that U.S. offers of missile defense cooperation to the Russians were "very forward leaning and open."

I said earlier that security is indivisible. The location of the proposed defense installations in Poland and the Czech Republic is optimal for covering the most Alliance territory possible. We are currently working with NATO to explore how a U.S. long-range missile defense system could work with NATO missile defense systems.

The U.S. proposed system is designed to counter long-range threats from the Middle East and would be able to protect all NATO countries facing such threat. However, some Allied countries could still face threats from shorter and medium-ranged missiles. For these countries to be protected, they would require short- and medium- range missile defense systems. These systems are more mobile than the system we are proposing to build in Europe and can be deployed relatively quickly if a need should arise.

Again, U.S. and NATO efforts are complementary and could work together to form a more effective defense for Europe. We would be able to link NATO systems with the ones we plan to deploy in order to ensure interoperability. We have raised this idea of cooperation with NATO and hope that the alliance will agree to it.

In sum, we have made progress with our European allies, with NATO, and potentially with Russia about our proposed missile defense system in Europe. NATO agrees that the threat of ballistic missiles is real and is currently debating its next steps on missile defense. Discussions with Russia continue; we have proposed various opportunities for cooperation on missile defense and are awaiting their considered response. We believe that a missile defense system in Europe would greatly increase the overall security of Europe.

Thank you for your attention. I appreciate the opportunity to be here and I look forward to your questions.

Mr. Wexler. Mr. Rood, please.

STATEMENT OF THE HONORABLE JOHN C. ROOD, ASSISTANT SECRETARY, BUREAU OF INTERNATIONAL SECURITY AND NONPROLIFERATION, U.S. DEPARTMENT OF STATE

Mr. Rood. Thank you, Chairman Wexler, Chairman Sherman, Mr. Royce. Thank you for the opportunity to appear before the committee today.

Since the end of the Cold War, we have observed the proliferation of weapons of mass destruction and ballistic missiles. The proliferation of these capabilities has continued despite the best efforts of the United States and our allies, including notable successes in Libya and in shutting down the A.Q. Khan network. Today, roughly two dozen countries possess ballistic missiles of varying ranges. The trend is toward missiles of increasing ranges and greater sophistication. Of particular concern are missile programs underway in Iran and North Korea. As the director of the Defense Intelligence Agency, Lieutenant General Maples, testified to the Senate in February:

> "North Korea continues to develop the Taepo Dong 2, which could reach parts of the United States and is capable of carrying a nuclear payload. On 4–5 July 2006, North Korea conducted seven widely published launches. Despite the failure of the Taepo Dong 2, North Korea successfully tested six theater ballistic missiles, demonstrating the capability to target U.S. Forces and our allies in South Korea and Japan."

Of course, you are familiar with North Korea's conduct of a nuclear test last October.

We continue to see Iran field additional ballistic missiles capable of reaching states in the region, such as Israel, and to pursue the development of more advanced missiles with even longer ranges. The Intelligence Community assesses Iran would be able to develop an ICBM capable of reaching the United States and all regions of Europe before 2015 if it chose to do so. And I would point out that Iran has acquired missiles from North Korea in the past, and it could do so in the future, potentially acquiring missiles with even longer ranges, quicker than the Intelligence Community estimate.

Iranian intentions are also of concern. For example, in October 2005, President Ahmedinejad called for Israel to be "wiped off the map." That same speech called for achieving a "world without America." These statements take on greater significance given Iran's missile efforts and its pursuit of nuclear weapons in defiance of the international community and U.N. Security Council resolutions.

It is important to note that our NATO allies are also concerned about the proliferation of ballistic missiles. As NATO Secretary General Jaap de Hoop Scheffer said on April 19th, after a North Atlantic Council meeting, "There is absolutely a shared threat per-ception. Allies all agree a threat from ballistic missiles exists."

Missile defenses are an important response to these threats but are one element of the administration's broader counterproliferation effort. We have pursued a number of efforts to secure materials and technology at their sources through cooperative threat reduction efforts and export control assistance. We have worked to curb trade in these dangerous technologies through the use of financial measures, support for the missile technology control regime, and efforts like the Proliferation Security Initiative. In addition, we have pursued active multilateral diplomacy at the U.N. Security Council and in groupings like the Six Party Talks with North Korea.

Missile defenses reduce incentives for missile proliferation by undermining the military utility and attractiveness of these weapons. Missile defenses are part of contemporary deterrence and promote stability, as we saw last summer when we activated our system for the first time in response to North Korea's missile launch preparations. In that case, our missile defense system allowed our national leadership to consider a wider, more flexible range of responses to a potential attack.

To help address these threats, we have proposed fielding ten ground-based interceptors in Poland and a radar in the Czech Republic. Such missile defenses would build upon the initial capabilities we have fielded in Alaska, California, and elsewhere and improve our ability to defend the United States from a missile attack from the Middle East. Such additional assets would also have the capability of providing missile defense coverage to most of Europe against long-range missiles.

We continue to consult with the Russian Government regarding its concerns. Such deployments are not directed at Russia but, rather, are intended to address the emerging threat from the Middle East. The ten interceptors and radar we hope to field in Europe would have little or no capability against Russia's large, strategic, offensive force which could overwhelm the United States system's limited number of interceptors, regardless of their location.

In theoretical one-on-one engagements, the United States interceptors in Europe would have little or no capability to intercept Russian ICBMs launched at the United States, as the U.S. interceptors are too slow to catch Russian missiles.

The NATO Secretary General commented after the April 19 NATO-Russia Council meeting:

> "The allies were convinced and are convinced that there are no implications of the United States system for the strategic balance. Ten interceptors will not and cannot affect the strategic balance, and ten interceptors cannot pose a threat to Russia."

On April 17th, I led an interagency delegation to Moscow to consult with our Russian colleagues and offer new proposals for cooperation between the United States and Russia across the full spectrum of missile defense activities. This proposal was a follow- up to President Bush's March 28th phone conversation with President Putin.

Mr. Chairman, I plan to lead an interagency team to Warsaw and Prague in late May to begin the formal negotiations on the placement of missile defense facilities in those countries. As we embark on this endeavor, I would urge you and your colleagues to support the President's fiscal year 2008 budget request of $310 million for the placement of missile defense capabilities in Europe.

Thank you again for the opportunity to testify before you today.

Mr. Wexler. Thank you, Mr. Rood.

[The prepared statement of Mr. Rood follows:]

Prepared Statement of the Honorable John C. Rood, Assistant Secretary, Bureau of International Security and Nonproliferation, U.S. Department of State

Mr. Chairman, thank you for the opportunity to testify before you today.

A New Strategic Environment

Since the end of the Cold War, we have observed the proliferation of weapons of mass destruction (WMD) and ballistic missiles. The proliferation of these capabilities has continued despite the best efforts of the United States and our allies, including notable successes in Libya and in shutting down the A.Q. Khan network. Today, roughly two dozen countries possess ballistic missiles of varying ranges. The trend is toward missiles of increasing ranges, payloads, lethality, and sophistication.

Of particular concern are the missile programs underway in North Korea and Iran. As the Director of the Defense Intelligence Agency, LTG Michael Maples testified to the Senate on January 11, 2007, "North Korea has an ambitious ballistic missile development program and has exported missiles and missile technology to other countries, including Iran. . . ." General Maples also testified on February 27, 2007, to the Senate that "North Korea continues to develop the Taepo Dong 2, which could reach parts of the United States and is capable of carrying a nuclear payload. On 4–5 July 2006, North Korea conducted seven widely-published launches . . . Despite the failure of the Taepo Dong 2, North Korea successfully tested six theater ballistic missiles, demonstrating the capability to target U.S. forces and our allies in South Korea and Japan." And of course, North Korea conducted a nuclear test in October. In Iran, we continue to see that government field additional ballistic missiles that are capable of reaching states in the region such as Israel, and the continued development of more advanced missiles with longer ranges. The Intelligence Community assesses that Iran would be able to develop an ICBM capable of reaching the United States and all regions of Europe before 2015 if it chose to do so. And, I would point out that Iran has acquired ballistic missiles from North Korea in the past and note the possibility that it could do so again in the future, potentially acquiring missiles with even longer ranges.

Iranian intentions are also of concern. For example, in October 2005 President Ahmedinejad called for Israel to be "wiped off the map" and in that same speech called for achieving "a world without America." These statements obviously take on greater significance given our concerns about Iran's ballistic missile efforts and its pursuit of nuclear weapons in defiance of the international community, UN Security Council resolutions, and its international obligations.

Mr. Chairman, it is important to note that our NATO Allies are also concerned about the proliferation of ballistic missiles. As NATO Secretary General Jaap de Hoop Scheffer observed after the April 19, 2007, North Atlantic Council meeting, "There is absolutely a shared threat perception . . . Allies all agree a threat from ballistic missiles exists."

Deterrence and Defense in the Twenty-First Century

Missile defenses are an important response to the threats that I have just described, but are just one element of the Administration's broader counter-proliferation effort. Under the National Strategy to Combat Weapons of Mass Destruction, the Administration has pursued a number of efforts in this area to secure materials and technology at their sources through cooperative threat reduction efforts and export control assistance. We have worked to curb the trade in these dangerous technologies through use of financial measures, support for the Missile Technology Control Regime, and efforts like the Proliferation Security Initiative (PSI), which today includes over 80 countries which have conducted dozens of successful interdictions of missile and WMD-related items. In addition, we have pursued active multilateral diplomacy at the UN Security Council and in groupings like the Six Party Talks with North Korea.

Missile defenses reduce incentives for missile proliferation by undermining the military utility and attractiveness of these weapons. Missile defenses are part of contemporary deterrence and promote stability, as we saw last summer, when we activated our system for the first time in response to North Korean missile launch preparations. In that case, our missile defense system allowed our national leadership to consider a wider, more flexible range of responses to a potential attack.

The Fielding of Missile Defenses in Europe

To help address the threats that I outlined, the Administration has proposed fielding 10 ground-based interceptors in Poland and a radar in the Czech Republic. Such missile defenses would build upon the initial capabilities we have fielded in Alaska, California, and elsewhere, and improve our ability to defend the United States from missile attack from the Middle East. Such additional assets deployed in Poland and the Czech Republic would also have the capability of providing missile defense coverage to most of Europe against intermediate- and intercontinental-range ballistic missiles.

Russian Concerns

We continue to consult with the Russian Government regarding its concerns about the potential fielding of U.S. missile defense capabilities in Europe. Such deployments are not directed at Russia but rather are intended to address the emerging missile threat from the Middle East. The 10 interceptors we hope to field in Poland and the radar in the Czech Republic would have little or no capability against Russia's large strategic offensive force, which could overwhelm the U.S. system's limited number of interceptors regardless of their location. In theoretical one-on-one engagements, U.S. interceptors located in Europe would have little or no capability to intercept Russian ICBMs launched at the United States as the U.S. interceptors are too slow to catch Russian ballistic missiles.

As NATO Secretary General Jaap de Hoop Scheffer commented after the April 19 NATO-Russia Council meeting, "The Allies were convinced and are convinced that there are no implications of the United States system for the strategic balance . . .Ten interceptors will not, and cannot affect the strategic balance and ten interceptors cannot pose a threat to Russia."

On April 17, I led an interagency delegation to Moscow to consult with our Russian colleagues on this issue and to offer some new proposals for missile defense cooperation between the United States and Russia across the full spectrum of missile defense activities—including experimentation with new concepts and technologies, research and development of missile defense systems and components, and work to improve the capability of our forces to successfully conduct cooperative missile defense operations during peacekeeping or other joint military operations. This proposal was a follow-up to President Bush's March 28 phone conversation with President Putin. In the week after my visit, Secretary of Defense Gates led another interagency delegation to Moscow to discuss opportunities for cooperation on missile defense. It is our hope that through the transparency and confidence-building measures that we have proposed, as well as potential missile defense cooperation, that we can address Russian concerns.

Way Ahead

Mr. Chairman, we will continue to discuss this issue with our European and Russian colleagues. In addition, I plan to lead an interagency team to Warsaw and Prague in late May to begin formal negotiations on the placement of missile defense facilities in those countries. If successful, these agreements would enable us to improve the security of the United States and our allies by giving us the capability to defend against the real and growing missile threat from the Middle East. As we embark on this endeavor, I would urge you and your colleagues to support the President's FY 2008 request of $310 million for the placement of missile defense capabilities in Europe.

Thank you again for the opportunity to testify today and for holding this hearing on this important topic.

Mr. Wexler. Thank you both, gentlemen. I will begin.

As I have said on several occasions, Ambassador Fried, I do not think there is a more intellectually honest, shrewd, capable diplomat that our country is fortunate to have the service of than you. The argument that you present today, however, is somewhat incredulous. So help me understand why I am wrong and you are right.

First of all, there is not anything I, and I think most Members of Congress, would not do to assist our ally Israel in her defense of an external threat, particularly from Iran. But with all due respect, if I understand it correctly, a Ground-based Midcourse Defense System stationed in Poland and the Czech Republic, or anywhere else in Europe, will have no defense effect with respect to protecting or assisting Israel from protecting herself from Iran.

So, while we appreciate the description of the threat presented by Iran—and agree—this proposal for a missile defense system in Europe, unless you tell me otherwise, would seem to add zero in terms of defense capability for Israel versus Iran. It seems to me to be a somewhat deceptive argument to, in any way, bolster the cause for the European system by throwing in the threat to Israel.

Second, both gentlemen have very articulately outlined the arguments that have been made to our NATO allies, through the process of NATO, as to why this is a justified response.

Given the very complete descriptions that you have provided and the response by Mr. Jaap de Hoop Scheffer and the apparent responses of our allies in NATO, that begs the question: Why not do it through NATO? If the reception is so good, then do it through NATO. Why on a bilateral basis?

The third aspect that I would raise in terms of the capability and the testing of the system is, if I understand it correctly, that the system we have developed/deployed in Alaska and California is a three-part system. The system that is to be proposed to be deployed in Europe is a two-stage configuration, different than what we have in Alaska and in California. If I understand it correctly, the two- stage configuration has not been tested at all.

If that is the case, how can we make any assertion as to the reliability of the two-stage system?

Please.

Ambassador Fried. Mr. Chairman, the question about the relationship to Israel brings me back 30 years to deterrence theory and strategic nuclear issues that I studied many, many years ago. Let us start, though, with Ahmedinejad's statement which I quoted to you.

He may be an extremist, but he is not stupid. What he was telling the Europeans is Iran may be in a position to threaten Israel, and I will make sure that Iran is in a position to threaten you so that you cannot come to Israel's assistance. In classic nuclear strategy, the purpose of ballistic missiles was not simply to attack; it was to undercut the political will of your adversary, divide your enemies, and isolate your genuine target.

The situation we want to avoid is one where Europe would be in a position of absolute vulnerability to an Iranian nuclear arsenal, even a small one, thereby decoupling transatlantic security and also giving Iran an ability to use its other forces in support for terrorism in the Middle East and perhaps, at some point, conventional forces to threaten Israel. We do not want Iran to be able to use a nuclear arsenal to extend its power or to threaten Europe. That is the relationship, the configuration, that we wish to avoid. That is the first answer.

Secondly, NATO. There are, actually, very few NATO-wide systems. NATO brings together national military systems. The only current existing NATO system is an AWACS system. The Bush administration has proposed and the allies have accepted a C–17 transport system, a NATO-like system. The NATO missile defense system that is already being developed would bring together national mid-range missile defense systems. In our conception—and John and I have agreed that this is something we are still thinking through—NATO could bring together national systems, short/midrange systems, plus the American system, if it is agreed with the Poles and Czechs, so that you would have an integrated and complete missile defense system which would cover all of the Alliance.

Now, we have discussed this with NATO, and especially in the last 3 weeks, we have seen a real change in the attitude of European governments as we have presented more comprehensively what could be a genuinely multilateral approach by integrating national systems and NATO systems and, hopefully, even a system with Russia, depending on the Russian view. And we hope to be able to work through NATO and do this as multilaterally as possible, but it is certainly well within NATO standard practice that the Alliance helps integrate national systems. That is not unusual at all.

Mr. Rood. Mr. Chairman, may I respond to a couple of the points that you made?

Mr. Wexler. Of course.

Mr. Rood. You had talked about Israel's security and our concerns about it, and I think we in the administration are obviously very concerned about our friends and allies' security, but what I would urge you to think about here in the missile defense area is that we and the Israelis have taken a similar approach to the development of missile defenses. There were some concerns expressed by the members about perhaps rushing systems to the field too soon. Are they adequately tested?

In Israel, we have a joint program with them called the Arrow Missile Defense System. That system was very important for Israel's security, and Israel took an approach in their development and fielding like we have in the United States. You will recall they began fielding the system, deploying it, in 2000 when they put out a radar before they had any interceptors. They began with the deployment of the first interceptor as soon as the first interceptor was available, while testing was continuing, because they face a real and growing threat, as we do in the United States.

That is why we moved in the early part of this administration to begin putting capabilities in the field, in Alaska and California, while our very robust test program continued. The Israelis have continued with their test program, and it will continue for some time. We think it is a rigorous program. In some cases, they have used simulated targets. Their tests are always done in controlled conditions, as our tests are. That is the reason for experimentation. You need to know the results of that testing.

I would urge you in your review of the administration's budget request, whether it be the Arrow program or ours, to show support for that approach, because we do face these real and growing threats. Had we not taken that approach, we would not have had a missile defense system last summer that we could activate in the face of North Korean launch preparation activity with an unknown payload and unknown intentions. In that case, missile defense has proved very stabilizing.

One of the other points that was made in the members' opening comments was that the fielding of missile defenses might increase the risk of terrorists smuggling a nuclear weapon into the United States. I would say again, in Israel they have faced this issue as we have. What you saw last summer is a terrorist group, Hezbollah. Its weapon of choice was one of rockets and missiles, and the reason was Israel lacked a defense against those shorter- range systems. They are working to put that in place now. They feel as though that is a gap that they would like to fill. But I would not say that because one threat exists and you deal with it that you do not have to deal with another. We have to deal with both of those, the possibility that nuclear weapons could be smuggled into the United States.

That is why we have the Domestic Nuclear Detection Office, at the Department of Homeland Security, and other efforts; and we need to do better at those things, but clearly, we cannot ignore the fact that our adversaries are investing in ballistic missiles with long ranges and not deal with that threat as well.

So thank you, Mr. Chairman.

Mr. Wexler. I appreciate both of the gentlemen's answers. I will now go to Mr. Royce, but I would just ask either gentleman, in the context of this hearing, if you could address, where it may be appropriate, the difference between the two-stage configuration and the three-stage configuration in the testing.

Mr. Royce, please.

Mr. Royce. Thank you, Mr. Chairman.

I was in Israel in August to witness the lack of effectiveness in terms of being able to respond to these rockets and to the missile attacks, including the missile attacks on one of the Israeli ships, and the consequences of that were very, very grave. I was in Haifa when the town was attacked, and I went down afterwards to the trauma hospital, which was also targeted, and saw the consequences there. There were about 500 people hospitalized in that trauma center.

I wanted to make a couple of points. The first is, since 2001, the Missile Defense Agency has had 26 successful missile intercepts; 15 of the last 16 flight tests have been successful.

My second point is that it will not work if we do not fund it. Missile defense is a system of systems that is constantly being upgraded and improved, and we have to recognize that.

I would like to focus on the Iranian threat for a moment, and I would like to focus on it because one of the consequences of being in Israel at that time was finding out that, in terms of those firing those missiles, not only were many of the missiles Syrian—all of the missiles were either Syrian- or Iranian-manufactured—but some of the missiles were actually fired by Iranian crews. In particular, we know that the missile that hit the Israeli ship off the coast of Israel was fired by an Iranian crew, and we also know that, as positions were overrun, Iranian IDs were found on many of the combatants. So I would like to focus on that threat.

What are the trend lines in the Iranian program? That is my first question because, according to unclassified U.S. intelligence assessments, including the assessment you gave today, they may be able to develop long-range ballistic missile capabilities by 2015.

Here is the point I would like to make. What confidence do you have in 2015? Because I recall the North Korean Taepo Dong 1 missile, and we had unclassified material on that. That missile was launched in 1998, and as I recall, that was many years ahead of the intelligence estimates of when it would be launched. So my first question: How confident are you that it is going to take all the way to 2015 for them to have that capability in Iran?

Mr. Rood. Well, I think, Mr. Royce, you raise an important question, which is our intelligence estimates are based on projections of when Iran could acquire this capability on its own, perhaps with some foreign assistance. A key determinant of how rapidly Iran might progress, of course, would be that foreign assistance, but as I mentioned in my testimony, there is also the possibility that Iran could procure a completed system from North Korea as it has done in the past. North Korea possesses ICBM-range missiles. It is certainly possible that another sale like that could occur in the future. We in the United States would take other efforts to try to prevent that, but that would potentially move the date up further beyond 2015, but depending on the amount of foreign assistance Iran might receive, you might also see that time frame move up.

To the third point, these are estimates by intelligence analysts trying to project trends in the future. Estimates are sometimes not accurate, despite the best efforts of those making them, and so missile defense provides a means by which we could hedge against that concern. I would point out that we are hoping to complete the fielding of these assets in Europe by 2013, just slightly before when the threat might emerge from Iran in 2015. We prefer to be ahead of the threats. There are some who would say wait until the threat is fully present before we would deploy something. We would prefer to have defense capabilities in advance of when our adversaries can threaten us.

Mr. Royce. As I say, I was there for about a week in Haifa during that struggle between Hezbollah and Israel, and during that period of time, I saw what happened to Haifa. Those missiles could not reach Tel Aviv or Jerusalem. I can only imagine what would have happened to that state if they had had that capability.

As you say, they could not reach this on their own or perhaps with North Korea, but I want to throw out another possibility here because, more than once, the International Institute for Strategic Studies out of London has proved right on this, and Mark Fitzpatrick is a pretty well-respected voice on Iran's nuclear missile programs. He told the *Financial Times* the Iranians are developing a long-range missile with Russian technology, and of course, Russian technology as opposed to North Korean technology is a real shot in the arm here.

I wanted to know if you thought that might be an accurate statement, or if you knew of any other sources for outside support besides Russia and Iran. From your comment, I think we can conclude that 2015 is a bit deceptive, especially in light of what we found in North Korea about the capability for them to bring their system on line before we anticipated it.

Before we go to your answer, also a House Armed Services subcommittee has withheld funding for the interceptors in Poland but has provided funding for the Czech Republic. We will see how this develops. But if this holds that they cut off the funds, how does that affect, first, operational capabilities of the system; and second, how will that affect your negotiations with the Poles?

Those were my questions, Mr. Chairman.

Mr. Rood. Congressman, I have also visited Haifa recently and have met with the mayor and others there, and I think it is important to bear in mind the effect that those attacks had with rockets and missiles on the population there. The mayor of Haifa told me he and his people had not had to experience this sort of threat despite all of the difficulties that have occurred in that region in the world over time. Even now, many months after that conflict has occurred, he told me that there are children; other members of the society are still coping with the after-effects of those attacks, and this is an important thing that the municipality is trying to deal with.

Obviously, the ability to provide a defense and not have to weather a barrage of rockets and missiles like that is clearly preferable in terms of the manner of dealing with that threat.

With respect to your other questions about the Iranians and their receipt of foreign aid, I would say ballistic missile-related co-operation from entities in China, North Korea, and Russia over the years has helped Iran move forward toward its goal of becoming self-sufficient in the production of ballistic missiles. That is a real concern for us because of the expertise that can be transferred and the effect that can have, then, not only for the Iranian program but on what expertise and capabilities Iran might provide to other states.

Finally, with respect to your question about the House Armed Services Committee's action yesterday, we obviously would like to see the Congress fully fund the President's request. I think if we were left in the situation where at the opening of the negotiations the Congress were moving to cut those, obviously that will undermine the negotiations. It will present issues for us in our discussions with those allies, and at a time when the NATO allies have responded so positively to our recent discussions, I would urge against taking such a step.

Mr. Royce. Well, I know the vote in the last Congress was 301 against cutting off those funds, 124 in favor.

I would just say, of course, if Russia is aiding Iran in this, its opposition to our deployment of a missile defense system is somewhat audacious, especially in light of the former Defense Minister, who at the time was Sergei Ivanov, admitted—and this was in April—that the deployment posed no medium-term threat to Russia.

So the Russians understand what we are trying to do here; it is to offset what Iran is developing. And I think, in light of that, we have to be especially vigilant about their support, given their past activities of the Iranian programs.

Thank you very much.

Mr. Wexler. Thank you very much.

I, too, was in Israel during the second week of the war. The only point I would like to make is that a ballistic missile defense system is not designed in any way, if I understand it correctly, to protect against the short-range system and rockets that were hailed upon Israel during the last war. That is not to say it will happen in the future.

Mr. Royce. That is correct, Mr. Chairman.

Mr. Wexler. Right.

Chairman Sherman.

Mr. Sherman. Thank you.

Mr. Rood, my staff tried to secure you for hearings our subcommittee was going to have on proliferation in general. We were told that, as is the custom, you are unavailable to testify until you are confirmed as Under Secretary. I am thrilled to see you here.

Can you commit to coming back later this month or sometime in June for hearings on general proliferation issues?

Mr. Rood. I would be happy to try to work with your staff to look at a time and the appropriate venue and so on.

Mr. Sherman. We will get something that works for schedules.

Mr. Rood, you say that the system that is going to be deployed in Poland and in the Czech Republic would be useless against Russian missiles because it is too slow to catch them. Does that mean that that defense system would be utterly useless against an accidental Russian launch?

Mr. Rood. Mr. Chairman, the interceptors that would be placed in Poland and in the Czech Republic, based on our operation of the system, will not be fast enough to—they will have little or no capability against Russian ICBMs.

When we do the modeling—the Missile Defense Agency does this—from the time that we can detect——

Mr. Sherman. Well, I have got limited time.

You are saying that whether it is a deliberate Russian launch or whether it is an accidental Russian launch, it is highly unlikely that this system would be hitting a Russian missile, correct?

Mr. Rood. As for the use of the interceptors in Poland and in the Czech Republic, those interceptors would have little or no capability against Russian ICBMs launched against the United States.

Mr. Sherman. Even an accidental launch. They are little to no use against an accidental launch.

Mr. Rood. However, the system that we have deployed in Alaska and in California would have some capability against that.

Mr. Sherman. Well, our focus here, joined by the chair of the Europe Subcommittee, is Europe.

So, by using the term "little or no," you are basically saying that it would have a little bit of an effect against an intentional Russian launch, that they would lose a little bit of their intentional nuclear capacity.

Why wouldn't they be worried about that? Why do they go to the cost of building, say, 100 missiles if 20 percent of them or 10 percent of them or a little portion of them, if you will, is going to be destroyed by our system? Wouldn't that worry them?

Mr. Rood. I would not say it is 10 or 20 percent. Remember, the Russians have thousands of nuclear warheads, and so ten interceptors would have little or no capability against those. But the part that I would say is——

Mr. Sherman. Now we are told that the Iranians are getting Russian technology. Why would a Russian-designed missile launched from Iran—why would that missile be susceptible to this defense system while a Russian-designed missile out of Russia would not be susceptible?

Mr. Rood. That is because the geography is very different, and therefore, the placement of the interceptors and radar in the Czech Republic and Poland have been chosen in order to optimize the coverage of both the United States and Europe against a long-range missile attack. Because of the geometry and the location of those facilities, it would have a very good capability against entering——

Mr. Sherman. Aren't there some Russian facilities and missiles located in the same region of the world as Iran; that is to say, Central Asia?

Mr. Rood. Russian ICBM facilities in Central Asia outside of Russia?

Mr. Sherman. No. Siberia and the Urals in non-European Russia.

Mr. Rood. The Russians have missile facilities in their Far East, yes.

Mr. Sherman. Well, not the Far East but the middle, what they do not call the "Middle East." The middle of Russia, right snap dab in the middle, is pretty much directly north of Iran.

Let me go on to another line of questioning. It is my understanding that these missiles placed in the Czech Republic and in Poland are optimally located in order to defend the NATO population of Europe. And the majority of the NATO population lives in Europe, and that is the reason we would put them there rather than in Canada or closer to home or in other places. And we are told that the Europeans really want us to do this because—and you keep quoting the same statement—they acknowledge that ballistic missiles are a threat. Well, there are lots of threats and lots of ways to respond to them, but in all of my conversations with Europeans off the record, with the exception of Poles and Czechs, they hate this system.

If it is there predominantly to defend the European NATO population, how much money are Germany and France willing to put up to pay for a system that does more to protect Paris than it does to protect Chicago?

Mr. Rood. I think in the first part of your question——

Mr. Sherman. Have they offered any money so far, sir?

Mr. Rood. If I can address your question, in the first year of the administration, we thought it was important to move beyond a unilateral approach to missile defense, to pursue missile defense cooperation with our friends and allies. That is why we dropped the "N" from National Missile Defense to make clear that we were interested in cooperation with our allies.

Mr. Sherman. Mr. Secretary, I am going to reclaim my time. I am just going to ask which European countries have offered how much money, and if you cannot respond with the name of a country and an amount of money, I will assume that no European country has offered a specific amount of money, with the exception of the basing rights being provided perhaps by the Czechs and Poles.

Mr. Rood. Well, I think what we have seen is that our allies who we are planning to negotiate this system with are interested in making a contribution. It is meaningful that they would host these facilities on their territory. Real estate and other things are important contributions, and it is important that we not overlook the fact——

Mr. Sherman. So that is with regard to the Poles and Czechs. As to France, Germany, and the nations of old Europe, the reason we would say that the majority of the NATO population lives in Europe is because of the population of Western Europe.

Which country west of the old Warsaw Pact has announced that they are going to contribute materially to this system which is better designed to defend Berlin and to defend Paris than it is to defend Chicago?

Mr. Rood. I would take issue with your characterization that the system is better designed to protect Berlin than it is Chicago. I think that we see the system as very effective in protecting the United States and that that is a key purpose of it. It will significantly improve the defense of the United States if we are able to have interceptors and a radar in Europe, because it significantly improves the battle space and performance of the system. We would be happy to have some simulations and other things shown to you to demonstrate——

Mr. Sherman. In any case——

Mr. Rood. But with respect to your point——

Mr. Sherman.—you came here and told us how much it would defend Europe, how it would liberate Europe to help Israel in a time of danger; and yet you cannot identify a single euro that will be contributed by any of the nations of the richer part of Europe, by Western Europe.

Mr. Rood. We are told we have not asked those countries to contribute.

Mr. Sherman. Why not? We are trying to run a country here with a huge deficit. Would you really come to Congress and say, "Give us the money for this system. Yet, we have not bothered to send a letter to Paris or to Berlin, asking for a penny or a euro"? I mean, come on.

Is there any fiscal responsibility if there are a few—if there is money there, ask for it, and the only reason not to ask for it is if you are convinced that they are going to laugh at your letter. Based on my private conversations with you—I mean I try to be polite in public, but based on the private conversations, the reason you have not invested a postage stamp to ask for a euro is you figure it is not even worth the cost of a postage stamp.

Is there any evidence that old Europe is going to contribute significantly to the cost of this program? Which, by the way, it is not just a few hundred million dollars. That is just the beginning.

Do you have an answer?

Ambassador Fried. Well, I would just point out that the NATO program, the Active Layered Theatre Ballistic Missile Defense program, is funded at NATO at 700 million euros, about $1 billion.

Mr. Sherman. Excuse me. We are here focusing on the program to put missile defense in Poland and in the Czech Republic. Has any nation in Western Europe offered a euro for that program?

Ambassador Fried. As my colleague said, we have not asked them about this program, but they are funding, without our assistance, their own national shorter-range programs.

Mr. Sherman. How could you possibly, representing a government with a huge budget deficit, come to us and ask for hundreds of millions of dollars when among the chief beneficiaries are Western Europe, and you have not bothered to ask them for a single euro?

Let me shift off to something else, and that is this theory that we are somehow defending Israel by allowing Europe to come to Israel's aid in its hour of need.

First of all, I think those of us familiar with European attitudes and actions toward Israel doubt very much whether European armies would be deployed to defend Israel in a time of need. But we are being told that the Europeans would be willing to do so, which seems odd because they have not now, and they do not face nuclear attack from Iran now. It is only if they had this missile defense system, which at best is like a 50/50 chance that you would lose Berlin.

Is there any evidence that Europeans, who have been able at the present time and in 1973 and in 1967 to send their armies to defend Israel at no risk of nuclear attack, would be willing to do so in the future when they face nuclear attack, perhaps, but they had the "might work, might not work, never been tested in battle" system that we plan to deploy in Poland and in the Czech Republic?

Ambassador Fried. I would be far more comfortable working with Europe to deal with potential Iranian pressures and threats in the Middle East if Europe were not absolutely vulnerable to potential Iranian ballistic missile attacks. Yes, I do think that is not only intuitively clear, I think it is a defensible strategic assertion. I would much rather—I would feel much more secure thinking about the Middle East if Europe were not under threat of an Iranian missile attack.

Mr. Sherman. I am reclaiming my time.

I will point out in Europe today—if I can just have 30 seconds. Mr. WEXLER. Sure.

Mr. Sherman. I just want to point out that it is somewhat disingenuous to have an administration that has just wanted missile defense so badly, for any reason or for no reason, that we are told that we are doing it to deal with the Iranians, knowing that this administration violates American law in order to protect foreign oil companies from a statute; namely, the Iran-Libya Sanctions Act, now the Iran Sanctions Act. When this administration has acquiesced in World Bank loans to Iran, it seems like the only thing we are actually going to do vis-a-vis Iran is to do something that the administration has just wanted to do really badly anyway.

With that, I yield back to the chairman.

Mr. Wexler. Thank you.

We have votes. If we could go to Mr. Royce for a quick question, then I have got a quick question. Then we will let the gentlemen respond to whatever they want to in total.

Mr. Royce. I appreciate it very much, Mr. Chairman.

It reads, just going to the page of the *Financial Times*, "'U.K. wants U.S. missile defense sites,' U.K. officials say. Tony Blair has pressed Washington to place at least some interceptors on British soil." It says, "'The U.K. Prime Minister is said to share U.S. concerns about the threat posed by missiles from states of concern. In the face of rogue states, this is something that can assist in Britain's defense,' a U.K. official said yesterday.''

One of the geographic realities is that the reason this should not be a concern to the Russians is because a Russian attack on the United States, because of its geographic position, comes over the polar caps, and that is why the Alaskan system and the other systems that we have to deal with or attempt to be a deterrent to a Russian threat.

But with Tehran's placement in an attack on Washington, DC, from Iran, the trajectory is over Warsaw, Poland to make that attack. So, if Iran were to attack Europe or to attack the United States, the placement of this system, where it would have to be placed, is in the Czech Republic and in Poland for maximum effectiveness. Also, the Danes have expressed their interest and some of their concerns.

I just want to go back to Ambassador Fried. Are there any remarks you might have in terms of why the Russians should not be concerned about the placement of this system?

Ambassador Fried. The ten unarmed interceptors planned for Poland are obviously not going to be an effective—will not effectively degrade any of the Russian strategic nuclear force. They physically, as John Rood said, cannot catch them. So I am comfortable being pretty categoric about the lack of any threat to the Russian offensive system.

Mr. Royce. We have the Russian Defense Minister on record with the same comment.

Ambassador Fried. I think there is no threat. I think the Russians know that. I think Secretary Gates heard two levels of concerns from the Russians when he was in Moscow. The first level was based on, perhaps, Russian misunderstanding of the capabilities of the system. The second level was based on Russian concerns that in the future this system could grow. Secretary Gates said he wanted to address those Russian concerns, and in addition to offering extensive cooperation with the Russians on missile defense, he said he looked forward to setting up experts' groups to discuss these Russians' mid- and longer-range concerns.

We have shared our proposals with the NATO allies. They were universally appreciative of our offer to the Russians, and we hope, despite the rhetoric, that the Russians will accept this.

Mr. Royce. In conclusion, I think they are just gaining diplomatic advantage in pressing this point, or we are pressing the point against them, not to assist Iran with their programs. And that looks to me like the real politic of what is going on in Europe with the Russian assertions.

Ambassador Fried. Well, it is true that, of some of us who remember the missile defense debates of 25 years ago or the Persia- 2 debates of the mid-1980s, there is something familiar about the Russian arguments designed to appeal to West Europeans, but I think we can get through that.

Mr. Wexler. Just very quickly, gentlemen, is it correct that the two-stage configuration system proposed for Europe has never been tested?

Mr. Rood. Congressman, the two-stage configuration that we are looking at has 98 percent of the same components as the three- stage configuration. So I would say that those components and that system have had testing as part of that.

The plan is to conduct two flight tests of the two-stage version prior to 2010. You will recall we are hoping to put in place these systems in Poland and in the Czech Republic by 2013, 3 years later. So that is, I guess, what I would offer in response to your question.

Mr. Wexler. So the two-stage system has not been tested, but your testimony is that it is comprised of almost all of the three- stage system; and therefore, testing of the two-stage system is not necessary? Or we can go forth with some degree of reliability without it?

Mr. Rood. My testimony would be that we not only think testing is required—we have planned two flight tests prior to 2010 of that system—but since there is a high degree of commonality in the components, that provides some additional assurance. If you have further questions, we can ask the director of testing.

Mr. Wexler. I will tell you what. We have probably got about 1 minute. I want to give you an opportunity to respond to Mr. Sherman's statement earlier.

I think you would probably appreciate a response.

Mr. Sherman. I would. But I would also point out that a chimp is 99 percent similar to a human being in its DNA, and one would expect that you would not test one and figure you did not need to test the other. And I would also point out that given the way we have shredded the ABM Treaty, Russian fears that that system will grow seem more than fanciful.

With that, I would like to hear from the witnesses.

Ambassador Fried. I was thinking, Chairman Sherman, why I was not entirely comfortable with the line of argument that on every NATO program there must be a bill presented and divided up.

When the European allies moved forces into Albania 10 years ago to stabilize it, they did so; and in doing so, they helped all of our security. Yet they did not ask us to pay a portion of the cost. When we deployed Persia-2—planned to deploy Persia-2 missiles into Europe in response to the Soviet deployment of SS–20s, we did so, or proposed to do so, on a national basis, without European contributions. When the Germans are developing their mid-range missile defense system and shorter-range systems, they do not ask us to foot the bill, even though their systems will help protect U.S. assets and U.S. Forces. When the Poles sent off an additional battalion for combat duty in Afghanistan, they swallowed tremendous costs, for which we are grateful.

In our Alliance, I look to a balance of costs. I do not think, at each stage for each program, we start sending bills to each other. That is not a full answer; but I think in an Alliance, we take on different kinds of responsibilities. We look for allies to do their share. The Dutch in the south of Afghanistan, the British, the Poles, the Czechs, and many others are doing their part. We think that our part might be fielding a missile defense system which will defend Europe, and an Alliance is solidarity, not divided bill-paying. At least that is my view.

Mr. Wexler. I want to thank the witnesses very much.

The joint subcommittees stands adjourned.

[Whereupon, at 2:54 p.m., the subcommittees were adjourned.]

In: Options for Deploying Missile Defenses in Europe
Editor: Melissa V. Jordan pp.45-51

ISBN: 978-1-60741-889-4
© 2010 Nova Science Publishers, Inc.

Chapter 4

KINETIC ENERGY KILL FOR BALLISTIC MISSILE DEFENSE: A STATUS OVERVIEW*

Steven A. Hildreth

SUMMARY

For some time, U.S. ballistic missile defense (BMD) programs have focused primarily on developing kinetic energy interceptors to destroy attacking ballistic missiles. These efforts have evolved over 30 years and have produced a significant amount of test data from which much can be learned. This chapter provides a broad overview of the U.S. investment in this approach to BMD.

The data on the U.S. flight test effort to develop a national missile defense (NMD) system remains mixed and ambiguous. There is no recognizable pattern to explain this record nor is there conclusive evidence of a learning curve over more than two decades of developmental testing. In addition, the test scenarios are considered by some not to be operational tests and could be more realistic in nature; they see these tests as more of a laboratory or developmental effort. Success and failure rates (and their technical causes) have shown relative consistency through this period.

The U.S. flight test effort to develop theater missile defense (TMD) systems appears more promising. In relative terms, developmental and operational testing of TMD systems has been more successful than the NMD effort. Nonetheless, TMD systems that evolved from mature, existing ground and sea-based air-defense systems have demonstrated greater test success than other TMD programs.

How effective has the U.S. investment been in developing kinetic energy BMD systems? Observers could make any number of arguments as to what the record means and what could be done to improve the effectiveness of systems under development and of those deployed. Some observers have suggested that the 110th Congress might review the U.S. investment in

---

* This is an edited, reformatted and augmented version of a CRS Report for Congress publication dated January 2007.

the kinetic energy concept to date to determine how best to proceed with the U.S. BMD effort in the coming years.

INTRODUCTION

The U.S. effort to develop and deploy ballistic missile defenses (BMD) based on the concept of hit-to-kill or kinetic energy kill[1] began three decades ago.[2] This effort gained momentum as the primary focus of the U.S. BMD program in the mid-1980s with the announcement of President Reagan's Strategic Defense Initiative (SDI).[3] Since that time, the United States has pursued numerous major kinetic energy BMD programs; these have produced hundreds of various flight test results. These test results and some very limited operational experience in wartime provide sufficient data for at least some conclusions regarding the decades-long U.S. investment in hit-to-kill as a concept for BMD. This overview report examines the U.S. investment in that concept, what that investment has produced, and raises various questions that might be considered. The development of BMD has shown important technological differences between efforts designed to attack and destroy short or medium-range ballistic missiles and those designed for long-range or intercontinental ballistic missiles.[4] Therefore, this chapter will review and distinguish between the program results of theater missile defense (TMD) and national missile defense (NMD).

CRS received historical flight test data[5] from the Missile Defense Agency (MDA) in June 2005.[6] It is important to note that for each of these flight tests there were various primary and multiple secondary objectives.[7] Such flight tests are inherently complex and relatively costly. Therefore, multiple test objectives are designed to maximize the potential benefit derived from each flight test. The determination as to whether each of these objectives was reached was made by each relevant agency or military branch. All of the references to flight test results in this chapter are derived from the Flight Tests Results memorandum provided by the MDA unless otherwise referenced. CRS currently is awaiting an update of the historical flight test data from MDA.

Summary of Analysis

Analysis of flight test data shows that the U.S. effort to develop, test, and deploy effective BMD systems based on this concept has produced mixed and ambiguous results. The actual performance in war-time of one kinetic-energy system currently deployed by the United States (i.e., the Patriot PAC-3) is similarly ambiguous. Further, it is not yet possible to assess the operational effectiveness the other deployed system (i.e., the National Defense System) against long-range ballistic missile threats.

LONG-RANGE BALLISTIC MISSILE DEFENSE

The United States has pursued four major kinetic energy interceptor long-range BMD or NMD programs since the early 1980s: Homing Overlay Experiment (HOE), Exoatmospheric

Reentry Interceptor Subsystem (ERIS), National Missile Defense (NMD), and Ground-based Midcourse Defense (GMD). Each of these is briefly discussed below.

The Army developed HOE in the late 1970s and early 1980s to test the viability of the emerging hit-to-kill concept. It conducted four intercept flight tests in 1983 and 1984. Three of the tests failed to intercept the intended target,[8] but the fourth was considered a success. The Army did not identify any secondary flight test objectives. Nonetheless, the nascent SDI program then viewed the single reported success as evidence of the promise of non-nuclear BMD interceptor technologies.

The technologies tested in HOE served as the basis for its successor program, ERIS. ERIS went through a lengthy development program before flight testing began in 1991 with the first of four intercept flight tests. Although the first was considered a successful intercept of the target, the following three intercept attempts through 1992 failed to destroy their intended targets.[9] Even so, officials concluded that half of the primary and secondary test flight objectives were accomplished, and that the primary BMD concept being pursued held significant promise.

The NMD program followed ERIS with a series of eight flight tests from 1997 to 2001. The first three were planned "fly-by" tests. There were no intercept attempt objectives. The first one failed to launch; however, the other two were deemed successful in their primary objectives. No secondary objectives were identified. Of the five planned intercept attempts, three reportedly intercepted their intended targets; one ended in failure because the interceptor kill vehicle did not deploy and the other failed because the on-board sensors designed to track and intercept the target failed. Officials concluded that 17 of the 20 primary objectives were met or partially met and all the secondary objectives by the planned intercept tests were met.

The current GMD program (NMD's successor) began flight testing in 2002. Since that time six flight tests have taken place. Five of these flight tests were planned intercept attempts, with three resulting in failure to intercept.[10] Officials concluded that about 80% of the program's 40 or so primary intercept flight test objectives were met; all the secondary objectives were met fully or partially. In 2004, the GMD undertook a new configuration with a different booster and interceptor. It flew a successful integration flight test (non-intercept test) in early 2004 with all primary and secondary objectives met. This system was deployed in Alaska and California in 2004 and declared operational after eight missiles were placed in silos. Subsequently, two planned intercept flight tests in December 2004 and February 2005 failed to launch. The currently deployed system thus remains to be tested successfully against targets it might be expected to intercept. In September 2006, a successful flight test exercise of the GMD system too place. Although not a primary objective of the data collection test, an intercept of the target warhead was achieved. Flight tests whose primary objectives are intercepts were scheduled for later in 2006, but have been delayed into 2007.

Each of the four NMD programs were different, but they built on the limited successes of their predecessors. Of the eighteen or so attempted intercepts since the early 1 980s, seven of them were considered successful, or roughly a 39% intercept rate in tests. Officials cited several reasons, including program hardware and software, as well as interceptor silo and target launch failures.[11] From that, there do not appear to be any recognizable patterns that emerge to account for the mostly unsuccessful history of the effort. Nor is there conclusive evidence of a learning curve, such as increased success over time relative to the first tests of the concept 20 years ago.

Program supporters can point to limited evidence that, under controlled conditions, there is reason to support the contention that kinetic energy interceptor technology for use against long-range ballistic missiles holds promise. Critics of the flight test effort to date,[12] whether they support missile defense or not in general, can raise questions about the success rate and the realism of the testing effort, given a generation of U.S. investment in its development.

Can kinetic energy interceptor technologies for use against long-range ballistic missiles be developed successfully and deployed as an effective part of the U.S. military posture? The answer appears to be ambiguous at this juncture. Can the now- deployed NMD system protect the United States from long-range ballistic missile attacks? Currently, there is insufficient empirical data to support a clear answer.

THEATER MISSILE DEFENSE (TMD)

There have been a number of major kinetic-energy TMD programs since the early 1990s: Extended Range Intercept Technology (ERINT), Flexible Lightweight Agile Guided Experiment/Small Radar Homing Intercept Technology (FLAGE/SRHIT), Navy Lightweight Exoatmospheric Projectile (LEAP), the Navy Aegis BMD, Patriot PAC-3, and Theater High Altitude Area Defense (THAAD). Each of these are briefly examined below.

The Army's FLAGE/SRHIT program conducted eight flight tests from 1984-1987 to prove the feasibility of lower atmosphere intercepts. Five of these flight tests were planned intercept attempts. From the data provided by MDA all the primary and secondary test objectives in the series were achieved. The targets included stationary targets in the atmosphere and an air-launched target. Only one target, however, was a short-range missile. The degree to which any conclusions might be drawn regarding very short-range hit-to-kill in this effort is therefore limited.

Building on the SRHIT effort, the Army's ERINT flight test program (1992-1994) conducted five flight tests. Three of these were planned intercepts; two of these three flight tests successfully intercepted their targets (the failure cited was hardware related). Despite the missed intercept, the Army concluded that all of its primary test objectives for the three tests were met fully or partially, and that all but one of the 26 secondary objectives in the three tests were met. As far as the two non-intercept flight tests were concerned, the Army determined that all of its primary and secondary flight test objectives were met.

The Navy developed its own indigenous LEAP program, which flight tested from 1992-1995. Three non-intercept flight tests achieved all primary and secondary objectives. Of the five planned intercept tests, only the second was considered a successful intercept, however. Failures were due to various hardware, software, and launch problems. Even so, the Navy determined that it achieved about 82% of its primary objectives (18 of 22) and all of its secondary objectives in these tests.

Building on some of its previous efforts in SRHIT and ERINT, the Army's THAAD program nevertheless experienced significant challenges from 1995 to 1999. After three relatively successful non-intercept flight tests (almost all of the primary and secondary test objectives were partially or fully met), THAAD failed to intercept in seven of its nine planned attempts. However, the THAAD intercept flight test program met about half of its primary and secondary objectives. Because the last two intercepts were successful (the last being in

1999), the Department of Defense and Congress agreed to further develop, but revamp, the THAAD program. The current THAAD program is a redesign of the former THAAD system. Recently, the program conducted its first flight test (non-intercept) to examine the launch, boost, and fly-out functions of the THAAD missile. MDA officials considered this test successful.[13]

The Army's Patriot (Phased Array Tracking to Intercept of Target) program has a history dating to the 1960s as an air-defense weapon. Only in the mid-to-late 1 980s at the insistence of Congress was the program given a specific anti-missile role.[14]

Using a focused explosive charge (non-nuclear and not hit-to-kill technology), Patriot PAC-2's (Patriot Antitactical Capability) 1991 Desert Storm performance remains controversial. After the war, Patriot improvements for missile defense were widely supported. Testing of the Patriot PAC-3 with a kinetic energy interceptor began in 1997. After the initial two successful non-intercept flight tests (most of the objectives were met), the Patriot PAC-3 attempted 27 intercept tests, of which 21 (about 78%) were considered successful intercepts. Additionally, some 92% of the primary intercept test objectives were met, as well as almost all of the known secondary objectives. In terms of actual wartime use, the Patriot PAC-3 was used in Operation Iraqi Freedom (OIF) in 2003, but its role was very limited (four missiles fired in two successful engagements) and thus, while suggestive of significant promise, its operational effectiveness remains uncertain based on limited empirical data.[15]

Building on its previous efforts as well,[16] the Navy (as of mid-2005) had conducted six (of seven) successful intercept tests of its Aegis BMD (or Navy sea- based) program using the Standard Missile-3 (SM-3) Block 1 missile (2002-2005).[17] The most recent test included in the data sheets provided to CRS was against a warhead target that separated from the booster rocket itself, in contrast to earlier intercept tests against SCUD-type ballistic missiles. The most recent flight test intercept attempt (in December 2006) was not completed due to technical problems aboard the Aegis cruiser involved prior to the launch of the two interceptor missiles themselves.

Primarily because of the Patriot PAC-3 flight test and operational record and the more recent Navy BMD program, the concept of hit-to-kill for TMD appears promising. Older TMD efforts were not as suggestive, and the foundation for the current THAAD program is based mostly on prior test failures. Nonetheless, because there is no flight test data yet on the current THAAD program, nothing conclusive can be said about its potential future for success. And, although the Patriot PAC-3 shows promise, some might note that the Patriot system itself has been evolving for about 40 years now. Additionally, much of the Navy infrastructure and technology supporting the Aegis SM-3 is decades old and is comparable in evolution to the Patriot air and missile defense system.

CONCLUSION

A central question might be: at this stage how well is the United States doing in developing effective ballistic missile defenses based on this kinetic energy kill concept? Since the announcement of the SDI program in the mid-1980s the United States has spent about $100 billion on missile defense with a primary focus on the kinetic energy or hit-to-kill concept. U.S. programs began looking at that concept a decade earlier into the mid-1970s.

Supporters of hit-to-kill could argue that what the United States is striving to do has indeed proven to be challenging, but that progress is being made. Furthermore, success measured in terms of operationally effective deployed BMD systems based on this concept, loom on the horizon. They could also argue that threats posed from the proliferation of ballistic missiles and weapons of mass destruction (WMD) must be addressed by developing effective BMD systems.

Supporters and skeptics could argue the need for an independent, comprehensive evaluation of the test record to determine whether any systemic or conceptual challenges are impeding the U.S. effort. Although some defense officials have provided testimony and private and government agencies have looked in detail at a few of these tests, some might argue that a comprehensive and independent review of the entire record to date has not been undertaken and is warranted.[18]

Other observers might argue that alternatives should be pursued as a hedge against the possible failure of this concept for either NMD or TMD. Such alternatives could be military in nature, such as reducing the emphasis on BMD in favor of increased emphasis on counter-force (i.e., attacking and destroying enemy missile systems before their missile could be launched). Alternatives also could focus on other ways to mitigate ballistic missile proliferation (e.g., arms control). Some alternatives, such as a return to nuclear BMD concepts or emphasis toward more exotic technologies (e.g., lasers or weapons in space) might face opposition on political or technical grounds.

Still other observers could argue that in general the United States needs to make a more concerted effort to increase developmental testing across the board, before these systems are ready for more realistic testing regimes. They could argue that almost all the testing to date is of a developmental nature and that an operational testing regimen has not been developed, but remains essential. Only then, they could argue, could assessments to confirm the validity of the hit-to-kill concept for BMD be made with confidence.

End Notes

[1] Kinetic energy kill interceptors seek to destroy targets through a direct collision at high speeds. The force of the impact destroys the attacking missile or warhead, renders it inoperable, or diverts it from its intended target. With such an approach, a near-miss has the same effect as a large miss distance: the targeted warhead or missile is not destroyed. From its beginnings, kinetic energy kill concepts held the promise of destroying attacking missiles without the potential collateral effects of nuclear weapons explosions inherent in earlier BMD concepts and deployed systems.

[2] During the 1960s and early 1970s, the United States developed and tested a nuclear BMD interceptor capability. This system was deployed in North Dakota for a short time in 1975- 1976. This system was dismantled for many reasons, including congressional and military concerns over its cost ineffectiveness in the face of a potentially massive nuclear attack, concerns over the adverse effects that nuclear detonations would have on nearby ground based BMD radars, and growing support for agreed upon limitations of U.S. and Soviet long-range nuclear arsenals. In the FY1976 defense budget, the Army initiated a program to examine alternatives to nuclear BMD. A couple years later, this effort led to the first specific kinetic energy program that sought to avoid the problems of nuclear effects on ground-based BMD interceptors by seeking to place guidance and other sensors on a nonnuclear missile interceptor itself.

[3] On March 23, 1983, President Reagan delivered a policy address announcing the establishment of the Strategic Defense Initiative (SDI) or what was quickly dubbed by others the "Star Wars" program. In his speech the President expressed his vision that the nation's scientists could develop the means of rendering "nuclear weapons impotent and obsolete." Various contemporary and historical accounts confirm that the President intended the development of U.S. BMD to be non-nuclear as well. Initial funding for the SDI program began in FY1985.

[4] For instance, some of the technological challenges are different because of where the final engagement occurs (within the atmosphere or in space) and because the closing velocities of these engagements can vary significantly (between shorter and longer range attacking missiles).

[5] There are any number of tests on systems, sub-systems and components prior to any flight test of the actual missile and interceptor itself. Pre-flight test data are not included as part of this chapter.

[6] MDA, "Congressional Research Service Inquiry: Flight Test Results," June 21, 2005. For Official Use Only.

[7] For illustration, an intercept flight test might have as primary objectives to: 1) demonstrate integration of system elements; 2) demonstrate sensor operations; and 3) demonstrate kill vehicle performance (intercept the target). Secondary objectives might include 1) demonstrate test monitoring; 2) provide risk reduction for future tests; and 3) collect data for model verification. Most primary and secondary objectives could be met, even if the intercept objective failed, for instance.

[8] Two failed tests were deemed failures because of hardware related problems. The other intercept flight test reportedly failed due to software errors in the on-board computer.

[9] Each of the three failures was due to a different reason: the interceptor failed to launch, the target failed to launch, and the third attempt missed its intended target.

[10] In one test, the kill vehicle did not separate from the booster rocket, in the other two launch attempts the ground-based interceptor did not launch (once because of a software problem and more recently because of a problem with the missile silo).

[11] Although the causes of failures are varied (i.e., they include hardware, software, and interceptor and target launch problems) and do not necessarily suggest any systemic causes such as system integration, some might suggest that quality control throughout the manufacturing, systems integration and test preparation process could be a common root cause.

[12] On occasion, private organizations and others such as the Government Accountability Office (GAO) have released analyses of some of these tests. Sometimes they drew similar conclusions as those provided by the Missile Defense Agency. On other occasions, they took issue with the flight test results. Although many consider these efforts useful and constructive, because such studies lack a common framework for analysis and also do not examine all of the tests cited, their potential significance or meaning for the overall 30-year research effort is unclear. For instance, see GAO. BMD: Information on Theater High Altitude Area Defense (THAAD) and Other Theater Missile Defense Systems. GAO/NSIAD-94-167, May 3, 1994; GAO. BMD: Records Indicate Deception Program did not Affect 1984 Test Results; GAO/NSIAD-94-2 19, July 1994; and Federation of American Scientists, Chronology of Hit-to-Kill Missile Tests, by George Lewis, April 16, 1997, [http://www.fas.org].

[13] Missile Defense Agency Bills Last Week's THAAD Flight Test a Success, Inside the Pentagon, December 1, 2005.

[14] U.S. Library of Congress. Congressional Research Service. The Patriot Air Defense System and the Search for an Antitactical Ballistic Missile Defense. CRS Report 91-45 6F, by Steven A. Hildreth and Paul Zinsmeister, June 16, 1991.

[15] Nine Iraqi ballistic missiles were targeted by Patriot. Another six were launched but not targeted by Patriot because they were projected to land in areas that would not cause harm. The missiles that Iraq fired in 2003 were slower flying and of shorter range than those fired in 1991. The Defense Department concluded that the Patriot system successfully intercepted all nine missiles it targeted. Seven of the intercepts, however, were made with the older Patriot PAC-2 system (which still used a proximity warhead to destroy its target), while the remaining two were intercepted by the newer PAC-3. One Iraqi cruise missile reportedly eluded the Patriot radar and hit a sea wall in Kuwait City. And the Patriot system was also involved in three friendly fire incidents that resulted in the loss of a U.S. and British aircraft.

[16] The Navy program has evolved over several decades from a sea-based air defense and cruise missile defense capability to include ballistic missile defense.

[17] Sea-based Missile Defense "Hit To Kill" Intercept Achieved, News Release, Missile Defense Agency, November 17, 2005.

[18] One such review, performed by experts for the MDA, examined the flight test record of the NMD program and concluded among other things inadequate quality control in the flight test record was a factor. See Missile Defense Setbacks Stall Program, CNN.com, July 11, 2005.

In: Options for Deploying Missile Defenses in Europe
Editor: Melissa V. Jordan pp.53-74

ISBN: 978-1-60741-889-4
© 2010 Nova Science Publishers, Inc.

Chapter 5

LONG-RANGE BALLISTIC MISSILE DEFENSE IN EUROPE[*]

Steven A. Hildreth and Carl Ek

SUMMARY

Successive U.S. governments have urged the creation of an anti-missile system to protect against long-range ballistic missile threats from adversary states. The Bush Administration believed that North Korea and Iran represent strategic threats, and questioned whether they could be deterred by conventional means. The Bush Administration's position on this issue remained unchanged, even after the intelligence community assessed that the Iranian nuclear weapons program halted in 2003. The Bush Administration built long-range missile defense bases in Alaska and California to protect against adversary missile threats, especially North Korea. Although the system has been tested, most agree that further testing is necessary. The Bush Administration proposed deploying a ground-based mid-course defense (GMD) element of the larger Ballistic Missile Defense System (BMDS) in Europe to defend against an Iranian missile threat. The system would include 10 interceptors in Poland, a radar in the Czech Republic, and another radar deployed in a country closer to Iran, all to be completed by 2013 at a reported cost of at least $4 billion.

The proposed U.S. system has encountered resistance in some European countries and beyond. Critics in Poland and the Czech Republic assert that neither country currently faces a notable threat from Iran, but that if American GMD facilities were installed, both countries might be targeted by missiles from rogue states—and possibly from Russia. The Bush Administration signed agreements with both countries permitting GMD facilities to be stationed on their territory; however, the two countries' parliaments decided to wait to ratify the accords until after the Obama Administration clarified its intentions on missile defense

---

[*] This is an edited, reformatted and augmented version of a CRS Report for Congress publication dated January 2009.

policy. NATO has deliberated long-range missile defense, and has taken actions that many interpreted as an endorsement of the U.S. GMD system.

The GMD plan has also affected U.S.-Russia relations. Former President Putin and his successor, Vladimir Medvedev, have argued that the proposal would reignite the arms race and upset U.S.- Russian-European security relations. U.S. officials dispute Russia's objections, noting that the interceptors are intended to take out Iranian missiles aimed at Europe or the United States and could not possibly act as a deterrent against Russia. Some argue that Russia has been attempting to foment discord among NATO allies. In mid-2007, Russia offered to cooperate on missile defense, proposing the use of a Russian-leased radar in Azerbaijan, but urging that U.S. facilities not be built in Eastern Europe. President Bush welcomed the idea in principle, but insisted upon the need for the European sites. Despite ongoing discussions over the issue, sharp Russian criticism of the program has continued. Medvedev has said that Russia might deploy Iskander tactical missiles to Kaliningrad, but later stated that Moscow would not do so if the United States reversed its plan to emplace GMD facilities in Poland and the Czech Republic.

For FY2008, Congress examined the European GMD proposal and eliminated proposed funding for initial site construction pending formal agreement with Poland and the Czech Republic, independent studies on missile defense options for Europe, and DOD certification of the proposed interceptor. The FY2009 request for the European site was $712 million, which Congress largely supported with funding for site construction available only after Czech and Polish ratification.

INTRODUCTION

In the FY2008 defense budget, the Bush Administration requested about $310 million to begin design, construction, and deployment of a ground-based midcourse defense (GMD) element of the Ballistic Missile Defense System (BMDS) in Europe.[1] According to the Administration, the proposed GMD European capability would help defend U.S. forces stationed in Europe, U.S. friends and allies in the region, as well as to defend the United States against long-range ballistic missile threats, namely from Iran. For FY2009, the Administration requested $712 million for development, fielding, and military construction of the European GMD element.

The proposed system would include 10 silo-based interceptors to be deployed in Poland, a fixed radar installation in the Czech Republic, and another transportable radar to be deployed in a country closer to Iran. Deployment of the GMD European capability is scheduled to be completed by 2013 at a current estimated cost of $4 billion (includes fielding and Operation and Support), according to the Bush Administration.

The prospect of a GMD capability based in Europe raises a number of significant international security and foreign policy questions. Central to the debate for many is how the proposed U.S. system might affect U.S.-European-Russian relations. For FY2008, Congress eliminated funding to start construction of the European site pending final approval of international agreements with Poland and the Czech Republic and an independent study of alternative missile defense options for Europe.[2] Congress largely supported the Administration's request for FY2009, but restricted funding for site construction until after the Polish and Czech Parliaments ratify the agreements reached with the Bush Administration. Congress continued to withhold funding for deployment of the ground-based interceptor missiles until after the Secretary of Defense certifies to Congress that those interceptor missiles will work effectively.

The Obama Administration

During the 2008 presidential campaign, Senator Obama said he supported the deployment of ballistic missile defenses that were operationally effective. In her January 2009 nomination hearings for Undersecretary of Defense for Policy, Michele Flournoy said the Obama Administration will review plans to deploy elements of a missile defense system in Europe.[3] Flournoy said the plans should be reviewed as part of the QDR (Quadrennial Defense Review) and "in the broader security context of Europe, including our relations with Russia," noting that any final policy decision should consider it in the interest of the United States if Washington and Moscow could agree to cooperate on missile defense. Flournoy also said the final contours of any decision would require close consultations between the Administration and Congress. At his nomination hearing before the Senate Armed Services Committee for Deputy Secretary of Defense, William Lynn responded to a question suggesting he would support making the MDA's budgetary, acquisition, testing, and policy processes more open and similar to the military services. "I think that all our military programs should be managed through those regular processes," he said, and "that would include missile defense. I would think any exceptions should be rare and fully justified."[4] Representative Ellen Tauscher (D-Calif.), head of the House Armed Services Strategic Forces subcommittee, reportedly predicted such changes would be made in the new administration.[5] On the White House website, the Obama Administration says it "will support missile defense, but ensure that it is developed in a way that is pragmatic and cost- effective; and, most importantly, does not divert resources from other national security priorities until we are positive the technology will protect the American public."[6]

THE THREAT

The Bush Administration argued that North Korea and Iran constituted major strategic threats. North Korea claims to have tested a nuclear device and has a ballistic missile program. The Bush Administration argued that Iran continues to acquire and develop ballistic missiles of various ranges.[7] Until recently, the Bush Administration argued that Iran had an active nuclear weapons development program. In November 2007, a U.S. National Intelligence Estimate (NIE) stated that "in Fall 2003, Tehran halted its nuclear weapons program," but that Iran is also keeping open the option to develop nuclear weapons at some point. The Iranian nuclear weapons program reportedly also included developing a warhead that could fit atop an Iranian ballistic missile.[8]

The Bush Administration regarded both countries as unpredictable and dangerous, and did not believe they could be constrained by traditional forms of military deterrence, diplomacy, or arms control. On a trip to attend a meeting of NATO foreign ministers in early

December 2007, Secretary of State Rice told reporters: "I don't see that the NIE changes the course that we're on" to deploy a European missile defense system.[9] Accompanying her on the trip, Undersecretary of State John Rood, lead U.S. negotiator for the European missile defense talks, added: "the missile threat from Iran continues to progress and to cause us to be very concerned.... Missile defense would be useful regardless of what kind of payload, whether that be conventional, chemical, biological, or nuclear."[10]

According to long-standing unclassified U.S. intelligence assessments, Iran may be able to *test* an ICBM (Intercontinental Ballistic Missile) or long-range ballistic missile capability by 2015 if it receives foreign assistance, such as from Russia or China. Many in Congress and elsewhere share this specific assessment, or that the potential threat may not emerge by 2015 but is sufficiently worrisome to begin addressing it now. Many therefore believe it prudent to move forward with plans to deploy a long-range missile defense system in Europe to defend U.S. forward deployed forces in Europe, friends and allies, and the United States against long-range ballistic missile threats. Some in the larger international security policy and ballistic missile proliferation community argue that evidence of an Iranian ICBM program is scant and unpersuasive. Additionally, the Iranian government reports (which cannot be verified) that Iran has a limited missile capability with a range of about 1,200 miles[11] and that it has stopped development of ICBM range missiles.

Although some Europeans have expressed concern about Iran's suspected nuclear weapons program, some U.S. friends and allies in Europe question the Administration's assessment of Iran's potential ICBM threat. Hence, some question the need for a GMD element of the U.S. BMDS in Europe. In December 2008, the European Council of the European Union approved a two-year study of ballistic missile proliferation trends.

THE SYSTEM

The U.S. Department of Defense began deploying long-range missile interceptors in Alaska and California in late 2004 to address long-range missile threats primarily from North Korea. Currently, the U.S. GMD element of the BMDS includes about more than two dozen silo-based interceptors in Alaska and several in California. As part of an integrated Ballistic Missile Defense System (BMDS) capability, the United States also has a number of ground-based radars in operation around the world, space-based assets supporting the BMDS mission, command and control networks throughout the United States and the Pacific, as well as ground-mobile and sea- based systems for shorter-range BMD.

What remains necessary as part of the global BMDS, according to the Bush Administration, is an ability in the European theater to defend against intermediate-to-long-range ballistic missiles launched from Iran. The Department of Defense (DOD) argues it is important to U.S. national security interests to deploy a GMD capability in Europe to optimize defensive coverage of the United States and Europe against potential threats both into Europe and against the United States.

There have not been a large number of intercept flight tests of the deployed GMD element. Nonetheless, the Bush Administration and many U.S. military leaders expressed confidence in the deployed system.[12] Most agree there is the need for further operational testing. Some observers continue to question how much confidence there should be in the system's potential operational or combat effectiveness based on the types of tests conducted and the test results to date.

The current GMD program began flight tests in 2002. This effort was built on several earlier long-range BMD programs with decidedly mixed results themselves since the early 1980s. Since 2002, some GMD intercept flight tests have taken place with mixed results.[13] In each of these tests, most all other flight test objectives were met.

In 2002, the GMD moved to the operational booster and interceptor. The interceptor system flew two developmental tests in 2003 and 2004, and the GMD element of the BMDS was deployed in late 2004 in Alaska and California. Two planned intercept flight tests of the new configuration for December 2004 and February 2005 were not successful. After technical review, the interceptor successfully demonstrated a booster fly-out in 2005. In September 2006, a successful flight test exercise of the GMD element as deployed took place. (Although a missile intercept was not planned as the primary objective of this data collection test, an intercept opportunity occurred and the target warhead was successfully intercepted.) Additional intercept flight tests of the deployed element whose primary objectives were intercepts of long-range ballistic missile targets were originally scheduled for later in 2006, but then subsequently postponed. Then a May 2007 intercept test was scrubbed when the target missile failed to launch as planned. A follow-on attempt scheduled for summer 2007 was completed successfully on September 29, 2007. The Missile Defense Agency reported a successful intercept in December 2008, but some were critical of this assessment as the test objective was for the intercept to occur amidst a field of decoys, which decoys failed to deploy from the test target.

Supporters and many military officials express confidence in the deployed system, but others continue to question the system's potential effectiveness based on the mixed intercept flight test record. Most observers agree, however, that additional, successful flight testing is necessary. Supporters add that a significant number of non-flight tests and activities are conducted that demonstrate with high confidence the ability of the GMD element to perform its intended mission.[14]

What would the European element of the BMDS look like? The proposal is to deploy up to 10 Ground-based Interceptors (GBI) in silos at a former military base in Poland. It should be noted that the proposed GBI for the European GMD site will not be identical to the GBIs deployed now in Alaska and California. Although there is significant commonality of hardware, there are some differences. For example, the European GBI will consist of two rocket stages in contrast to the three-stage GBI deployed today.[15] This particular 2-stage configuration has not been tested and is a basis for additional questions about the proposed system's effectiveness. Proponents of the system would argue that the 2-stage version is fundamentally the same as the 3-stage system, however.[16] In Europe, the GBI reportedly will not need the third stage to achieve the range needed to intercept its intended target.[17] This issue has raised the question for some observers as to whether other U.S. systems designed for shorter or medium-range ballistic missile threats, such as Patriot, THAAD (Terminal High Altitude Area Defense), or Aegis (sea-based BMD) might be more appropriate for addressing the current and prospective Iranian ballistic missile threat to Europe. DOD's Missile Defense Agency (MDA) believes these systems would not be adequate to counter prospective Iranian ballistic missile threats over the mid-term and longer.

Deployment of the silos and interceptors in Poland is scheduled to begin in 2011 with completion in 2013. A final decision on specific locations took into consideration detailed site and environmental analyses, as well as an overall security and support assessment. The field of the 10 interceptors itself is likely to comprise an area somewhat larger than a football field. The area of supporting infrastructure is likely to be similar to a small military installation. In addition, an American X-Band radar (a narrow-beam, midcourse tracking radar), that was being used in the Pacific missile test range, would be refurbished and transported to a fixed site at a military training base in the Czech Republic. The X-Band radar with its large, ball-shaped radome (radar dome) is several stories in height. A second, transportable forward acquisition radar would be deployed in a country to be determined, but closer to Iran. Some European press accounts once mentioned the Caucasus region, but the Bush Administration never publicly indicated where this radar might be located. Additionally, the proposed GMD European capability would include a communications network and support infrastructure (e.g., power generation, security and force protection systems, etc.) A few hundred U.S. personnel would be engaged in securing and operating both the interceptor and radar sites. The Administration intends for the United States to have full command authority over the system.

The FY2008 request was $310.4 million for the proposed European GMD across several program elements of the Missile Defense Agency (MDA) budget. The total reported GMD costs for the European site are about $4 billion (FY2007-FY2013), including Operation and Support costs through 2013. Although relatively small in U.S. defense budget terms, the FY2008 request represented a significant commitment to the proposed European system. The FY2009 request was for $712 million.

In 2007, both the House and Senate Armed Services Committees asked for studies of alternatives to the Administration's proposed European GMD deployment (see "Congressional Actions"). This classified review was provided to Congress in August 2008. Some, such as Representative Tauscher, suggested the Administration consider instead a combination of sea-based (Aegis SM3) and land-based systems (PAC-3, THAAD). MDA Director General Henry Obering has argued that most of the current Aegis fleet would be required to defend Europe, and that the cost would be considerably greater than the current Bush Administration proposal.[18] MDA's assessments, however, assume the need for 24/7 coverage. Assessments based on deployment on a contingency basis or crisis reduce significantly the estimated cost of such alternatives. Separately, the Center for Naval Analyses (a federally funded research center) is conducting an analysis of alternatives for the Navy's next big surface combatant ship.[19] That review reportedly includes recommendations about future naval BMD requirements that might bear on any discussion of alternatives to the proposed European GMD plan.

THE LOCATION

In 2002 the Bush Administration began informal talks with the governments of Poland and the Czech Republic over the possibility of establishing missile defense facilities on their territory. Discussion of a more concrete plan—placing radar in the Czech Republic and interceptor launchers in Poland—was reported in the summer of 2006. The issue was increasingly debated in both countries. In January 2007, the U.S. government requested that formal negotiations begin. Agreements have been struck with both countries, and if the Polish and Czech parliaments approve the projects, construction on the sites could begin relatively soon, according to MDA officials. The two governments have grappled with several issues as the debate has evolved.

Poland

Some analysts maintain that in Poland the notion of stationing American GMD facilities was more or less accepted early on in the discussions and that the main questions subsequently have revolved around what the United States might provide Warsaw in return. Some Poles believe their country should receive additional security guarantees in exchange for assuming a larger risk of being targeted by rogue state missiles because of the presence of the U.S. launchers on their soil. In addition, many Poles are concerned about Russia's response. Both of the past two Polish governments reportedly requested that the United States provide batteries of Patriot missiles to shield Poland against short- and medium-range missiles.[20]

Formal negotiations on the base agreement, which will require the approval of the Polish parliament, began in early 2007 under the populist-nationalist Law and Justice (PiS) party, led by Jaroslaw Kaczynski. As talks began, Civic Alliance (PO), then the leading opposition party, had questions about the system—particularly the command and control aspects—and urged the government to ensure that it be integrated into a future NATO missile defense program. The former ruling leftist party supported deployment of the missiles, but also called for greater transparency in the decision-making process. The smaller parties of the governing coalition expressed some skepticism, mainly for reasons of sovereignty, and indicated support for a public referendum.[21]

In snap elections on October 21, 2007, Poles turned out PiS and replaced it with a center-right two-party coalition led by PO; its leader, Donald Tusk, became prime minister. During the campaign, Tusk indicated that his government would not be as compliant toward the United States as PiS, and that it would seek to bargain more actively on missile defense.

As he left office, former Prime Minister Kaczynski urged the incoming government to approve the missile defense proposal, arguing that an agreement would strengthen relations with the United States. In a post-election news conference, however, Tusk was cautious about the plan: "If we recognize that the anti-missile shield clearly enhances our security, then we will be open to negotiations.... If we recognize, jointly in talks with our partners from the European Union and NATO, that this is not an unambiguous project, then we will think it over." Two weeks later, however, newly minted Defense Minister Bogdan Klich stated that Poland should again "weigh the benefits and costs of this project for Poland. And if that balance results unfavorably, we should draw a conclusion from those results."[22] Foreign Minister Radek Sikorski later indicated that the new government would discuss the project with Russia.

Talks between Warsaw and Washington resumed in early 2008. Some observers forecast that the new Polish government would strongly renew the argument for the United States to provide additional air and/or short-range missile defenses.[23] On February 2, 2008, during a visit by Sikorski to Washington, D.C., U.S. Secretary of State Rice voiced support for strengthening Poland's air defenses. Although there was said to be agreement "in principle" on the missile defense issue, an accord was not signed when Prime Minister Tusk visited the United States in the following month.[24]

The major sticking point in the negotiations was the question of U.S. assistance for Poland's military "modernization," mainly in the form of PAC-3 air defense. During Prime Minister Tusk's visit to Washington DC in March 2008, however, President Bush declared, "Before my watch is over we will have assessed [Poland's] needs and come up with a modernization plan that's concrete and tangible." Nevertheless, the meeting of the two leaders did not result in a deal being struck. In addition, Poland has been anxious that the two projects not be too explicitly linked, for fear of further alienating Russia. Concerning the likely future of the program, Polish Ambassador to the United States Robert Kupiecki in spring 2008 told a Polish parliamentary committee that "there are serious reasons to think that the project will be continued" by Bush's successor, no matter whom it might be. A Czech newspaper reported that MDA Director Obering "said [on April 2 that] the United States will be interested in stationing the radar in the Czech Republic even if it does not reach agreement with Poland."[25] What this might have meant for the overall system without the interceptors sited in Poland was not clear. However, some suggested that the radar would be useful if used in conjunction with other medium-range BMD systems, such as Aegis, in the absence of GMD interceptors based in Poland. In addition, Bush Administration officials reportedly held discussions on the interceptor basing issue with the government of Lithuania.[26] In early July, the Polish media reported that a meeting in Washington between Foreign Minister Sikorski and Secretary Rice failed to produce an agreement.[27]

In a surprise move on August 14, Polish and U.S. government officials initialed an agreement; the formal accord was signed six days later by Rice and Sikorski. Some observers believe that the negotiations, which had stalled in July, received impetus from concerns over Russia's military incursion into South Ossetia in early August. While some U.S. officials denied an explicit linkage between the two events, U.S. Defense Secretary Gates on August 15 commented that Russia's neighbors have "a higher incentive to stand with us now than they did before, now that they have seen what the Russians have done in Georgia."[28] Under the agreement, Poland received from the United States enhanced security guarantees, which Minister Sikorski likened to a "kind of reinforcement of Article 5 [the NATO treaty's mutual defense clause]."[29] The United States also pledged to help modernize Poland's armed forces, in part by providing a battery of Patriot air defense missiles, which reportedly would be re-deployed from Germany and would initially be manned by U.S. military personnel.

Polls have consistently indicated that a majority of Poles disapprove of a missile defense base being established in their country. Most objections appear to be based on concerns over sovereignty, as well as over the belief that the presence of the system would diminish rather than increase national security and might harm relations with neighboring states and Russia. However, the Russian military action in Georgia and its subsequent threats to place tactical missiles in Kaliningrad (see below) may have increased support in Poland for the missile shield – and for the battery of Patriots.[30]

The Polish parliament did not immediately ratify the agreement. The speaker of the Polish parliament, Bronislaw Komorowski, said that he would not "rush" the vote, and added that "it would be worth knowing if the election result in the U.S. would have an influence on the U.S. attitude towards this program." In an August 19 news conference, Prime Minister Tusk said that he had requested Foreign Minister Sikorski to discuss missile defense with "both candidates John McCain and Barack Obama – and both conversations, although less decisively in the second case, indicated support for the project."[31] President Kaczynski's office criticized Prime Minister Tusk for delaying ratification until after elections. Despite the delay, U.S.-Polish negotiations on GMD continued. In addition, the Poles continued to hold high-level discussions with Moscow.[32]

Shortly after the U.S. elections, President-elect Obama spoke by phone with President Kaczynski; there was apparent confusion on the Polish side over whether or not President-elect Obama had made a commitment to continue with the GMD plan. During a meeting with residents of the village near which the interceptors would be based, U.S. Ambassador to Poland Victor Ashe reportedly said that the GMD project would likely be in suspension until such time as the Obama Administration had formulated its policies.[33]

In a mid-November 2008 interview, Foreign Minister Sikorski estimated the chances of the system's continuation at more than 50 percent. He added, however, that budgetary pressure might lead to the project being "put on hold" – a regrettable possibility, in his view. Sikorski has also noted that, "[t]here are clauses in the agreement that say it can be cancelled if there's no financing." During an address delivered in Washington in late November, Sikorski said that he hoped the GMD project would continue, as it was a sign of transatlantic cooperation. He also implied that hosting the interceptor base would bolster Poland's security, commenting that "everyone agrees that countries that have U.S. soldiers on their territory do not get invaded."[34] Polish President Kacyznski and Foreign Minister Sikorski both recently have expressed hope publically that the Obama Administration will continue the program.[35]

Some observers believe that Polish MPs, like their Czech counterparts, are reluctant to approve a treaty that may not be acted upon. Olaf Osica, a fellow at Warsaw's Natolin European Center, commented that "[o]ne of the worst scenarios for the Polish government would be if the agreement is ratified and then it turns out that Americans are no longer committed to it."[36]

Czech Republic

In September 2002, the Czech defense minister, a member of the Social Democratic Party (CS SD), announced that he had "offered the United States the opportunity to deploy the missile defense system on Czech soil."[37] In June 2006, inconclusive elections toppled the CSSD government and replaced it with a shaky coalition led by the center-right Civic Democratic Party (ODS). As with the outgoing government, the new one voiced support for GMD. However, the CSSD, now in opposition, began to backpedal on its support as polls showed increasing public skepticism, and by mid-2006 only the ODS was unambiguously backing deployment. When a relatively stable ODS-led government was finally formed in January 2007, the ODS apparently persuaded its coalition partners to support GMD (the Greens made their agreement contingent upon NATO approval). In January 2007, it was announced that the United States had requested that official negotiations be started, and in March the Czech government formally agreed to launch talks.

In October 2007, U.S. Defense Secretary Robert Gates visited Prague to discuss several issues— including the planned radar installation—with Czech leaders. During the visit, he reportedly proposed that, in the interest of transparency, Russia be allowed to station personnel at the radar site. Czech Prime Minister Topolanek had no immediate comment but appeared to concur with Gates's observation that the presence of Russians on Czech territory would have to be approved by Czechs first. Gates also suggested that activation of the missile defense system could be delayed until such time as there was "... definitive proof of the threat—in other words, Iranian missile testing and so on." On the same day, however, President Bush delivered a speech in which he called the need for the missile defense project "urgent." Some analysts argued that the U.S. proposal to include Russia might complicate Topolanek's efforts to secure approval for an eventual agreement with the United States.[38] On March 19, 2008, a State Department official announced that the Czech Republic had agreed to join in proposing to Russia an agreement that would permit reciprocal inspections of missile defense radar facilities. However, during an April 7 interview, Czech Foreign Minister Schwarzenberg said, "If Russians want to check something on our soil, they will have to speak with us first."[39]

On December 5, 2007, the Czech Foreign Ministry issued a statement asserting that the U.S. intelligence community's conclusion that Iran had suspended its nuclear weapons program in 2003 would not affect Prague's decision to host the radar facility, as the threat has the potential to re-emerge in the future.[40] In late January 2008, Jiri Paroubek, leader of the opposition CSSD party, argued that, because of the high and increasing public resistance to the radar, the government should freeze negotiations until after the results of the November 2008 U.S. presidential elections were known. He also urged that Prime Minister Topolanek report on the substance of his upcoming talks on the issue with President Bush.[41]

During a visit to Washington in late February 2008, Topolanek said that the two sides were "three words" away from an agreement. On April 3, 2008, during the NATO summit in Bucharest, Czech media reported that Foreign Minister Karel Schwarzenberg had announced that Prague and Washington had reached an accord over the terms of the proposed U.S. radar base, and that a treaty would be signed in May. The signing was postponed due to scheduling conflicts, and finally took place on July 8, during a visit by Secretary of State Rice. As part of the deal, the United States reportedly agreed to provide ballistic missile defense—from Aegis system-equipped U.S. Navy vessels—for the Czech Republic.[42]

The agreement must now be ratified by the parliament, and approval is not a foregone conclusion. In April, Schwarzenberg said that he thought "the conclusions of the NATO summit regarding US MD should be sufficient for the junior government Green party to vote in favor of the radar." However, a Czech newspaper stated that "[a]t the moment the government lacks at least five votes." Although the Green Party leadership reportedly called for its members to oppose the radar despite the NATO summit declaration, some members reportedly intend to support the project.[43] On July 9, 2008, Czech Deputy Foreign Minister Tomas Pojar expressed confidence that parliament would ratify the treaty by the end of the year or early in 2009, and added that "it is probable that the [ratification] vote will be after the election in the United States, however, that does not mean that it would be after the new (U.S.) President takes office."

At the end of October, the Czechs announced that ratification would take place after the inauguration of the next President. Prime Minister Topolanek explained that "We want a delay to make sure about the attitude of the new American administration." In mid-November, Miloslav Vlcek, chairman of the lower house of parliament – a member of the opposition CCSD – confirmed that a ratification vote would not be held until after Barack Obama had been inaugurated; in addition, he expressed doubts that the treaty would be approved, and also suggested that the radar deployment might face a constitutional challenge.

Although the Czech Senate on November 26 ratified the agreement by a vote of 49-31, it must still pass the chamber of deputies, where approval is less certain.[44] Parties on both sides of the issue are hopeful that the Obama Administration will validate their position on missile defense.[45]

Public opinion surveys consistently have shown strong (60%-70%) opposition to the plan among Czechs, who share many of their Polish neighbors' concerns.[46] Some Czech officials believe that public disfavor may be the result of a lack of knowledge about the program, and argue that the U.S. government has not provided sufficient information about the planned facilities. The CSSD called for a public referendum on the issue, and on September 2, 2008, joined with the Polish Social Democrats in opposition to the missile defense agreements.[47]

POLICY ISSUES

U.S. proponents of the missile defense program note that the bases being planned would be part of a limited defensive system, not an offensive one. The missiles would not have explosive payloads, and would be launched only in the event that the United States or its friends or allies were under actual attack. Critics respond that Europe does not currently face a significant threat from Iran or its potential surrogates, but that Polish and Czech participation in the European GMD element would create such a threat. If American GMD facilities were installed, they argue, both countries would likely be targeted by terrorists, as well as by missiles from rogue states— and possibly from Russia—in the event of a future confrontation.

Debate in Poland and the Czech Republic

Some proponents of the proposed GMD European capability system assert that cooperation would help consolidate bilateral relations with the United States. In Poland in particular there is a sense, based in part on historical experience, that the United States is the only major ally that can be relied upon. Therefore, some Poles argue, it would be beneficial to strengthen the relationship by becoming an important U.S. partner through joining the missile defense system. In addition, some Czechs and Poles believe that the missile defense sites would become a prestigious symbol of the two countries' enhanced role in defending Europe. Some would argue that the Czechs and the Poles see this formal U.S. military presence as an ultimate security guarantee against Russia; when asked shortly before Poland's October 21, 2007, parliamentary elections about the missile defense issue, former Prime Minister Kaczynski singled out Russia as a threat.[48]

Opponents, however, contend that this is not a valid reason for accepting missile defense facilities because the two countries, which joined NATO in 1999, already enjoy a security guarantee through the alliance's mutual defense clause. Polish missile defense skeptics also maintain that their country does not need to improve its bilateral security relationship with the United States because it has already shown its loyalty through its significant contributions to the military operations in Iraq and Afghanistan and the global war on terrorism. Some Polish and Czech political leaders reason that the United States may proceed with missile defense with or without them, so they may as well be on board. However, the missile bases are unpopular among the Czech and Polish public, and any government that agreed to host such facilities might lose political support. In addition, some Czechs and Poles may be speculating whether it would be worthwhile to expend political capital on the GMD bases, as the issue may become moot. If GMD proponents are voted out of office in the United States and the project is discontinued, "Poland will become an international laughingstock."[49] A Czech member of parliament noted that, if the U.S. Congress determines not to fund a European arm of missile defense, "[t]he USA will thus solve the problem for us."[50]

Some Czechs and Poles have argued that the extra-territorial status of the proposed bases would impinge upon national sovereignty. However, the Czech position is that the base "would be under the Czech Republic's jurisdiction."[51] In addition, some have raised questions over command and control—who would decide when to push the launch button and what would the notification system be? Polish and Czech government leaders reportedly acknowledge that the time between the detection of the launch of a missile by a hostile regime and the need to fire off an interceptor would be so brief as to preclude government-to-government consultations.

Opponents have also cautioned that the interception of a nuclear-tipped missile over Polish or Czech territory could result in a rain of deadly debris. Supporters argue that an enemy missile would not be intercepted over Eastern Europe, and that even if it were, the tremendous kinetic energy of impact would cause both projectiles to be obliterated and any debris burnt upon atmospheric reentry. Skeptics note, however, that testing of these systems is never performed over populated areas.

European Response

The proposed U.S. system has encountered resistance in some European countries and beyond. Some critics claim that the program is another manifestation of American unilateralism and argue that, because of opposition by major European partners, Polish and Czech participation in the GMD program could damage those countries' relations with fellow EU members.[52] Supporters, however, counter that the establishment of a missile defense system would protect Europe as well as the United States.

Some European leaders have asserted that the Bush Administration did not consult sufficiently with European allies or with Russia on its GMD plans. German Foreign Minister Frank-Walter Steinmeier faulted the Bush Administration for failing to adequately discuss the proposal with affected countries. Former French President Chirac cautioned against the creation of "new divisions in Europe." Bush Administration officials, however, maintained that these arguments were disingenuous, as they had held wide-ranging discussions on GMD with European governments, and with Russia, both bilaterally and in the framework of the NATO-Russia Council.[53] In addition, critics charged that establishing a European GMD base to counter Iranian missiles implied a tacit assumption on the part of the Bush Administration that diplomatic efforts to curb Iran's nuclear and ballistic missile aspirations were doomed to failure, and that Iran's future leaders would be undeterred by the prospect of nuclear annihilation. Finally, an analyst with the Swedish Transnational Foundation Research Center has argued that the U.S. missile defense system is being built in order to enable the use of a first strike.[54]

Europeans also have raised questions about the technical feasibility of the program as well as its cost-effectiveness. According to a wire service report, "Luxembourg's Foreign Minister Jean Asselborn called the U.S. [missile defense] plan an 'incomprehensible' waste of money.... "[55]

Other European leaders, however, including those of Denmark and Britain, indicated that they supported the missile defense project as a means to protect Europe from threats from rogue states. In addition, some European allies do not appear to be averse to the missile defense concept *per se*. Foreign Minister Steinmeier indicated that Germany and other countries were interested in building a comparable system, but lacked the technological know-how.[56]

NATO has also been deliberating strategic missile defenses. A feasibility study of such a program called for in the 2002 Prague Summit was completed in 2005. In the final communiqué of their 2006 Riga summit, NATO leaders declared the alliance study had concluded that long-range BMD is "technically feasible within the limitations and assumptions of the study," and called for "continued work on the political and military implications of missile defence for the Alliance including an update on missile threat developments." Supporters contend that the U.S. facilities currently under negotiation in Eastern Europe are intended to be a good fit—and therefore not inconsistent with—any future NATO missile defense. However, other policymakers have recommended that the establishment of any anti-missile system in Europe should proceed solely under NATO auspices rather than on a bilateral basis with just two NATO partners. U.S. officials maintain that "the more NATO is involved in [GMD], the better."[57]

Some observers have suggested that the Bush Administration chose not to work primarily through NATO because consensus agreement on the system was unlikely. However, in mid-June 2007, alliance defense ministers did agree to conduct a study of a complementary "bolt-on" anti-missile capability that would protect the southeastern part of alliance territory that would not be covered by the planned U.S. interceptors. American officials interpreted the move as an implied endorsement of the U.S. GMD plan and an adaptation of NATO plans to fit the proposed U.S. system. In addition, NATO Secretary General Jaap de Hoop Scheffer stated "The roadmap on missile defense is now clear.... It's practical, and it's agreed by all."[58]

The Bush Administration hoped that NATO would endorse missile defense at its 2008 summit meeting, held April 2-4 in Bucharest, Romania.[59] The Summit Declaration stated that the alliance acknowledges that ballistic missile proliferation poses an increasing threat. It further affirmed that missile defense is part of a "broader response," and that the proposed U.S. system would make a "substantial contribution" to the protection of the alliance. It declared that the alliance is "exploring ways to link [the U.S. assets] with current NATO efforts" to couple with "any future NATO-wide missile defense architecture." The declaration also directed the development, by the time of the 2009 summit, of "options" for anti-missile defense of any alliance territory that would not be covered by the planned U.S. installations. These options would be prepared "to inform any future political decision." In addition, the document declared support for ongoing efforts to "strengthen NATO-Russia missile defense cooperation," and announced readiness to look for ways to link "United States, NATO and Russian missile defense systems at an appropriate time." Finally, alliance members stated that they are "deeply concerned" over the "proliferation risks" implied by the nuclear and ballistic missile programs of Iran and North Korea, and called upon those countries to comply with pertinent UN Security Council resolutions.[60]

The Bush Administration interpreted the Summit Declaration as an endorsement of its missile defense project; Secretary of State Condoleezza Rice hailed the statement as a "breakthrough document." Concerning the question of whether ballistic missiles from rogue states were a threat, National Security Advisor Stephen Hadley declared, "I think that debate ended today."[61]

Representative Tauscher welcomed "NATO's acknowledgment of the contribution that the long- range interceptor site could make to Alliance security" and to make "cooperation with NATO a cornerstone of its missile defense proposal."[62]

In the final communiqué of their December 3, 2008 meeting, the foreign ministers of NATO member states reiterated the language on missile defense that had been included in the Bucharest summit declaration, while also noting "as a relevant development the signature of agreements by the Czech Republic and the Republic of Poland with the United States regarding those assets." The communiqué also called upon Moscow "to refrain from confrontational statements, including assertions of a sphere of influence, and from threats to the security of Allies and Partners, such as the one concerning the possible deployment of short-range missiles in the Kaliningrad region." (see below.) The latter statement was likely included at Warsaw's insistence.[63]

European opponents of the proposed U.S. plan also contend that statements by Russian officials are evidence that deployment of the U.S. system would damage Western relations with Russia. At a February 2007 security conference in Munich, former President Putin strongly criticized GMD, maintaining that it would lead to "an inevitable arms race." Russia has threatened to abrogate the 1987 Intermediate-Range Nuclear Forces (INF) Treaty, which eliminated this class of U.S. and then-Soviet missiles that were stationed in Europe. Putin also announced that Russia had suspended compliance with the Conventional Forces in Europe (CFE) Treaty,[64] and on another occasion indicated Russia might now target Poland and the Czech Republic and transfer medium-range ballistic missiles to the Russian exclave of Kaliningrad. Some U.S. and European officials dismissed Russia's alleged concerns and have noted that Moscow has known of this plan for years and has even been invited to participate.[65] GMD proponents maintain that the interceptors are intended to take out launched Iranian missiles aimed at European or American targets and could not possibly act as a deterrent against Russia, which has hundreds of missiles and thousands of warheads. The chief of the Czech general staff has noted that "by simple arithmetic, Russian generals can see that U.S. missile defenses cannot imperil Moscow's arsenal." Some Russians contend, however, that the modest GMD facilities planned for Eastern Europe are likely just the harbinger of a more ambitious program.

Russian officials have also argued that North Korean or Iranian missiles would not likely enter European airspace, and that the real reason for GMD is to emplace U.S. radar in eastern Europe to monitor Russian missile sites and naval operations. A Czech military officer dismissed the charge of electronic espionage as "absolute nonsense," arguing that "the radar monitors the already launched missiles, and it cannot monitor what is going on the ground"— a task that is already being performed by U.S. surveillance satellites.[66]

Some argue that Russia has other motives for raising alarms about the U.S. missile defense system: to foment discord among NATO member states, and to draw attention away from Russia's suppression of domestic dissent, its aggressive foreign policy actions, and its nuclear technology cooperation with Iran. Observers note that Russia blustered about NATO expansion, too, and argue that Russia's veiled threats may actually stiffen resolve in Prague and Warsaw. Some observers note, however, that Russian acceptance of NATO expansion was conditioned on a tacit understanding that NATO or U.S. military expansion into the new member states would not occur. The European GMD in this regard is seen as unacceptable to Russia.

On June 7, 2007, during the G-8 meeting in Germany, Putin offered to partner with the United States on missile defense, and suggested that a Soviet-era radar facility in Azerbaijan be used to help track and target hostile missiles that might be launched from the Middle East. President Bush responded by calling the proposal an "interesting suggestion," and welcomed the apparent policy shift. The following day, Putin suggested that GMD interceptors be "placed in the south, in U.S. NATO allies such as Turkey, or even Iraq ... [or] on sea platforms." Military and political representatives from both countries have met to discuss the proposal, but some experts point out that Azerbaijan is technically not the ideal place to locate the radar because it would be too close to potential Iranian launch sites; they also argue that the radar is outmoded.

In the meantime, Putin urged the United States not to deploy elements of GMD until his offer had been examined. One week later, however, U.S. Defense Secretary Robert Gates stated that even if the United States were to accept Russia's offer to share use of the Azeri radar, that facility would be regarded as "an additional capability" to complement the proposed GMD sites planned for Europe.[67] In late July 2007, MDA Director Obering said the United States was looking at the proposal very seriously. He said the Azeri radar could be useful for early detection of missile launches, but that it does not have the tracking ability to guide an interceptor missile to a target— which the proposed Czech radar would be able to do.

At a July 1-2, 2007, meeting in Kennebunkport, ME, Putin expanded on his counterproposal by recommending that missile defense be coordinated through offices in Brussels and Moscow. He also suggested the possible use of radar in south Russia and said that cooperation could be expanded to other European countries through the use of the NATO-Russia council—eliminating, he added, the need for facilities in Poland and the Czech Republic. President Bush reportedly responded positively to Putin's new proposal, but insisted on the need for the Eastern European sites.[68]

Despite ongoing discussions over the issue, Russian criticism of the program has continued, edged, at times, with sarcasm. During an October 2007 visit to Moscow by Secretaries Gates and Rice, President Putin remarked "of course we can sometime in the future decide that some antimissile defense system should be established somewhere on the moon." Putin later likened the U.S. placement of the missile defense facilities in central Europe to the 1962 Cuban missile crisis—a comparison disputed by U.S. officials. In late November 2007, Russia rejected a written U.S. proposal on the project, arguing that it failed to include the points Secretary Gates had discussed a month earlier, including "joint assessment of threats, ... Russian experts' presence at missile shield's sites, [and] readiness to keep the system non-operational if there is no actual missile threat.... "[69] In December, the chief of Russia's army suggested that the launching of U.S. missile defense interceptors against Iranian missiles might inadvertently provoke a counter launch of Russian ICBMs aimed at the United States. However, critics assert that a Russian counterstrike could not be prompted so easily and mistakenly. In February 2008, Putin reiterated earlier warnings that, if construction commenced on the missile defense facilities, Russia would re-target ICBMs toward the missile sites.[70]

During President Bush's post-Bucharest meeting with Putin at the Russian resort of Sochi, the two leaders reportedly sought to find common ground on missile defense; they agreed to introduce greater transparency in the project, and to explore possible confidence-building measures. In the meantime, Russia remains opposed to the proposed European bases. The two sides agreed to "intensify" their dialogue on missile defense cooperation. After the meeting, however, Iran's ambassador to Poland warned that if the missile defense system is installed, "the United States will acquire supremacy over Russian nuclear forces."[71]

Following the signing of the U.S.-Poland agreement, Russia once more vociferously objected to the missile defense plan. On August 16, a highly placed Russian general officer stated that Poland's acceptance of the interceptors could make it a target for a nuclear attack. Later, newly inaugurated President Dmity Medvedev reiterated Russia's conviction that the interceptors constitute a threat, and added that Moscow "will have to respond to it in some way, naturally using military means." On August 20, it was also announced that the governments of Russia and Belarus had launched discussions on the establishment of a joint air defense system; the move was interpreted by ITAR-TASS as a "retaliatory measure" in response to the planned U.S. missile defense system.[72]

The day after the U.S. elections, in his State of the Federation speech, President Medvedev said that Russia would deploy short-range Iskander missiles to the Russian exclave of Kaliningrad, which borders Poland and Lithuania, if the U.S. GMD system is built. However, Medvedev later told a French newspaper that it the United States does not deploy the system, Russia would not transfer its missiles to Kaliningrad. Prime Minister Putin later reiterated that Russia would scrap its plans for the Iskanders if the United States cancelled its European GMD project.[73] Some observers believe that the announcement created more concern in central than in western Europe. Shortly thereafter, however, European Commission President Jose Manuel Barroso stated that "cold war rhetoric" was "stupid," and U.S. Defense Secretary Gates states that "such provocative remarks are unnecessary and misguided."[74]

In mid-November 2008, French President Nicolas Sarkozy recommended that the U.S. and Russian plans be discussed by NATO and the OSCE in the spring of 2009, and that, "until then we should not talk about missile or shield deployments which lead to nothing for security, which complicate things and rather make things go backwards." Czech Deputy Prime Minister Alexandr Vondra criticized Sarkozy's remarks as inappropriate, and Polish Prime Minister Tusk stated that GMD was a Polish-U.S. project, and that "I don't think that third countries, even such good friends as France, can have a particular right to express themselves on this issue." Sarkozy later appeared to backtrack somewhat, saying "every country is sovereign to decide whether it hosts an anti-missile shield or not."[75]

Some observers believe that the ongoing dialog between Russia and the United States may help reduce tensions. Eventual Russian cooperation in missile defense could remove a significant impediment to the program and could dampen criticism by European and other leaders. It also may open the door to a more favorable attitude by NATO toward missile defense.

CONGRESSIONAL ACTIONS

Fiscal Year 2009

For FY2009, the Bush Administration requested $712 million for the European GMD Element. The reported cost of the European element is $4 billion (FY2008-FY2013), according to the Administration, which includes fielding and Operation and Support costs.

On May 14, 2008, the House Armed Services Committee approved its version of the FY2009 defense authorization bill (H.R. 5658). The committee provided $341 million for the proposed European GMD site, reducing the total by $371 million ($231 million in R&D funding and $140 million in Military Construction). The committee expressed concerns about the slower-thanexpected pace of the Iranian long-range missile program, the effectiveness of the GMD system based on program testing results, the ability to spend the proposed funds, and the lack of signed and ratified agreements with Poland and the Czech Republic.

On April 30, 2008, the Senate Armed Services Committee approved its version of the FY2009 defense authorization bill (S. 3001). The committee provided full funding for the European GMD Element, but noted that certain conditions have to be met before those funds could be expended: (1) military construction funds cannot be spent until the European governments give final approval (including parliamentary approval) of any deployment agreement, and 45 days have elapsed after Congress has received a required report that provides an independent analysis of the proposed European site and alternatives, and (2) acquisition and deployment funds, other than for long-lead procurement, cannot be expended until the Secretary of Defense (with input from the Dir., Operational Test and Operations) certifies to Congress that the proposed interceptor has demonstrated a high probability of accomplishing its mission in an operationally effective manner.

President Bush signed a continuing resolution into law on September 30, 2008 (P.L. 110-329), which incorporated defense appropriations and authorizing language for FY2009. According to a Press Release from the Senate Appropriations Committee dated September 24, 2008, Congress provided $467 million for the European BMD sites and development and testing of the two-stage interceptor. According to authorizing language,[76] funding for the Czech radar and site will then be available only after the Czech Parliament has ratified the basing agreement reached with the United States and a status of forces agreement (SOFA) to allow for such deployment and stationing of U.S. troops is in place. Funding for the Polish interceptor site will only be available after both the Czech and Polish parliaments ratify the agreements reached with the United States, and a SOFA with Poland is also in place for the site. Additionally, deployment of operational GBIs is prohibited until after the Secretary of Defense (after receiving the views of the Director of Operational Test and Evaluation) submits to Congress a report certifying that the proposed interceptor to be deployed "has demonstrated, through successful, operationally realistic flight testing, a high probability of working in an operationally effective manner and the ability to accomplish the mission."

Fiscal Year 2008

In its report on the FY2008 defense authorization bill, the House Armed Services Committee cited its concern from last year (FY2007) that investment in the European BMD site was premature.[77] In part, the Committee's concerns focus on the need to complete scheduled integrated end-to-end testing of the system now deployed in Alaska and California. Additionally, the Committee notes its reluctance to fund the European site without formal agreements with Poland and the Czech Republic and without knowing the terms under which the estimated $4 billion program costs would be expended. Therefore, the Committee recommended that no funds be approved for FY2008 for construction of the European GMD site.[78] The Committee did, however, recommend $42.7 million to continue procurement of ten additional GMD interceptors that could be deployed to the European site or for expanded inventory at the GMD site in Alaska (as noted in MDA budget documents). Also, the Committee expressed concern over the testing plan and risk reduction strategy for the proposed two-stage GMD interceptor for Europe. The Committee further directed that two studies be done: (1) the Secretary of Defense and the Secretary of State are to submit a report to Congress by January 31, 2008, to include how the Administration will obtain NATO's support for the European GMD proposal, and how other missile defense capabilities such as Aegis and THAAD (Terminal High Altitude Area Defense) could contribute to the missile defense protection of Europe; and (2) an independent assessment of European missile defense options should be done in a timely manner.

In the Senate defense authorization bill, the Armed Services Committee recommended limiting the availability of funding for the European GMD site until two conditions were met: (1) completion of bilateral agreements with Poland and the Czech Republic; and (2) 45 days have elapsed following the receipt by Congress of a report from an FFRDC (federally funded research and development center) to conduct an independent assessment of options for missile defense of Europe.[79] The Committee recommended a reduction of $85 million for site activation and construction activities for the proposed European GMD deployment. The Committee also limited FY2008 funding for acquisition or deployment of operational interceptor missiles for the European system until the Secretary of Defense certified to Congress that the proposed interceptor to be deployed had demonstrated, through successful, operationally realistic flight testing, that it had a high probability of working in an operationally effective manner. The Committee noted that the proposed 2-stage version of the interceptor has not been developed and was not scheduled to be tested until 2010.[80] Therefore, the Committee noted, it could be several years before it is known if the proposed interceptor will work in an operationally effective manner. The Committee indicated that it would not limit site surveys, studies, analysis, planning and design for the proposed European GMD site, but that construction and deployment could not take place prior to ratification of formal bilateral agreements, which MDA estimates would not take place before 2009. Finally, the Committee notes there were a number of near-term missile defense options to provide defense of Europe against short-range, medium-range and future intermediate-range ballistic missiles, such as the Patriot PAC-3, the Aegis BMD system, and THAAD.

In floor debate, the Senate approved an amendment by Senator Sessions (90-5) to the defense authorization bill stating that the policy of the United States is to develop and deploy an effective defense system against the threat of an Iranian nuclear missile attack against the United States and its European allies. Further debate and passage of the defense authorization bill was postponed at the time by the Majority Leader until after debate over Iraq war funding.

On November 13, 2007, President Bush signed into law the FY2008 Defense Appropriations Bill (H.R. 3222; P.L. 110-114). This bill eliminated the proposed $85 million for FY2008 for the European missile defense site construction, but permitted $225 million for studies, analyses, etc. of the proposed European GMD element.

The House passed the FY2008 National Defense Authorization bill (H.R. 1585) on May 17, 2007. The Senate passed its version on October 1, 2007. House and Senate negotiators filed the defense authorization report on December 6, 2007. The House adopted the report on December 12, 2007. The Conference Report contained a number of provisions pertaining to the proposed European GMD element. First, it cut the $85 million requested for site activation and construction activities. This left about $225 million to fund surveys, studies, analysis, etc. related to the European GMD element in FY2008. Second, the Conference Report required an independent assessment of the proposed deployment of long-range missile defense interceptors and associated radar in Europe and a second independent analysis of missile defense options in Europe before site construction and activation could begin. The conferees noted that if the Polish and Czech governments gave final approval to any successfully completed agreements during FY2008, the Department of Defense had the option of submitting a reprogramming request for those funds ($85 million) to begin site construction in Europe. Third, the conferees strongly supported the need to work closely and in coordination with NATO on missile defense issues. Finally, the defense authorization bill required that the Secretary of Defense certify that the proposed two- stage interceptor "has demonstrated, through successful, operationally realistic flight testing, a high probability of working in an operationally effective manner" before funds could be authorized for the acquisition or deployment of operational missiles for the European site.

End Notes

[1] Some were calling for such an effort in Europe before the Administration formally requested funding in early 2007. For instance, in October 2006, Sen. Sessions noted NATO steps in developing an Alliance-wide theater missile defense capability, and encouraged the deployment of a U.S. long-range missile defense system in Europe. See "U.S. Missile Defense Site in Europe Needed to Support Alliance Strategy," *Space News*, October 9, 2006, p. 19.

[2] "Rep. Ellen Tauscher Applauds House Passage of Defense Authorization Bill," Press Release, Office of Rep. Ellen Tauscher, December 12, 2007.

[3] Andrew Gray, "U.S. to Review Europe Missile Shield Under Obama," *Reuters News*, January 15, 2009.

[4] *Defense Daily*, January 16, 2009.

[5] Ibid.

[6] http://www.whitehouse.gov/agenda/defense

[7] CRS Report RS22758, *Iran's Ballistic Missile Programs: An Overview*, by Steven A. Hildreth.

[8] David Sanger and Steven Lee Meyers "Details in Military Notes Led to Shift on Iran, U.S. Says," *New York Times*, December 6, 2007

[9] "Iran Report Won't Slow Missile Defense," *CBS News*, Brussels, Belgium, December 6, 2007.

[10] "U.S.: Iran Still Poses Missile Threat," *Associated Press*, December 6, 2007.

[11] There are reports that Iran is developing other medium-range ballistic missiles with ranges greater than those now deployed, but short of what is considered ICBM range (i.e., more than 5,500 kilometers).

[12] For instance: (1) General Cartwright, Commander, U.S. Strategic Command, said the July 4, 2006 North Korean missile tests spurred a limited operational activation of the BMD System. "We learned that the ballistic missile defense system, procedures, and personnel performed well, and demonstrated a credible operational missile defense capability for homeland defense." Testimony before the Senate Armed Services Committee, March

21, 2007; (2) Admiral Mullen, on his nomination hearing to be Chairman of the Joint Chiefs of Staff, said he believes the U.S. "Has a viable initial operational capability and we are maturing the system toward a full operational capability." "Answers to Advanced Policy Questions," Senate Armed Services Committee, July 26, 2007; and (3) Dr. Charles McQueary, Director, Operational Test and Evaluation, said: "I can state that the ballistic missile defense system has demonstrated a limited capability against a simple foreign threat. Coupled with the successes of other element-level testing and MDA's integrated ground tests, the BMD system is definitely maturing. My assessment is bolstered by the fact that the MDA is increasing the operational realism of each successive test." Testimony before the Senate Armed Services Committee, April 11, 2007.

[13] Two tests in March and October 2002 using an older interceptor successfully intercepted their intended targets. Three flight tests (IFT-10, IFT-13c and IFT-14) using the GBI in planned intercept attempts failed in those attempts for various reasons: (1) December 2002, the kill vehicle failed to deploy; (2) December 2004, the GBI launch aborted due to a software error in the interceptor; and (3) February 2005, the GBI did not launch due to problems with the test facility launch equipment. In the May 2007 flight test, the target missile second stage booster failed in flight, so the interceptor was not launched as planned. In September 2006 and 2007 successful intercepts were achieved.

[14] The Bush Administration maintained that since 2002 it has fielded a long-range BMD capability where none existed previously. Furthermore, the United States now has operationally capable upgraded early warning radars, command, control and battle management systems, Navy cruisers and destroyers capable of conducting long-range ballistic missile search and track missions, and about 20 GBI fielded in Alaska and California. This element of the BMDS was transitioned to alert in July 2006 when North Korea launched several ballistic missiles, including a long-range ballistic missile.

[15] Boost Vehicle Plus. Report to Congress. March 1, 2007. Missile Defense Agency. For Official Use Only.

[16] The Orbital Boost Vehicle 2 (OBV/2) is a modification of the existing, tested OBV/3 achieved by removing the 3rd stage from the existing missile.

[17] More accurately, according to MDA, two stages provide the enhanced performance and burnout velocity required for the mission.

[18] See http://www.armscontrolwonk.com/1539/how-many-aegis-ships-to-defend-nato.

[19] "U.S. May Build 25,000-ton Cruiser, Analysis of Alternatives Sees Nuclear BMD Vessel," *Defense News*, July 23, 2007, by Christopher P. Cavas.

[20] U.S. Missiles in Poland—Risks and Benefits. *Rzeczpospolita*. In *BBC European Monitoring*. November 15, 2005. Sikorski Exit Is Bad For MD Bid. *Oxford Analytica*. February 8, 2007.

[21] Polish Politician Weighs Up Pros and Cons Of US Radar Plan. *Gazeta Wyborcza*, February 5, 2007. In: *BBC Monitoring European*. February 6, 2007. See also: Don't Take Poland For Granted. Radek Sikorski [former Polish Defense Minister and current Foreign Minister]. *Washington Post*. March 21, 2007.

[22] Poland's Likely Next Prime Minister Open To Talks On U.S. Missile Defense. *Poland Business Newswire*. November 6, 2007. Poland's New Defense Chief Wants To Reconsider U.S. Missile Defense Request. *AP*. November 19, 2007.

[23] Poland Said Likely To Launch Tough Missile Defence Talks With USA. *Gazeta Wyborcza* [in: *BBC Monitoring European.*] December 5, 2007.

[24] "Poland Says U.S. Shield a 'Foregone Conclusion.'" *Reuters*. July 16, 2007. Poland Signals Doubts About Planned U.S. Missile-Defense Bases On Its Territory. *New York Times*. January 7, 2008. No Poland-US Missile Deal Next Month: Defense Minister. *AFP*. February 2, 2008.

[25] Bush, Poland's Tusk Discuss Missile Shield Plans. *Agence France Presse*. March 10, 2008. Game For US Shield Begins. *Polish News Bulletin*. March 14, 2008. Next U.S. Pres. Unlikely To Axe Proposed Central European Missile Defense Project—Polish Diplomat. *Poland Business Newswire*. April 2, 2008. Czech, USA Agree On Main Treaty On U.S. Radar On Czech Soil. *CTK Daily News*. April 3, 2008.

[26] As Poles Balk, U.S. Eyes Lithuania As Site For Missile Shield. *New York Times*. June 19, 2008.

[27] No Progress On Shield Talks. *Polish News Bulletin*. July 8, 2008. Date Of US-Poland Treaty On Missile Base Still Unknown. *Poland This Week*. July 11, 2008.

[28] Russian Relations In Doubt, Gates Says. Washington Post. August 15, 2008.

[29] US Missile Deal Gives Poland Patriots, Bolstered Defence Ties. *AFP*. August 20, 2008. Some analysts, however, have argued that the agreement's special security guarantee may be questioned by other NATO allies, especially in central Europe. See Implications of the U.S.-Polish Defense Pact. By William L. T. Schirano. Center for European Policy Analysis. August 29, 2008.

[30] With Russia Rising, Poles Look West. *New York Times*. August 21, 2008.

[31] Polish Lower House Speaker Refuses To Rush Ratification Of Polish-U.S. Missile Shield Deal. *Poland Business Newswire*. August 20, 2008. U.S. Presidential Candidates endorse Missile Shield Project, Obama Less Enthusiastic – Polish PM. *Poland Business Newswire*. August 19, 2008.

[32] Czechs See Anti-missile radar Ratified By Year-end. *Reuters*. July 9, 2008.

[33] U.S. Ambassador: Decision On Missile Shield Suspended. *Polish News Bulletin*. November 26, 2008.

[34] Poland Won't Lobby Obama On Missile Defense. *Washington Post*. November 20, 2008. Sikorski: New US Administration May Put on Hold Anti-missile Shield Project. *Polish News Bulletin*. November 13, 2008.

[35] Polish President Hopes Obama As U.S. President Will Treat Missile Shield As "Necessary." *Polish Business Newswire.* January 19, 2009.

[36] Obama, Democrats Likely To Pare back Missile Defense Plans To Save Money. *CQ Today.* November 17, 2008.

[37] Czech Republic Seeks Joining Missile Defence Shield Project. *BBC Monitoring European.* September 17, 2002.

[38] US May Delay Missile Defense System. *AP.* October 23, 2007. Administration Diverges On Missile Defense. *Washington Post.* October 24, 2007. Gates Causes Missile Defence Flap. *Oxford Analytica.* October 24, 2007.

[39] US Offers Mutual MD Checks. *Oxford Analytica.* March 20, 2008.

[40] Czechs Say Report On Iran Nuclear Program Not To Influence Missile Defense Talks. *Associated Press.* December 5, 2007.

[41] *Select Briefing Europe East.* Center for Strategic and International Studies. Vol. 5, No. 3. February 1, 2008.

[42] Czechs, USA Agree Radar Treaty To Be Signed In May. *BBC Monitoring European.* April 3, 2008. U.S. To Give Czechs Ballistic Missile Defense. *Washington Post.* July 16, 2008.

[43] Czech Minister Sees 'Virtually No Opposition' in NATO, EU to US Missile Shield. *BBC Monitoring European.* April 7, 2008. US Set To Sign Main Czech Radar Deal: Embassy. *AFP.* April 7, 2008. Czech Senator To Vote For Radar Base Against Greens' Call. *CTK Daily News.* April 15, 2008.

[44] Czech Govt Wants Vote On Missile Shield After US Election. *Agence France Presse.* October 29, 2008. US Base's Chance In Czech Parliament Diminishing – Vlcek in Russia. *CTK Daily News.* November 17, 2008. Czech MPs Delay U.S. Shield Deal Debate Until Obama's Inauguration. *RIA Novosti.* November 28, 2008. Missile Defense Deal With US Clears Czech Senate, Faces Tougher test In Lower Chamber. *Associated Press Newswires.* November 27, 2008.

[45] Czech Politicians Disagree On U.S. Radar Plans Under Obama. *CTK Daily News.* January 20, 2009.

[46] Czech Poll Indicates Number Of Missile Defense Radar Opponents Declines. *AP.* September 26, 2007. But see also: Many Czechs Love U.S., But Say 'Hold the Radar.' *New York Times.* October 1, 2007. Poll: 70 Percent of Czechs Oppose U.S. Missile Defense Plan. *Associated Press.* January 8, 2008. Majority of Czechs Against U.S. Anti-missile Radar System. *Poland Business Newswire.* July 9, 2008.

[47] Paroubek Says U.S. Ambassador Told Him On His Govt Talks On Base. *CTK Daily News.* July 8, 2007. Czech Opposition Leader Watns to Know Contents of Talks with Bush. *CTK Daily News.* January 30, 2008. Czech, Polish Socialists Reject U.S. Missile Defence Shield. *CTK Daily News.* September 2, 2008.

[48] Polish PM: Hosting U.S. Shield May Counter Russia. *Reuters.* October 18, 2007.

[49] Polish Daily: US Missile Defence in Poland Means 'Local Arms Race' With Belarus. *BBC Monitoring European.* November 18, 2005.

[50] USA Wants To Deploy Missile Defence Radar On Czech Territory—Foreign Minister. *CTV* [Czech news agency]. In: *BBC Monitoring European.* November 29, 2006.

[51] That Missile Debate of Ours. *Pravo.* September 9, 2006. In: *BBC Monitoring European.* September 12, 2006. Any US Missile Base On Czech Territory Subject To Czech Laws—Czech Ministry. *BBC Monitoring European.* August 18, 2006. State Security Council Okays US Radar. *Pravo.* In: *BBC European Monitoring.* January 26, 2006. Czech Premier Reminds Opposition Its Cabinet Started Talks On US Radar Base. *CTK Czech News Agency.* In: *BBC European Monitoring.* February 1, 2007.

[52] Missile Shield: Poland's Security Better Served By Supporting Ukraine's Western Ambitions Than By Building Another Maginot Line. *Polish News Bulletin.* December 22, 2005.

[53] Where Does Germany Stand? *Spiegel Online.* March 26, 2007. US Build Pressure On Europe Over Bases. *Financial Times.* February 21, 2007. France Calls For Dialogue on US Anti-Missile System. *Agence France Presse (AFP).* February 21, 2007. U.S. Officials Brief On Missile Defense. February 23, 2007. U.S. Embassy Warsaw.

[54] Swedish Expert Says US Missile Shield Meant To Allow Nuclear First Strike. *BBC Monitoring.* January 8, 20080.

[55] NATO Stepping Up Talks On Missile Defense Amid Concerns Over US Plans. *Associated Press.* March 12, 2007.

[56] Danish PM Supports US Anti-Missile Shield. *AFP.* March 7, 2007. Blair: We Need To Look At Missile Options. *Press Association National Newswire.* February 28, 2007. Europe Considers Missile Defense System: German Minister. *AFP.* February 19, 2007.

[57] This program should be distinguished from the theater missile defense system intended to protect deployed forces, which the alliance has already approved. See Riga Summit Declaration. NATO web page. http://www.nato.int/docu/pr/ 2006/p06-150e.htm Missile Defense and Europe. *Foreign Press Briefing.* U.S. Department of State. March 28, 2007.

[58] NATO Considers Missile Defenses For Southeastern Flank In Tandem With U.S. Shield. *Associated Press.* June 14, 2007. U.S. Wins NATO Backing On Missile Defense. *New York Times.* June 15, 2007.

[59] NATO Debates BMD Ahead Of April Bucharest Summit. *WMD Insights.* April, 2008.

[60] NATO Summit Declaration. April 3, 20008 http://www.nato.int/docu/pr/2008/p08-049e.html.

[61] NATO Backs U.S. Missile Shield. *Los Angeles Times.* April 4, 2008. NATO Endorses Europe Missile Shield. *New York Times.* April 4, 2008.

[62] Opening Statement, Chairman Ellen O. Tauscher, Strategic Forces Subcommittee, Hearing on the FY2009 Budget Request for Missile Defense Programs, April 17, 2008.

[63] Final communiqué. Meeting of the North Atlantic Council at the level of Foreign Ministers held at NATO Headquarters, Brussels. December 3, 2008. NATO website: http://www.nato.int/docu/pr/2008/p08-153e.html Poland Wants NATO To Declare Russian Placement Threat As Unacceptable – Sikorski. *Poland Business Newswire*. December 3, 2008.

[64] See CRS Report RL33865, *Arms Control and Nonproliferation: A Catalog of Treaties and Agreements*, by Amy F. Woolf, Paul K. Kerr, and Mary Beth Nikitin, section on Conventional Armed Forces in Europe Treaty. NATO "Very Concerned" At Russia Treaty Pullout. *Reuters*. July 16, 2007.

[65] Russia Sees Threat From US Plan For Missiles In Eastern Europe. *AFP*. January 22, 2007. Poland Government Leaders Meet On U.S. Missile Defense Proposal. *Associated Press*. February 12, 2007.

[66] U.S. Radar Not To Threaten Russia, China - Czech Chief Of Staff. *CTK Daily News*. January 25, 2007.

[67] Putin Wants Quick Answer On Alternative Antimissile Site. *RFE/RL Newsline*. June 11, 2007. Putin Surprises Bush With Plan On Missile Shield. *New York Times*. June 8, 2007. US Says Russia Offer Cannot Replace Missile Shield. *Reuters*. June 14, 2007.

[68] Putin Expands On His Missile Defense Plan. *New York Times*. July 3, 2007/ Putin Proposes Broader Cooperation On Missile Defense. *Washington Post*. July 3, 2007.

[69] Putin Dismisses US Missile Shield Plan. *Financial Times*. October 12, 2007. Russia Dismisses US Offer On Missile Defence. *AFP*. November 23, 2007. Russia Alleges U.S. "Rollback" On Anti-Missile Plan. *Washington Post*. December 6, 2007.

[70] US Missile Could Trigger Russian Strike: Russian Army Chief. *Agence Presse France*. December 15, 2007. Putin Repeats Threat To Aim Russian Rockets At U.S. Missile Defenses. *Associated Press Newswires*. February 14, 20080.

[71] Putin and Bush Narrow Some Differences. *Oxford Analytica*. April 7, 2008. U.S. To Gain Supremacy Over Russia With Central European Anti-missile Base—Iranian Ambassador. *Poland Business Newswire*. April 9, 2008. Fact Sheet: U.S.-Russia Strategic Framework Declaration. *News Press*. April 7, 2008.

[72] Russian Says Shield Makes Poland Target. *Washington Times*. August 16, 2008. Medvedev Sees Military Response To U.S. Missile Shield. *Reuters*. August 26, 2008. Moscow, Minsk To Build Air Def In Response To Missiles In Europe. *ITAR-TASS*. August 20, 2008.

[73] Putin Offers To End Stand-Off Over Missiles In Eastern Europe. *DPA/Deutsche Welle*. November 24, 2008.

[74] Europe Split Over Russia's Tough Talk On Missiles. *Washington Post*. November 9, 2008. Gates and European officials Criticize the Russian President For His Bellicose Remarks. *New York Times*. November 14, 2008.

[75] France urges Russia and US To End Missile Feud. *Agence France Presse*. November 14, 2008. Poles, Czechs Brush Aside Sarkozy Missile Plea. *Agence France Presse*. November 15, 2008. France "Overstepped Mandate" On Missile Shield. euobserver.com November 17, 2008.

[76] Congressional Record – House, September 24, 2008, p. H9103.

[77] National Defense Authorization Act for Fiscal Year 2008. Report of the House Armed Services Committee on H.R. 1585, May 11, 2007. House of Representatives. 1 10th Congress, 1st Session. H.Rept. 110-146, pp. 238-240.

[78] To preserve the opportunity to move forward with the research and development components of the European interceptor and radar site, the Committee recommended that $150 million for FY2008 be available. Upon completion of bilateral agreements and if further engagement with NATO on the proposed site can be demonstrated, the Committee notes that the Department of Defense has the option of submitting a reprogramming request to Congress in FY2008 to fund site preparation activities.

[79] National Defense Authorization Act for Fiscal Year 2008. Report of the Senate Armed Services Committee on S. 1547, June 5, 2007. Committee on Armed Services. U.S. Senate. 110th Congress, 1st Session. Report 110-77, pp. 140- 142.

[80] See footnote 9.

In: Options for Deploying Missile Defenses in Europe
Editor: Melissa V. Jordan pp.75-151

ISBN: 978-1-60741-889-4
© 2010 Nova Science Publishers, Inc.

Chapter 6

OPTIONS FOR DEPLOYING MISSILE DEFENSES IN EUROPE[*]

Congressional Budget Office

SUMMARY

As part of ongoing efforts to protect the United States and its allies from attack by ballistic missiles, the U.S. Missile Defense Agency (MDA) is working to deploy a missile defense system in Europe. As proposed, the system would be fielded by 2013 and would include interceptor missiles in silos to be built in Poland, a tracking radar in the Czech Republic, and another radar at an unspecified location near Iran. The goal of the system, according to MDA, is to "defend [U.S.] allies and deployed forces in Europe from limited Iranian long- range threats and expand protection of [the] U.S. homeland."[1]

MDA's proposed system is controversial. Some critics argue that testing of the system to date has been insufficient to verify that it will function as intended. Other critics argue that even if the system performs according to expectations, it is unnecessary given the current status of Iranian missile development and the likelihood of an Iranian missile attack on Europe or the United States. The United States has signed agreements with Poland and the Czech Republic to host the missile defense system, but those agreements have been the subject of debate in the host nations and have not yet been fully ratified by their parliaments. The system as proposed would not be able to defend some areas—including parts of North Atlantic Treaty Organization (NATO) member Turkey—that are within striking distance of missiles that Iran has tested or claims to have developed. The Russian government has also sharply protested the deployment by the United States of missile defenses in eastern Europe.

In this study, the Congressional Budget Office (CBO) compares the potential cost and performance of MDA's proposed European system with the cost and performance of three other options for deploying missile defenses in Europe, as follows:

---

[*] This is an edited, reformatted and augmented version of a Congressional Budget Office publication dated February 2009.

- Standard Missile-3 (SM-3) Block IIA interceptors located on U.S. Navy Aegis ballistic missile defense (BMD) ships operating at three locations around Europe, supported by two transportable forward- based radars (FBRs);

- Ground-based SM-3 Block IIA interceptors operating from mobile launchers located at two existing U.S. bases (Ramstein Air Force Base in Germany and Incirlik Air Force Base in Turkey), supported by two transportable forward-based radars; and

- Ground-based Kinetic Energy Interceptors (KEIs, a new high-acceleration interceptor MDA is developing that could be based either in silos or on mobile transporters), operating from mobile launchers located at two existing U.S. bases in Europe (Ramstein Air Force Base in Germany and Incirlik Air Force Base in Turkey), supported by two transportable forward- based radars.

CBO developed the alternatives using components that are already being planned rather than entirely new systems. Like MDA's proposal, the alternatives are all midcourse-phase defense systems, which would intercept an enemy missile after its rocket booster had burned out and the missile was "coasting" on a ballistic trajectory above the atmosphere. (For an introduction to ballistic missiles, see Appendix A.) CBO's analysis assumes that all the components of the proposed defenses and alternatives to them will perform according to MDA's current expectations. Many observers would argue that assumption is optimistic, however, because it has not been verified by testing.

Besides protecting parts of Europe, MDA's proposed European system is intended to give the United States an extra layer of defense against potential Iranian intercontinental ballistic missiles (ICBMs) beyond that provided by U.S.-based interceptors. CBO's analysis indicates that interceptors of the Ground-Based Midcourse Defense (GMD) system already in place at two bases in the United States—supported by radars currently slated to be incorporated into the system by 2012—would provide defensive coverage to more than 99 percent of the U.S. population against ICBMs from Iran. MDA's proposed European system would extend defensive coverage to the other 1 percent of the U.S. population. It would also provide redundant defense from a third interceptor site for all of the continental United States. Such redundancy gives system operators more flexibility: Interceptors launched from Europe against a U.S.-bound ICBM would engage the missile early in its trajectory, allowing operators to determine whether the intercept was successful and still have enough time to launch a second interceptor from the United States, if necessary.

CBO compared the proposed deployment and the alternatives to it on the basis of the defense of Europe that they would provide, the additional defense of the United States they would provide relative to the defense provided by the existing Ground-Based Midcourse Defense system, their costs, and when the alternatives could be available. Using those four criteria, CBO's analysis suggests the following:

- **Defense of Europe.** All of the alternatives CBO considered would provide defense of most of Europe roughly equivalent to the defense provided by MDA's proposal against most types of ballistic missiles that Iran is thought to have developed or could develop in the future. Because the alternatives CBO considered would locate interceptors closer to Iran than MDA's planned system, they would generally provide more extensive defense of southeastern Europe than would MDA's proposal. Moreover, because they would be composed of mobile or transportable components, deploying the alternative systems would not require building permanent facilities—including missile silos—at European sites. However, none of the systems that CBO analyzed, including the system proposed by MDA, would be capable of defending all of Europe against all of the threat missiles that Iran has either already tested or might develop.

- **Extended Defense of the United States.** MDA's proposed system would complement the coverage already available from U.S.-based interceptors by providing redundant defense from a third interceptor site for all of the continental United States. None of the alternatives considered by CBO provide as much additional defense of the United States. Deploying Kinetic Energy Interceptors would add defense from a third redundant interceptor site for about 75 percent of the U.S. population in range of ICBMs from Iran. Deploying land-based or sea-based Standard Missile-3 (SM-3) Block IIA interceptors would provide additional defense for about one-half or less of the U.S. population.

- **Costs.** For roughly the same cost as MDA's European system—a total of about $9 billion to $14 billion over 20 years—the United States could deploy either SM-3 interceptors or Kinetic Energy Interceptors at its existing bases in Germany and Turkey, supported by tracking radars in Azerbaijan and Qatar. At greater cost, the United States could deploy SM-3 interceptors on U.S. Navy ships and station them permanently at three locations in European waters. That system would cost almost twice as much as MDA's proposal—a total of about $18 billion to $26 billion over 20 years—largely because CBO assumed that the Navy would need to buy additional ships to operate it.

- **Availability.** The alternatives that CBO examined might not be available as early as MDA's proposed European system. MDA's plans call for that system to be fully fielded by 2013, although constraints that the Congress has placed on the availability of funds could delay its completion. Given the U.S. military's development schedules for various interceptors, the two alternative systems using SM-3 Block IIA interceptors could be available around 2015, but the system using Kinetic Energy Interceptors probably would not be available until sometime after 2018. Deploying the alternatives considered by CBO would require surmounting technical challenges similar to those associated with deploying MDA's proposed system.

MDA's Plans for European Missile Defenses

Developing defenses against ballistic missiles has long been a goal of the Department of Defense (DoD) and was particularly emphasized by the Bush Administration. Early U.S. efforts at missile defense (such as the 1960s-era Nike-Zeus program) were aimed at countering the vast Soviet missile arsenal. Recent efforts are more modest in scope. The National Missile Defense Act of 1999 states, "It is the policy of the United States to deploy as soon as is technologically possible an effective National Missile Defense system capable of defending the territory of the United States against limited ballistic missile attack (whether accidental, unauthorized, or deliberate)."[2]

DoD's Missile Defense Agency has the mission of "develop[ing] and field[ing] an integrated, layered, ballistic missile defense system to defend the United States, its deployed forces, allies, and friends against all ranges of enemy ballistic missiles in all phases of flight."[3] In its budget request for fiscal year 2009, MDA divided its efforts to fulfill that mission into a series of "blocks," each based on a particular desired capability:

- Block 1.0—Defend the United States from limited North Korean long-range threats;
- Block 2.0—Defend allies and deployed forces from short- to medium-range threats in one region or theater;
- Block 3.0—Expand defense of the United States to include limited Iranian long-range threats;
- Block 4.0—Defend allies and deployed forces in Europe from limited Iranian long-range threats and expand protection of the U.S. homeland; and
- Block 5.0—Expand defense of allies and deployed forces from short- to intermediate-range threats in two regions or theaters.[4]

Block 1.0 is nearing completion, and most of the work on Blocks 2.0 and 3.0 is expected to occur over the next two years. The other blocks are mainly in the planning and development stages.

The Block 4.0 program centers on establishing a European Interceptor Site (EIS) in Poland, where silos would be constructed to hold 10 ground-based, midcourse- phase interceptors. The EIS would be supported by the European Midcourse Radar (EMR), an X-band tracking radar that is slated to be moved from its current location in the Pacific to the Czech Republic. MDA's plans also call for deploying a forward-based short-wavelength radar somewhere closer to Iran. That radar would provide tracking earlier in the trajectory of an enemy missile (usually referred to as a threat missile) and thus would extend the area defended by the interceptors. MDA has not specified a location for the forward-based radar in its public statements.

In the President's 2009 budget, MDA requested total funding of $3.9 billion over the 2008–2013 period for the Block 4.0 system, including operations and support in those years.[5] That budget request was based on a plan in which both the EIS and EMR become operational in 2012 and all of the interceptors are in place in Poland by 2013. However, limits on the availability of funding that the Congress included in the 2009 defense authorization bill could delay the fielding of the system. Those limits make funding contingent on final approval of missile defense agreements with the countries hosting facilities and on certification by the Secretary of Defense that the proposed interceptor has successfully completed "operationally realistic" flight testing.

CONTROVERSIES ABOUT MDA'S PROPOSED SYSTEM

MDA argues that establishing a missile defense capability in Europe is necessary to address a ballistic missile threat that is "real and growing."[6] According to the agency's technical analysis, the proposed Block 4.0 system would provide additional defense of the United States against ICBMs launched from the Middle East and would defend most of Europe against medium- and intermediate-range missiles launched from the Middle East.[7] However, a number of observers have argued that the testing conducted to date has been insufficient to verify that the Block 4.0 system will function according to MDA's expectations.

Moreover, as proposed, the system would not defend some areas in southeastern Europe—including some member countries of NATO—against short- or medium- range missiles launched from Iran. Extending defensive coverage to those areas would require the United States or NATO to provide additional defensive systems. The Secretary General of NATO has emphasized the importance of complete coverage for NATO members, stating, "We have no A league or B league in NATO. Every NATO ally is entitled to the same kind of protection."[8] In a statement following the NATO summit in Bucharest in April 2008, NATO "recognise[d] the substantial contribution to the protection of Allies from long range ballistic missiles to be provided by the planned deployment of European based United States missile defence assets" but also called for developing "options for a comprehensive missile defence architecture to extend coverage to all Allied territory and populations not otherwise covered by the United States system."[9]

Russia has objected to the U.S. proposal to deploy missile defenses in Europe, questioning the immediacy of an Iranian threat and arguing that the proposed system is actually intended to defend against Russian missiles. The United States and Russia have held several rounds of high-level talks about the proposal. Those discussions have reportedly included the possibility of Russia's cooperation and the use of Russian radars in the system.[10] In April 2008, the two nations released a strategic framework declaration in which "the Russian side has made clear that it does not agree with the decision to establish" missile defense sites in Europe but that left open the door to negotiate about the issue and "to intensify our dialogue...on issues concerning [missile defense] cooperation both bilaterally and multilaterally."[11]

Although the U.S. Secretary of State signed an agreement with the Czech government in July 2008 to host the EMR and an agreement with the Polish government in August 2008 to host the EIS, neither of those agreements has been finalized. The parliaments of the Czech Republic and Poland need to ratify the agreements, and press reports indicate that a majority of the public in those countries opposes hosting the systems.[12] The agreement with the Polish government calls for basing a U.S. battery of Patriot Advanced Capability-3 (PAC-3) missiles in Poland; details about which existing PAC-3 battery will be moved to Poland have yet to be announced.[13]

Options for Missile Defenses in Europe

In this study, the Congressional Budget Office has attempted to address the following questions:

- How well does MDA's proposed system meet the agency's stated Block 4.0 goals?

- What other combinations of existing, planned, or potential missile defense systems could achieve all or part of those goals?

To answer those questions, CBO estimated the ability of the proposed system to defend both Europe and the United States against ballistic missiles fired from Iran and compared the system's cost and level of effectiveness with those of other defensive architectures that could be deployed in Europe. In addition, CBO examined the defensive capability that would be available from other systems that MDA is planning, even if no dedicated European missile defenses were deployed.

For the analysis, CBO assumed that the various systems would be capable of achieving their intended levels of operational effectiveness. However, a number of technical analyses have questioned the efficacy of planned systems, particularly if an adversary employs countermeasures designed to confuse missile defenses. CBO did not explicitly model the options' effectiveness when countermeasures are used. That issue and other caveats about the analysis are discussed at the end of the summary.

The results of the modeling described in this chapter depend on the assumptions that CBO made about the performance of the threat missiles and defensive systems and about the locations of components of those systems. Because many of the systems considered here are under development or are proxies for systems that could potentially be developed, their actual performance parameters are uncertain; different sets of assumptions would lead to different results. (For a discussion of the sensitivity of CBO's analysis to selected assumptions about performance, see Appendix B.)

Dedicated European Missile Defenses

To compare other systems with MDA's planned system, CBO constructed various alternatives that would use mobile interceptors located at sea or on existing U.S. bases in or around Europe. CBO designed the alternatives so that they would provide roughly equivalent levels of defense of Europe against most threats. The specifics of the four options that CBO analyzed are as follows:

- Option 1—The European capability proposed by MDA, consisting of 10 Ground-Based Interceptors permanently housed in silos to be constructed in Poland, an X-band radar in the Czech Republic, and a forward-based X-band radar at a location to be determined.[14] CBO assumed that the forward-based radar (FBR) would be located in Azerbaijan.[15] Current plans call for the system to be fully fielded by 2013.

- Option 2—A standing sea-based defense comprising Aegis ballistic missile defense ships of the U.S. Navy equipped with SM-3 Block IIA interceptors, which are slated to start entering the fleet around 2015. Those ships would maintain three stations—in the waters off Romania, eastern Italy, and Poland—and would be supported by forward-based transportable X-band radars in Azerbaijan and Qatar.

- Option 3—Land-based SM-3 Block IIA interceptors operating from mobile launchers at two existing U.S. bases: Ramstein Air Force Base in Germany and Incirlik Air Force Base in Turkey. Tracking would be provided by forward-based transportable X-band radars in Azerbaijan and Qatar. This system would be available around 2015.

- Option 4—Land-based Kinetic Energy Interceptors operating from mobile launchers at Ramstein and Incirlik Air Force Bases, supported by forward-based transportable X-band tracking radars in Azerbaijan and Qatar. Given the current development schedule for those interceptors, this system would probably not be available before 2018.

The location of the components of a missile defense system relative to the likely trajectories of enemy missiles is critical to the system's capability. In many cases, U.S.-bound missiles launched from Iran would fly over Russia rather than Europe (see Summary Figure 1)—for example, a trajectory from northwestern Iran to Los Angeles passes almost directly over Moscow. Placing the forward-based radar far enough east to track such trajectories is critical to providing defense of the western United States. CBO considered Azerbaijan a suitable location for an FBR for defense of both Europe and the United States, but using locations farther east (such as Afghanistan) could provide better tracking of ICBMs headed toward the United States. Interceptors located in Europe would generally have to fly north and/or east to intercept U.S.- bound missiles. The site of the intercept would vary according to the type of threat missile and interceptor; many potential intercepts would occur over Russia, Scandinavia, or the polar region.

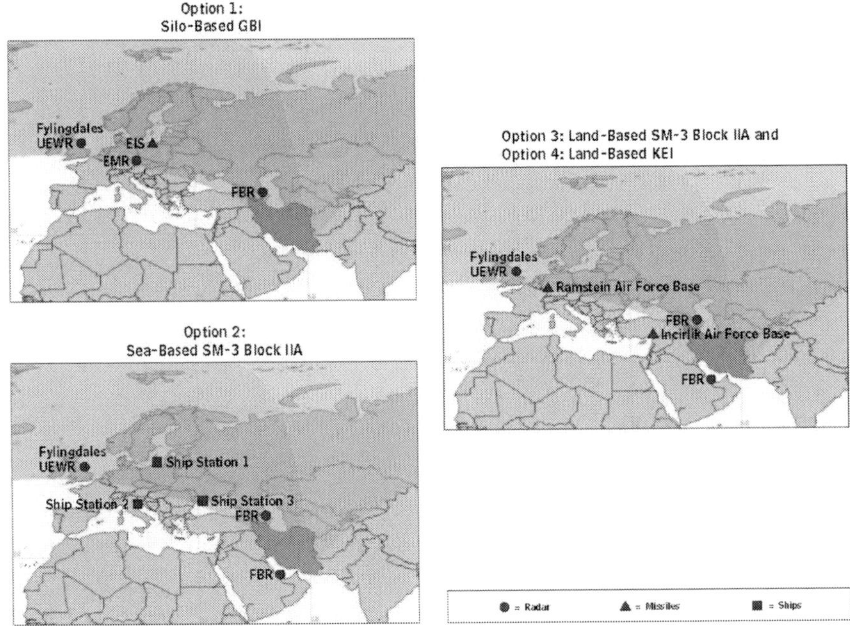

Source: Congressional Budget Office.

Notes: Blue shading indicates the range of trajectories of intercontinental ballistic missiles from Iran to the continental United States. Red shading indicates the additional range of trajectories for missiles targeting all of the United States, including Alaska and Hawaii. Iran is shown in dark gray.

GBI = Ground-Based Interceptor; UEWR = upgraded early-warning radar; EMR = European Midcourse Radar; EIS = European Interceptor Site; FBR = forward-based radar; SM = Standard Missile; KEI = Kinetic Energy Interceptor.

Summary Figure 1. Components of the Options for European Missile Defenses and Their Locations.

Most European-bound missiles launched from Iran could be tracked by an FBR in Azerbaijan. However, that radar could not track missiles launched from southeastern Iran toward the southernmost parts of Europe, such as Spain, southern Italy, and Greece. In Option 1, tracking by the European Midcourse Radar in the Czech Republic could be used for some of those trajectories. In Options 2, 3, and 4, CBO added the forward-based radar in Qatar to provide early tracking for those trajectories. Compared with Iranian missiles bound for the United States, missiles targeting Europe would fly more directly toward the interceptors, so the interceptors would generally fly south and/or east to engage those threats. Intercepts would most likely occur over Europe or the Mediterranean Sea.

Non-European Missile Defenses

The primary goal of this study is to compare the cost and performance of options for deploying missile defenses in Europe. Even without such defenses, however, midcourse-phase systems that are being deployed mainly in the United States and aboard U.S. Navy ships would be capable of defending parts of both Europe and the United States against Iranian missiles. In addition to the options listed above, CBO modeled the defense available from two portions of the overall U.S. missile defense system that are scheduled to be available around 2012:

- The Block 3.0 Ground-Based Midcourse Defense system, which will consist of Ground-Based Interceptors at Fort Greely in Alaska and Vandenberg Air Force Base in California, supported by tracking radars at multiple locations around the world.
- The near-term "surge" capability of Navy ships equipped with the Aegis BMD system using SM-3 Block IB interceptors, which are slated to start entering the fleet around 2011. (That system is an earlier version of the system in Option 2, with less capable interceptors and limits on communications that would mean intercepts could occur only within range of shipboard radars. Those limits increase the number of ships required, so this capability probably represents a temporary crisis-response defense rather than a standing defense.)

Costs of the Missile Defense Options

To estimate the total costs associated with each of the four European-based options, CBO calculated the potential costs for research and development, production of interceptors and radars, construction of physical infrastructure at missile defense sites, and operations over the assumed 20-year lifetime of a system (see Summary Table 1).[16] Overall, CBO estimates, Option 1 would cost between $9 billion and $13 billion; Option 2, between $18 billion and $22 billion; Option 3, between $9 billion and $13 billion; and Option 4, between $10 billion and $14 billion. (Those and other cost estimates in this chapter are in 2009 dollars.) The low number in each range of estimates represents the total cost if few technical difficulties arise in making a system fully operational. The high number accounts for the risk of cost growth by factoring in the extent to which costs have typically grown for similar systems in the past.[17]

The estimates described above do not include development costs for system components (such as various radars or interceptors) that MDA already plans to develop for applications not specific to European defense. The estimates also do not include the costs of any defense assistance or equipment that the United States might provide to the nations hosting missile defense sites, beyond that associated with the direct construction and operation of the sites themselves.

Capabilities of the Missile Defense Options

To compare the defensive capabilities of the various missile defense options, CBO modeled their ability to intercept missiles launched from Iran. The modeling focused on two types of missile threats:

Summary Table 1. Estimated Costs and Components of the Options for European Missile Defenses

	Option 1		Option 2		Option 3		Option 4	
	Low	High	Low	High	Low	High	Low	High
	Estimated Cost (Billions of 2009 dollars)							
R&D[a]	0.4	0.5	0.2	0.3	0.5	0.7	0	0
Production	2.8	3.2	9.5	10.4	2.1	2.6	3.2	4.1
Construction	1.1	1.4	0.3	0.3	0.5	0.7	0.5	0.7
Operations[b]	5.0	7.6	8.3	10.9	5.9	8.8	5.9	8.8
Total	**9.2**	**12.8**	**18.3**	**21.9**	**9.0**	**12.8**	**9.6**	**13.6**
	Deployed Components							
Interceptors	10 two-stage GBIs in Poland		30 SM-3 Block IIAs on ships at three stations		20 SM-3 Block IIAs at Ramstein and Incirlik Air Force Bases		20 KEIs at Ramstein and Incirlik Air Force Bases	
Sensors	UEWR in Fylingdales EMR in Czech Republic FBR in Azerbaijan		UEWR in Fylingdales FBR in Azerbaijan FBR in Qatar		UEWR in Fylingdales FBR in Azerbaijan FBR in Qatar		UEWR in Fylingdales FBR in Azerbaijan FBR in Qatar	

Source: Congressional Budget Office.

Notes: The low estimates assume that few technical difficulties arise in making a system fully operational; the high estimates account for the extent to which costs have typically grown for similar systems in the past.

GBI = Ground-Based Interceptor; SM = Standard Missile; KEI = Kinetic Energy Interceptor; UEWR = upgraded early-warning radar; EMR = European Midcourse Radar; FBR = forward-based radar.

a. The estimates for research and development (R&D) do not include development costs for components that the Missile Defense Agency (MDA) already plans to develop for applications not specific to European defense. For Option 4, no Europe-specific R&D would be necessary because the system would rely on components that already exist or that MDA is developing for general use.

b. Costs are estimated over 20 years.

- Near-term threats—that is, missiles that Iran has tested or claims to have developed, such as the Shahab-3, Shahab-3A, and Ashura. All of those missiles have ranges of about 2,000 kilometers or less, meaning they can reach only the southeastern portion of Europe, including parts of Bulgaria, Romania, and Greece (see Summary Figure 2).

- Potential future threats—that is, missiles that Iran could potentially develop or acquire, such as a liquid- fuel intermediate-range ballistic missile (IRBM), with a range of about 5,000 kilometers, and liquid- or solid-fuel ICBMs, with ranges of about 18,000 and 12,000 kilometers, respectively. In its modeling, CBO used several existing missiles developed by other countries as proxies for those potential future threats. All of those missiles would be capable of reaching anywhere in Europe, and the modeled ICBMs would also be capable of reaching the United States (see Summary Figure 2).

The primary measure of performance in CBO's analysis is the area that a given system would be able to defend against a particular type of missile. That defensive coverage is shown on maps that compare the areas defended by each option. CBO focused on two aspects of performance: defense of Europe against all modeled threats and defense of the United States against potential ICBM threats. (The methodology that CBO used to estimate the options' defensive capability is described in Appendix B.)

Defense of Europe

CBO's analysis supports the following observations about defending Europe against missiles launched from Iran:

- Missiles that Iran has tested or claims to have developed (the near-term threats in this study) are capable of reaching only the southeastern portion of Europe. If Iran developed or acquired IRBMs or ICBMs with performance similar to those produced by several other countries, those missiles would be capable of reaching all of Europe.

- The U.S.-based GMD Block 3.0 system will not provide any defense of Europe against missiles launched from Iran (see Summary Figure 3).

- Aegis BMD ships equipped with SM-3 Block IB interceptors and stationed around Europe would be capable of defending some of Europe against Iranian missiles; the extent of the area defended would depend on the type of threat. That capability could be available before any of the options for dedicated defenses in Europe considered in this analysis. However, given MDA's current plans, the Aegis BMD system would be limited until around 2015 to engaging targets only when they were within range of the ships' onboard SPY-1 radars at the time of intercept. Thus, as many as seven ship stations would be required to provide defensive coverage of much of Europe (albeit with gaps in coverage against some threats). Because two or more ships would be necessary to maintain constant coverage at a given station, that level of presence would probably be sustainable only for short periods with the 18 total ships that MDA plans to outfit for Aegis ballistic missile defense.

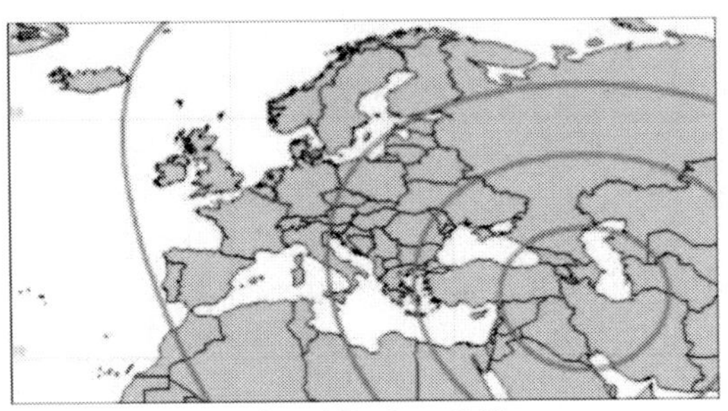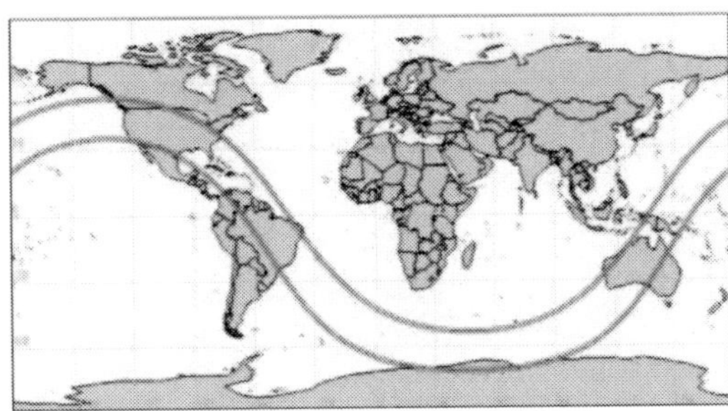

Source: Congressional Budget Office.

Notes: The ranges shown are for launches from northwestern Iran.

The ballistic missiles that Iran is thought to possess now have a maximum range of about 2,000 kilometers (km).

Summary Figure 2. Distances from a Potential Missile Launch Site in Iran.

- The European system proposed by MDA (Option 1) would cover most of Europe against Iranian missiles, with the extent of the defended area depending on the type of missile threat (see Summary Figure 4 for an IRBM threat). However, both CBO's and MDA's analyses indicate that the system's defense would generally not extend to all of southeastern Europe. Defending that area would require deploying additional systems.
- The other alternatives in this analysis (Options 2, 3, and 4) would provide broad defense of most of Europe against all modeled missile threats. All of those options include interceptor locations nearer to Iran than the proposed European Interceptor Site in Poland and thus would provide more extensive defense of southeastern Europe (see Summary Figure 4).
- None of the systems that CBO analyzed would be capable of defending all of Europe against all of the modeled threats.

(Detailed maps of the areas defended by the options and by a near-term Aegis BMD surge capability against all modeled threats are included in Chapter 3.)

Defense of the United States

CBO also modeled the capability of the four options to defend the United States against potential Iranian ICBMs. That defense would be redundant in the sense that it would be in addition to the defensive capability of the GMD Block 3.0 system, much of which is already in place and which MDA plans to complete by 2012.

CBO's analysis supports the following observations about defending the United States against missiles launched from Iran:

- None of the missiles that Iran has tested or claims to have developed are capable of reaching the United States. If Iran developed or acquired an ICBM with performance similar to those built by the United States or Russia, such a missile would be capable of reaching the United States.
- The GMD Block 3.0 system will provide defense for nearly 100 percent of the U.S. population within range of ICBMs from Iran (see Summary Table 2). In most cases,

that defense will be redundant in that both the interceptor site at Fort Greely and the one at Vandenberg Air Force Base will be able to cover a given area.

- Aegis BMD ships with SM-3 Block IB interceptors stationed around Europe would not provide any additional defense of the United States.

- The European system proposed by MDA (Option 1) would provide extra defense of the United States, extending coverage to the less than 1 percent of the U.S. population not covered by the GMD Block 3.0 system and providing defense from a third redundant interceptor site for most of the U.S. population (see Summary Figure 5). For ICBMs headed to the United States, engagement timelines would generally allow operators to assess the results of an attempted intercept from the European site before launching an interceptor from U.S. sites—a scenario referred to as "shoot-look-shoot."

- The options with sea-based and land-based SM-3 Block IIA interceptors (Options 2 and 3) would provide some additional defense of the United States against liquid-fuel ICBMs but none against solid-fuel ICBMs. Those options could provide about the same level of U.S. defense as MDA's proposed European system if they added launch sites for SM-3 Block IIA interceptors in the United States.

- Option 4, with its land-based Kinetic Energy Interceptors, would cover at least 75 percent of the U.S. population in range of ICBMs from Iran. With the modeled interceptor sites in Germany and Turkey, the additional U.S. defense provided by Option 4 would not be as extensive as that of MDA's proposed European system; using different or additional interceptor locations could change the area defended by Option 4. Intercept timelines would allow "shoot-look-shoot" between KEI intercepts from Europe and intercepts from existing GMD sites in the United States. Additionally, as modeled by CBO, the KEI would carry the Multiple Kill Vehicle, which MDA is currently developing to improve an interceptor's performance against countermeasures such as balloons or other mock reentry vehicles launched along with a threat warhead to act as decoys.[18]

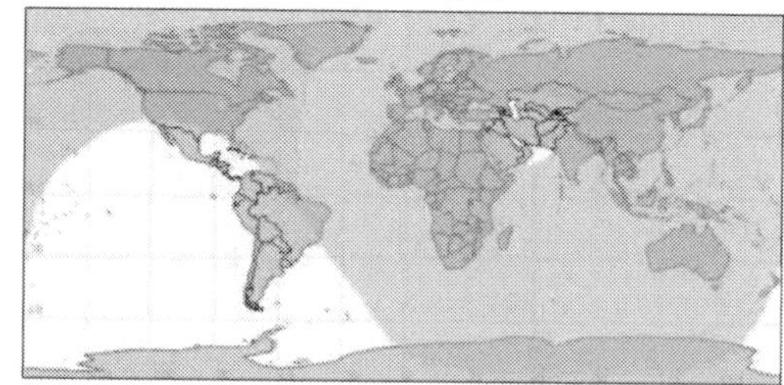

Source: Congressional Budget Office.

Notes: Blue shading indicates the area defended against a given missile threat. Red shading indicates undefended areas within range of that threat.

GMD = Ground-Based Midcourse Defense; ICBM = intercontinental ballistic missile.

Summary Figure 3. Areas Defended by the GMD Block 3.0 System Against ICBMs from Iran.

Issues Not Addressed in This Analysis

An analysis like the one CBO conducted for this study must necessarily include simplifying assumptions that limit the level of technical detail included in the model. Other issues, although relevant to the topic at hand, are beyond the scope of the analysis.

Technical Limitations

Some critics of proposed missile defense systems question their ability to reliably defend against missile threats from a determined adversary. One of the main issues in such criticisms is whether planned missile defenses will be able to overcome countermeasures. A 1999 National Intelligence Estimate on ballistic missile threats stated, "We assess that countries developing missiles also will respond to US theater and national missile defenses by deploying larger forces, penetration aids, and countermeasures.... These countries could develop countermeasures based on these [readily available] technologies by the time they flight test their missiles."[19] A number of more recent analyses argue that the current midcourse interceptors and radars fielded by MDA would not be capable of overcoming such countermeasures.[20]

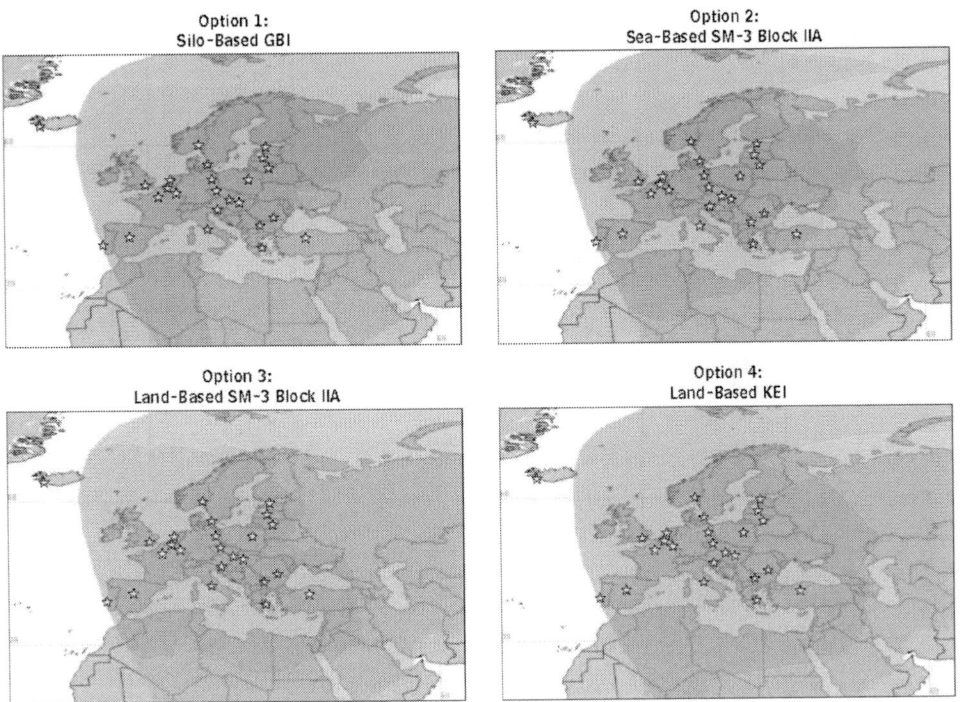

Source: Congressional Budget Office.

Notes: Blue shading indicates the area defended against a given missile threat. Red shading indicates selected undefended areas within range of that threat. Yellow stars show the locations of NATO capitals.

IRBM = intermediate-range ballistic missile; GBI = Ground-Based Interceptor; SM = Standard Missile; KEI = Kinetic Energy Interceptor; NATO = North Atlantic Treaty Organization.

Summary Figure 4. Areas Defended by the Missile Defense Options Against IRBMs from Iran.

Summary Table 2. Summary of the Options' Defensive Capabilities

Type of Missile Threat	GMD Block 3.0 System (Three-stage GBIs at two bases in the United States)	Near-Term "Crisis Response" Defense (SM-3 Block IBs on ships in seven locations)	Option 1 (Two-stage GBIs in Poland)	Option 2 (SM-3 Block IIAs on ships at three permanent stations)	Option 3 (SM-3 Block IIAs at two U.S. bases in Germany and Turkey)	Option 4 (KEIs at two U.S. bases in Germany and Turkey)
	With No Dedicated Defenses in Europe		**Options for Dedicated Defenses in Europe**			
	Defense of Europe (Percentage of threatened European NATO capitals defended)					
Shahab-3A (1 capital in range)	0	100	0	100	100	100
Ashura (3 capitals in range)	0	100	67	100	100	100
IRBM (23 capitals in range)	0	43	91	100	100	100
Liquid-Fuel ICBM (24 capitals in range)	0	71	75	88	46	71
Solid-Fuel ICBM (24 capitals in range)	0	63	92	100	100	100
	Defense of the United States (Percentage of threatened U.S. population defended)					
Liquid-Fuel ICBM						
(100 percent in range) Stand-alone defense	100	0	99	58	24	77
Defense combined with GMD Block 3.0 system	100	100	100	100	100	100
Solid-Fuel ICBM						
(85 percent in range) Stand-alone defense	100	0	100	1	0	89
Defense combined with GMD Block 3.0 system	100	100	100	100	100	100

Source: Congressional Budget Office.

Notes: GMD = Ground-Based Midcourse Defense; GBI = Ground-Based Interceptor; SM = Standard Missile; KEI = Kinetic Energy Interceptor; NATO = North Atlantic Treaty Organization; IRBM = intermediate-range ballistic missile; ICBM = intercontinental ballistic missile.

MDA is working on several projects to defeat countermeasures, including improving discrimination of actual weapon payloads from decoys and developing the Multiple Kill Vehicle to allow a single interceptor to engage several potential targets. Moreover, MDA is pursuing a layered defense, with systems designed to engage missiles during the boost, midcourse, and terminal phases of their flight. Since countermeasure techniques vary for different phases of flight, that approach is intended to reduce the susceptibility of the overall system to countermeasures and to allow multiple systems to engage the same threat missile, if necessary.

Because this chapter focuses on the proposed European midcourse-phase system, CBO considered only other midcourse systems as alternatives to limit the scope of the study. However, boost-phase and terminal-phase systems could also be used to achieve some of MDA's stated defensive goals. A previous CBO report examined missile defense with boost-phase interceptors.[21] Future CBO studies will also address boost-phase defense, including the Airborne Laser. Because of their nature, terminal-phase systems have a limited effective range and probably would be used as a supplement to boost- or midcourse- phase systems rather than as a sole defense.

For the midcourse architectures considered, CBO's technical analysis was based on unclassified performance parameters for the various radars and interceptors and assumed that the systems would work "as advertised." (A sensitivity analysis, which describes the extent to which the results would differ if actual performance deviated from the modeled parameters, is included in Appendix B.) In particular, CBO's estimation of whether an intercept could occur in a given scenario was based on a simulation of the ability of sensors to determine the ballistic trajectory of a threat missile (which, in CBO's model, requires only that the missile be within the sensor's assumed field of regard for a given length of time after the missile booster burns out) and the ability of the interceptor's booster to launch the kill vehicle onto a trajectory that passes close enough to the threat missile for an intercept to potentially occur (subject to constraints on intercept altitude and closing velocity). CBO did not model the detailed dynamics of the kill vehicle's maneuvers in the "end game" or the performance of the kill vehicle's sensor and guidance systems, nor did CBO estimate the probability of a successful intercept (beyond a simple yes or no). Thus, CBO's analysis did not quantify the value of system features designed to defeat countermeasures, such as improved discrimination or multiple kill vehicles, although the report includes a qualitative discussion of how such features vary among the options.

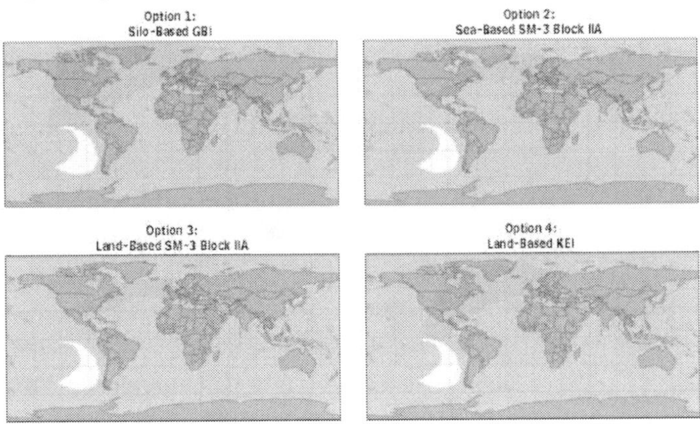

Source: Congressional Budget Office.

Notes: Blue shading indicates the area defended against a given missile threat. Red shading indicates undefended areas within range of that threat.

    ICBM = intercontinental ballistic missile; GBI = Ground-Based Interceptor; SM = Standard Missile; KEI = Kinetic Energy Interceptor.

Summary Figure 5. Areas Defended by the Missile Defense Options Against Liquid-Fuel ICBMs from Iran.

The Severity of Missile Threats from Iran

Another question often raised about MDA's plans for European missile defense is the viability and urgency of the Iranian missile threat—in particular, the threat to the United States. Developing long-range missiles capable of traveling the 10,000 or more kilometers from Iran to the United States would be a technical challenge, as would developing a nuclear weapon. (Presumably, an Iranian ICBM attack on the United States would use a nuclear warhead or other weapon of mass destruction rather than a conventional warhead.) In a 2006 report, DoD's National Air and Space Intelligence Center stated that "Iran has an extensive missile development program and has received support from entities in Russia, China, and North Korea," concluding that "Iran could have an ICBM capable of reaching the United States before 2015."[22] Previous assessments by various organizations have reached similar conclusions.

A National Intelligence Estimate from November 2007 addressed the issue of potential Iranian nuclear weapons, concluding that "Iran probably would be technically capable of producing enough [highly enriched uranium] for a weapon sometime during the 2010–2015 time frame." That report also stated that until fall 2003, Iranian military entities were working to develop a nuclear weapon, but those programs were subsequently halted. However, the report also judged that "Iran has the scientific, technical and industrial capacity eventually to produce nuclear weapons if it decides to do so."[23] Combining those two components to form a viable nuclear ICBM threat would present additional challenges. Citing the difficulties in adapting a nuclear weapon from a laboratory environment "in a concrete tunnel, [with] no G-loading, no vibration, no temperature extremes" to an ICBM, a former commander-in-chief of U.S. Strategic Command stated, "I would submit that the miniaturization of a nuclear warhead is probably the most significant challenge that any proliferant would have to face."[24]

CBO modeled the defensive capability of various missile defense options against shorter-range missiles that Iran has reportedly tested or claims to have developed and against potential future Iranian IRBMs or ICBMs. However, CBO did not attempt to assess whether or when Iran might be technically capable of fielding such threats. CBO's analysis was based on technical descriptions of current Iranian missiles and of proxy missiles developed by other countries available in unclassified literature. The proxy missiles were chosen to represent the various types of missiles that exist and could potentially be fielded by an adversary (a liquid-fuel IRBM capable of reaching all of Europe and liquid- and solid-fuel ICBMs capable of reaching the United States), each of which would present different challenges to a missile defense system. Any actual missiles in those categories that Iran fielded in the future would most likely differ in detail from the proxies that CBO selected.

Finally, some analysts question the need for extensive systems to defend the United States against ballistic missiles in the face of other, arguably more likely, threats. A recent National Intelligence Estimate addressed the potential of nonmissile threats to the United States (using, for example, ships, trucks, or airplanes as delivery mechanisms). It stated that although "[n]onmissile means of delivering weapons of mass destruction do not provide the same prestige or degree of deterrence and coercive diplomacy associated with ICBMs," nevertheless "the Intelligence Community judges that US territory is more likely to be attacked with WMD [weapons of mass destruction] using nonmissile means."[25] That conclusion was based on the arguments that nonmissile means are less expensive than ICBMs; can be developed and deployed covertly in an attempt to evade retaliation; would avoid missile defenses; and, with expected technology over the next 15 years, would be more reliable and much more accurate than ICBMs. CBO has not tried to analyze Iran's strategy or the relative likelihood of various threats. Rather, the scope of this analysis is to compare the expected performance of various missile defense options against a posited Iranian missile threat.

1. BALLISTIC MISSILES: THREATS AND DEFENSES

With their ability to strike at long range and to carry devastating weapons, ballistic missiles are both an attractive military option and a feared threat for many nations. In combat, missiles have several advantages over manned aircraft for attacking an adversary: They can fly above traditional air defenses and attack over long distances very quickly. Moreover, even without being used, missiles pose a threat that gives their owners a means to deter or coerce enemies. Since World War II—when Germany ushered in the modern era of missile warfare by using V-1 and V-2 rockets to attack Britain—the development and use of missiles have become widespread. Today, more than 20 countries field ballistic missile systems. (For a discussion of what makes a missile "ballistic" and other basic concepts of missile defense, see Appendix A.)

To counter such threats, the Department of Defense (DoD) has long been working to develop defenses against ballistic missiles. Early U.S. efforts (such as the 1960s-era Nike-Zeus program) were aimed at countering the Soviet Union's vast arsenal of missiles. Recent efforts are more modest in scope. The National Missile Defense Act of 1999 states, "It is the policy of the United States to deploy as soon as is technologically possible an effective National Missile Defense system capable of defending the territory of the United States against limited ballistic missile attack (whether accidental, unauthorized, or deliberate)."[26]

DoD's Missile Defense Agency (MDA), which oversees those efforts, has broken its goals into a series of "blocks." It is fielding those blocks more or less sequentially, with each new block extending the capability of the overall system:

- Block 1.0—Defend the United States from limited North Korean long-range threats;
- Block 2.0—Defend allies and deployed forces from short- to medium-range threats in one region or theater;
- Block 3.0—Expand defense of the United States to include limited Iranian long-range threats;
- Block 4.0—Defend allies and deployed forces in Europe from limited Iranian long-range threats and expand protection of the U.S. homeland; and
- Block 5.0—Expand defense of allies and deployed forces from short- to intermediate-range threats in two regions or theaters.[27]

MDA's planned Block 4.0 program—which is the focus of this study—envisions putting a missile defense system in Europe by 2013 that could disable or destroy ballistic missiles launched from Iran. The system would consist of interceptor missiles based in Poland, supported by a tracking radar in the Czech Republic and another at an undetermined location closer to Iran. This analysis looks at how well the proposed system would meet MDA's Block 4.0 goals and whether other combinations of existing, planned, or potential missile defense systems could achieve all or some of those goals. Specifically, the Congressional Budget Office (CBO) estimated the ability of MDA's proposed system to defend both Europe and the United States against various types of ballistic missiles fired from Iran. CBO then compared the cost and effec-tiveness of that system with the cost and effectiveness of other defensive architectures that could be deployed.

Current and Potential Missile Threats from Iran

Iran has a history of pursuing ballistic missile programs dating back to the 1970s. Those programs have involved Iran's developing missile systems itself and acquiring them from other countries. Iran has also used its missiles in combat: During the Iran-Iraq "War of the Cities" in the mid-1980s, it reportedly fired more than 600 ballistic missiles. According to unclassified reports, the missiles that Iran has deployed or tested so far appear to have a maximum range of roughly 2,000 kilometers (km).[28] But Iran reportedly has several projects aimed at developing or acquiring longer-range missiles, and Iranian officials have publicly discussed plans to develop a space-launch vehicle for putting satellites into orbit. That vehicle supposedly underwent developmental testing in February 2008. Space-launch technology, if developed, could easily be adapted to offensive ballistic missiles. Several recent assessments by the U.S. intelligence community have judged that by about 2015, Iran could be capable of developing and testing a missile with a long enough range to reach the United States.

For this analysis, CBO considered two types of Iranian missile threats: near-term threats—missiles that Iran has tested or claims to have developed—and potential future threats. To approximate future threats, CBO examined several existing missiles developed by other countries; they are intended to represent the types of missiles that Iran might be able to develop or acquire.

Ballistic missiles are generally categorized by the range over which they can operate. Several classification schemes exist. This chapter follows the categories that MDA uses:

- Short-range ballistic missiles are those with ranges up to 600 km;
- Medium-range ballistic missiles are those with ranges up to 1,300 km;
- Intermediate-range ballistic missiles (IRBMs) are those with ranges up to 5,500 km; and
- Intercontinental ballistic missiles (ICBMs) are those with ranges greater than 5,500 km.

Near-Term Iranian Threats

Iran reportedly has at least three types of intermediate- range ballistic missiles: Shahab-3, Shahab-3A, and Ashura. Their ranges vary from 1,300 km to about 2,000 km, which means that if launched from northwestern Iran, they would be capable of reaching the Black Sea region of southeastern Europe, but not central or western Europe (see Figure 1.1).[29]

The Shahab-3 is a single-stage, liquid-fuel missile with an estimated maximum range of 1,300 km (see Table 1.1). Reportedly, the missile is similar in design to North Korea's No-Dong missile, with the two countries cooperating on at least part of the development process. In turn, the No-Dong is thought to derive from the Russian Scud- B missile. Iran's Shahab-3 is believed to be about 16.5 meters (m) in length and 1.4 m in diameter, with a payload of around 1,200 kilograms (kg). The first reported test of the Shahab-3 was in 1998. According to a recent intelligence report, the system is now operational, with a total inventory of less than 20 launchers fielded.[30]

Numerous reports suggest that Iran has tried to increase the range of the Shahab-3 by adjusting its design. A new version with a redesigned nose-cone shape was reportedly displayed by Iran in 2004. That variant, designated Shahab-3A, is believed to be about a meter longer than the original version and to have an estimated range of about 1,700 km. An intelligence report from 2006 concluded that the Shahab-3A was still in development and not yet fielded at that time.[31]

In November 2007, Iran announced that it had developed a new missile, called the Ashura. According to Iranian statements, the Ashura has a range of about 2,000 km. The Ashura is thought to be a multiple-stage, solid-fuel missile, which represents a departure from the sort of incremental improvements previously made to the Shahab-3 to increase its range. Shortly after Iran announced that it had developed the Ashura, the director of MDA was quoted as saying that the Ashura was "different" and "surprises us."[32] To date, Iran has not claimed to have tested the Ashura, although some press reports indicate that an unsuccessful test occurred in November 2007.[33] In November 2008, Iran said that it had successfully tested a solid-fuel missile with the same range as the Ashura, although it referred to the missile as the Sejil.[34]

Because the claimed development of the Ashura is so recent, no unclassified source is available that gives technical parameters for the new missile. For the modeling in this analysis, CBO used an existing two-stage, solid-fuel missile with comparable range—the Chinese CSS-5—as a proxy for the Ashura.[35] Although that choice was primarily motivated by the availability of unclassified technical parameters for a missile of the same general description, it is possible that the Ashura and the CSS-5 share a common heritage. The 1998 Commission to Assess the Ballistic Missile Threats to the United States concluded that China had contributed extensively to Iran's solid-fuel missile program.

Another missile that might pose a near-term threat is the Musudan, a two-stage, liquid-fuel missile with an estimated maximum range of 3,000 km. The Musudan (also referred to as the BM-25) was developed by North Korea and reportedly was based on Russian R-27 missile technology. Some reports conclude that Iran acquired Musudan missiles from North Korea and may have carried out a flight test of them.[36] However, to date, Iran has not publicly claimed to have acquired or tested the Musudan.

CBO did not specifically look at how well possible missile defenses in Europe would defend against the Musudan. With its 3,000 km range, the Musudan would threaten more of central Europe than the near-term threats that CBO did examine, although it would not be capable of reaching most of western Europe (see Summary Figure 2 on page xvii). As a multiple-stage, liquid-fuel missile, it is similar to the potential future intermediate-range ballistic missile that CBO included in this analysis (see below). However, because the Musudan reportedly has a comparable burn time but a 2,000 km shorter range than that notional missile, it would probably present a less challenging threat to midcourse-phase missile defenses.

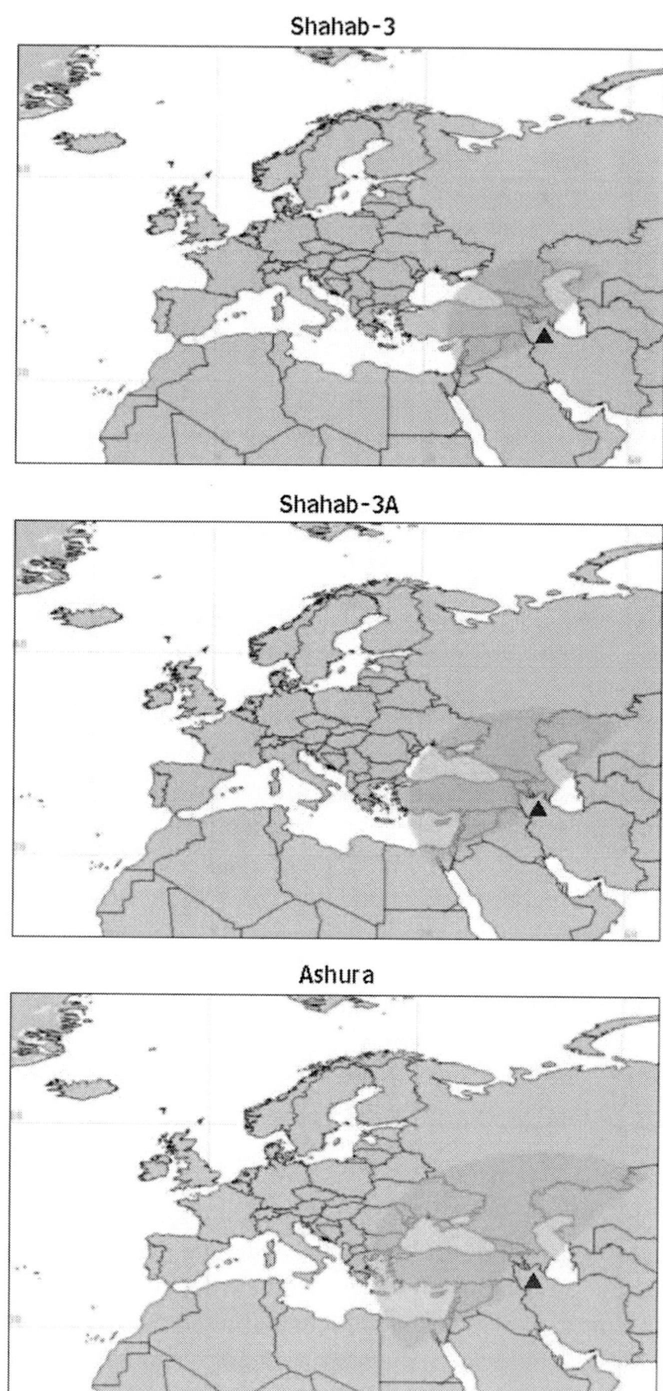

Source: Congressional Budget Office.

Note: Red shading indicates selected regions within range of a given missile launched from northwestern Iran. Missile symbol ▲ indicates the location of the modeled missile launch site in Iran.

Figure 1.1. Areas Within Range of Near-Term Missile Threats from Iran.

Table 1.1. Performance Parameters Assumed for Near-Term and Potential Future Missile Threats from Iran

	Number of Stages	Fuel Type	Maximum Burn Time (Seconds)	Nominal Maximum Burn-Out Velocity (Kilometers per second)	Nominal Maximum Range (Kilometers)
Missiles Posing a Near-Term Threat					
Shahab-3	1	Liquid	98	3.4	1,300
Shahab-3A	1	Liquid	98	3.7	1,700
Ashura	2	Solid	72	3.8	2,100
Missiles Posing a Potential Future Threat					
IRBM	2	Liquid	188	5.5	5,200
Liquid-Fuel ICBM	2	Liquid	329	7.6	17,800
Solid-Fuel ICBM	3	Solid	203	7.0	12,300

Source: Congressional Budget Office based on *Jane's Strategic Weapons Systems* (Coulsdon, Surrey, United Kingdom: Jane's Information Group, 2008); and Steven J. Isakowitz and others, *Space Launch Systems*, 4th ed. (Reston, Va.: American Institute for Aeronautics and Astronautics, 2004).
Note: IRBM = intermediate-range ballistic missile; ICBM = intercontinental ballistic missile.

Potential Future Iranian Threats

None of the missiles that Iran has claimed to have developed or tested is capable of threatening the northwestern half of Europe or the United States. To assess the capability of missile defenses to defend all of Europe and the United States, CBO posited three types of threats that Iran could field in the future:

- A liquid-fuel intermediate-range ballistic missile capable of reaching all of continental Europe, the United Kingdom, and Ireland;
- A liquid-fuel intercontinental ballistic missile capable of reaching all of the United States; and
- A solid-fuel ICBM capable of reaching most of the United States (see Figure 1.2).

In all of those cases, CBO used as proxies existing missiles that fit the general description. It did not attempt to assess when or whether Iran might be able to actually field such missiles.

As a stand-in for a potential Iranian IRBM threat to Europe, CBO used the Taepo-Dong 2 (also referred to as the Paektusan 2), a North Korean two-stage, liquid-fuel missile with a maximum range of more than 5,000 km. The Taepo-Dong 2 failed after about 40 seconds during its only known flight test, which was part of multiple missile launches that North Korea conducted in July 2006.

As a proxy for a potential Iranian liquid-fuel ICBM, CBO chose the Titan II, a two-stage missile first fielded by the United States in the early 1960s. Originally intended to serve as a nuclear-capable ICBM, the Titan II was later adapted as a space-launch vehicle for putting spacecraft into orbit. In CBO's modeling, the Titan II is assumed to have a payload of 3,700 kg and a maximum range of more than 17,000 km, making it capable of reaching almost anywhere on Earth.

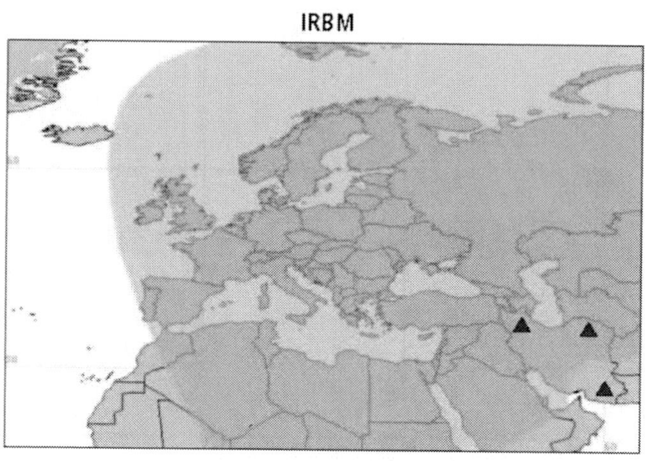

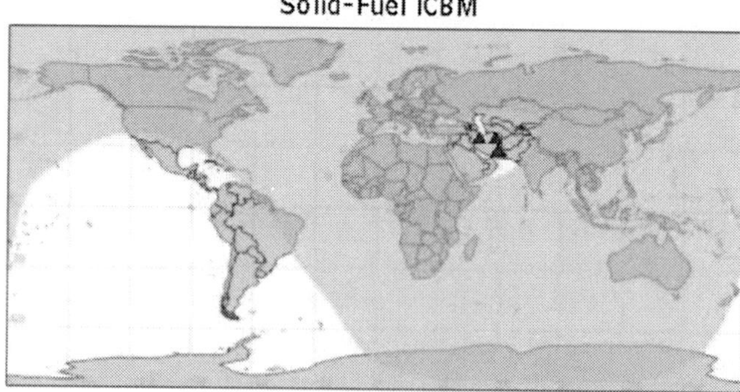

Source: Congressional Budget Office.

Notes: Red shading indicates regions within range of a given missile launched from any of the three modeled missile launch sites in Iran. Missile symbols ▲ indicate the locations of all of the missile launch sites in Iran used in this analysis.

IRBM = intermediate-range ballistic missile; ICBM = intercontinental ballistic missile.

Figure 1.2. Areas Within Range of Potential Future Missile Threats from Iran.

As a stand-in for a potential Iranian solid-fuel ICBM, CBO used the SS-25, a missile first fielded by the Soviet Union in the late 1980s. It is a road-mobile missile that is launched from a transporter-erector-launcher vehicle. As modeled by CBO, this missile has an estimated payload of 1,000 kg and a maximum range of around 12,000 km—capable of reaching most of the United States from Iran.

The Debate about Ballistic Missile Defenses

When faced with an adversary that possesses, or has indicated the intention to possess, ballistic missiles, nations have historically responded in various ways. For example, in the 1970s and 1980s, the United States and the Soviet Union negotiated agreements about the extent or capability of their inventories of ballistic missiles, such as the Intermediate-Range Nuclear Forces Treaty and agreements from the Strategic Arms Limitation Talks. In addition, nations that possess missile or warhead technology have negotiated agreements to refrain from sharing that technology with countries that do not already possess it. Examples of such agreements include the Missile Technology Control Regime and the Nuclear Non-Proliferation Treaty.

Another approach that nations have followed is trying to deter an adversary militarily from using (or perhaps even from fielding) ballistic missiles, either through conventional armed forces or through the deployment of a countering ballistic missile force. The ultimate example of that approach is the strategy of mutually assured destruction that the United States and the Soviet Union pursued during the Cold War. Another military option is to destroy or neutralize an adversary's missiles before they can be used. For example, U.S. and allied special forces reportedly captured Iraq's Scud missile sites before the main invasion of Iraq in 2003 so those missiles could not be used in combat.[37]

The approach that this study focuses on is fielding ballistic missile defenses to destroy an enemy missile after it is fired. The primary example of such defenses being employed in combat is the United States' use of Patriot missile interceptors against Iraqi Scud missiles during Operation Desert Storm in 1991.

Historically, the development of missile defenses has often been controversial. Advocates argue that the threat from ballistic missiles is growing despite efforts to control it through diplomacy. The United States' nuclear arsenal and conventional forces provide some measure of deterrence by enabling the country to make a devastating response to the launch of an enemy missile. But missile defenses are touted as a supplement to that deterrent: They could provide a means of defense against the potentially catastrophic effects of even a single missile attack, should deterrence fail. Moreover, some people argue that deterrence may not entirely succeed against threats from rogue nations, which seek to use missiles not "as operational weapons of war" but "primarily as weapons of coercive diplomacy, to complicate U.S. decision-making or limit our freedom to act in a crisis."[38] In such cases, advocates argue, the presence of missile defenses would give U.S. leaders more flexibility in their actions and perhaps discourage adversaries from pursuing offensive missiles in the first place.

Critics of missile defenses make a number of arguments against developing such defenses, including their potential to complicate deterrence and arms control agreements. The 1972 Anti-Ballistic Missile (ABM) treaty between the United States and the Soviet Union sought to reduce the effect of missile defenses on the deterrence calculus by limiting the number and nature of missile defenses that each country could field. In particular, the treaty outlawed any system with full national coverage, limiting each nation to a single missile defense site with a maximum of 100 ground-based interceptors.[39] No land- mobile, sea-based, or space-based interceptors were permitted. During the late 1990s—when the first tests of what would become the current Ground-Based Mid-course Defense (GMD) system were taking place— efforts were made to design a system that would be close enough to existing ABM treaty limitations on location and scope of coverage to fit within an amended treaty. Reportedly, one concern during that process was that if the United States withdrew from the ABM treaty, the Russians or Chinese might respond by expanding or improving their nuclear forces, which in turn could trigger expansion or improvement of India's and Pakistan's arsenals.[40] Nevertheless, the United States withdrew from the treaty, effective in June 2002, citing a need to "defend its homeland, its forces and its friends and allies" against missile threats from "terrorists and rogue states."[41] More recently, in response to the proposal to deploy a missile defense system in Europe, Russian leaders reportedly threatened to withdraw from some arms control treaties, such as the Intermediate-Range Nuclear Forces Treaty. They also pledged to move short-range missiles closer to the interceptor site in Poland if the defense system was deployed.[42]

Besides concerns about arms control, critics of missile defenses often cite the high cost of such systems and the technical challenges they must overcome to operate effectively. Since 1985, appropriations for MDA and its predecessor missile defense organizations have totaled about $144 billion, an average of $6.0 billion per year (in 2009 dollars). Since 2002, after the U.S. withdrawal from the ABM treaty, annual appropriations for MDA have averaged about $9.0 billion. President Bush's 2009 budget request called for the average level of annual spending to rise slightly, to $9.2 billion, through 2013. Developing cost-effective missile defenses is also technologically challenging, particularly when the missiles being targeted are equipped with countermeasures designed to foil defense systems. The various technical obstacles that different kinds of missile defense systems face are described in more detail below.

Technical Challenges to Ballistic Missile Defenses

Missile defense systems are generally categorized by where in a missile's flight they are designed to engage the missile. Missile flight is generally split into three phases:

- The **boost phase,** which lasts from launch until the booster stops firing (and generally separates from the weapon payload). The length of this phase can vary from one minute or less for short- and medium-range ballistic missiles to several minutes for intermediate- range and intercontinental ballistic missiles.
- The **midcourse phase,** during which the payload coasts on a ballistic trajectory, usually outside the atmosphere, toward its target. This phase is by far the longest and can last from less than 10 minutes to about 40 minutes, depending on the range of the missile.

- The **terminal phase,** which begins when the payload reenters the atmosphere (nominally at an altitude of 100 km) on its way toward the target. This phase generally lasts for less than a minute.

The U.S. missile defense systems now under development generally use one of two technological approaches to engaging enemy missiles: directed-energy (laser) beams or interceptor missiles. Laser-based systems are designed to engage the booster of an enemy missile (usually referred to as a threat missile) by burning a hole in its outer casing. Thus, such systems are limited to boost-phase defense, before the payload separates from the booster. (A payload typically includes a warhead encased in a reentry vehicle. Because such vehicles are hardened to resist the heat of reentering the atmosphere at high speed, destroying them with a laser beam would be very challenging.)

Interceptors, by contrast, can engage threat missiles during any phase of flight, either by striking the booster or the payload directly (referred to as hit-to-kill or kinetic kill) or by causing a high-explosive or nuclear detonation near the missile. Intercepting a missile during its boost phase has the advantage that the booster is still attached to the payload and is still burning, presenting a relatively large, hot target that is easy for both radar and infrared sensors to detect. However, because the boost phase is short, interceptors need to have high acceleration and be located close to the launch site of the missile they are targeting.

Intercepts in the midcourse phase have the advantage of a longer time frame, so interceptors can be launched from locations farther from the launch site of the threat missile and still be able to reach the missile in time. However, once the payload separates from the booster, it is considerably smaller than the full missile, presenting a more challenging target for hit-to-kill interceptors and making tracking with radar more difficult. In addition, nations have developed numerous countermeasures to foil midcourse defenses. They include deploying decoys to confuse interceptors; encasing the warhead in a balloon or an oversized reentry vehicle to hide it (also potentially to cool it and mask its thermal signature); deploying jammers, chaff, or flares to reduce sensors' ability to track the warhead; splitting the warhead into numerous submunitions to make complete destruction more difficult; and enabling the reentry vehicle to maneuver so it can depart from the expected ballistic trajectory. Some current or planned midcourse-phase defense programs include, or intend to develop, various means to address countermeasures. The efficacy of such counter- countermeasures has not yet been evaluated with flight tests against target missiles equipped with countermeasures.

Intercepts in the terminal phase have the advantage that many of those countermeasures will not survive reentry into the atmosphere. In addition, terminal-phase interceptors are deployed near the areas being protected rather than the potential launch sites of enemy missiles, reducing the political and logistical issues associated with basing defenses in other countries. However, the time scale for intercept during the terminal phase is very short, and the warhead is moving very fast.

Although each phase of a missile's flight presents unique challenges to missile defenses, all types of defenses must go through several critical steps before actually engaging a missile. First, the defense must become aware that the threat missile has been launched. U.S. systems generally detect launches by using infrared sensors on satellites, although land- or air-based infrared sensors or radar might also be used.

Second, the defense must determine the trajectory of the threat missile. That knowledge allows operators to predict the intended target, the flight time of the missile, and its position as a function of time along the trajectory. The missile's trajectory is generally measured with radar, although infrared satellites can provide some tracking capability, particularly during the boost phase. Before the missile's booster burns out, predictions of the full trajectory are very uncertain.[43] The velocity and acceleration of the missile can change quickly as stages burn out and new ones start to fire, so predicting the trajectory even on short time scales is difficult. Once the booster has burned out and the missile has entered the ballistic (midcourse) phase, its future position can be estimated much more reliably. Nevertheless, because of the inherent limitations of sensors operating over long range, there is always some uncertainty in the predicted position of the missile. To reduce that uncertainty, most missile defense systems are designed to allow communication between the tracking sensors and the engagement system, so the trajectory prediction can be refined during the engagement. Generally, the interceptor itself carries some sensors, often contained in a so-called kill vehicle that separates from the interceptor booster and maneuvers to adjust the trajectory to the intercept.[44]

Third, on the basis of the predicted trajectory of the threat missile, operators must choose the parameters of the defensive engagement. Because most U.S. missile defense systems use interceptors, this step consists of determining the optimum trajectory for the interceptor to intersect with the trajectory of the threat missile. That choice is constrained by the time required for the interceptor to fly to the intercept point. It may also be restricted by the interceptor's or kill vehicle's limits on intercept altitude (both maximum and minimum intercept altitudes are possible) and by constraints on the intercept geometry (such as limits on the relative velocity between the interceptor and the threat missile that is required to make a kinetic kill or on the angle between the trajectories that will allow the interceptor's sensors to operate).[45] For directed-energy weapons, such as the Airborne Laser, other criteria go into selecting the optimum engagement position. They include constraints on the distance to the threat missile, the angle between the laser beam and the missile's body, and the altitude of the engagement.

The timeline for the three steps described above—and the time available for the engagement itself—depends on the type of missile being targeted, the phase of flight in which the engagement will occur, the location of the missile defense system's components relative to the launch site, and the range over which the components can operate effectively. The various types of missiles with which Iran might pose a threat to Europe or the United States vary widely in their burnout times, total flight times, and distances flown during those times (see Figure 1.3). Thus, the placement of the sensors and interceptor launch sites is critical to a system's ability to engage all types of threat missiles.

- Sensors need to be close enough to the launch site to begin tracking a missile early in its trajectory. But ideally, they should not be so close that a longer-range missile passes through and out of the sensors' field of regard before its booster burns out.
- Sites for launching interceptors need to be far enough away from the potential launch sites of threat missiles that the defense has time to react and the interceptor has time to fly to the intercept point before the threat missile has passed too far beyond the interceptor launch site. (Such "tail-chase" engagements put the defense at a disadvantage unless the interceptor is significantly faster than the threat missile.) However, for boost-phase intercepts, interceptor launch sites must be close enough to the launch sites of threat missiles that an interceptor can fly out to engage a missile before the missile's booster has burned out.

To meet their defensive goals, both boost-phase and midcourse-phase missile defenses may need to cover threat-missile trajectories with a wide range of azimuth angles (the angle of the trajectory relative to north). For missiles launched onto trajectories that point away from the interceptor site, a trade-off comes into play: If the interceptor site is too close to the launch site, the interceptor may not have time to reach those trajectories before the threat missile passes the interceptor site, resulting in a tail-chase engagement. But if the interceptor site is too far away from the threat missile's launch site, the interceptor may not have enough range or speed to reach the missile. If the range of azimuths that threat missiles could use is sufficiently large, multiple interceptor sites may be needed to defend the full desired area.

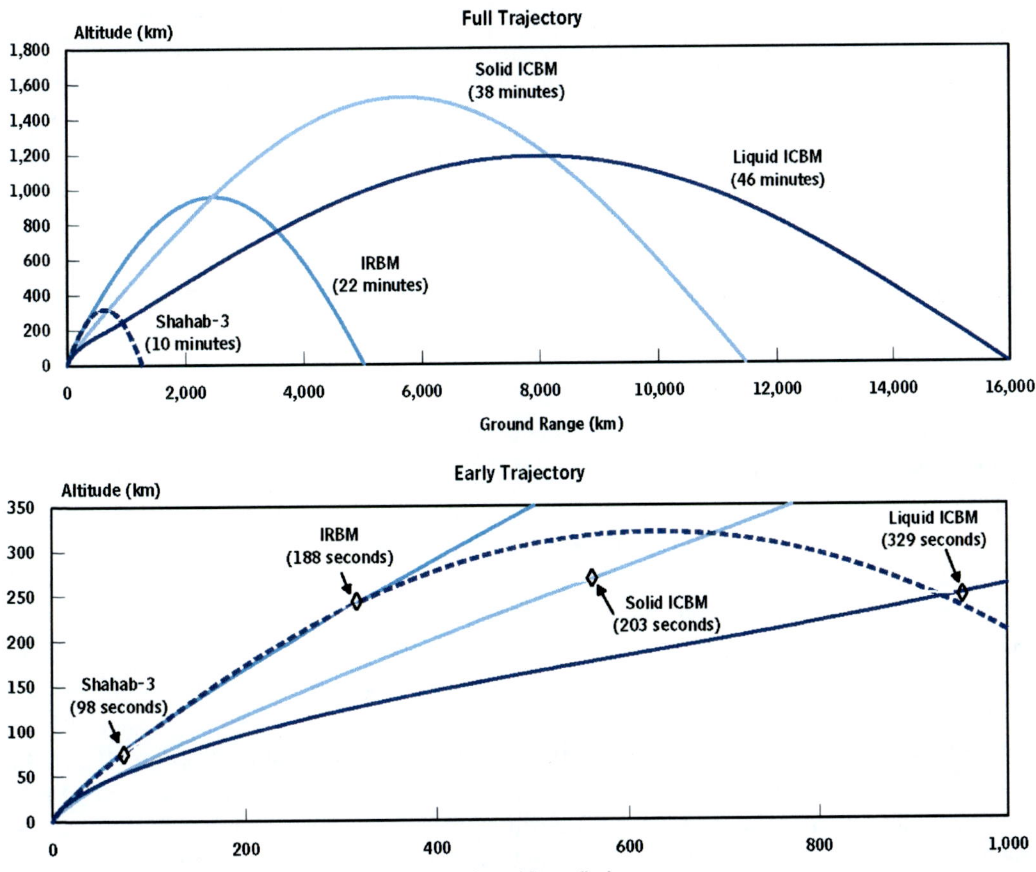

Source: Congressional Budget Office.

Notes: The upper panel shows the full trajectories and total flight times for the various types of missiles; the lower panel shows detail of the missiles' trajectories near the launch site as well as their burnout times and position at burnout (diamond-shaped symbols).

km = kilometers; IRBM = intermediate-range ballistic missile; ICBM = intercontinental ballistic missile.

Figure 1.3. Altitude Versus Ground Range for Various Types of Missile Threats.

Current and Planned Components of U.S. Missile Defenses

Under the ABM treaty, defenses against long-range missiles were limited to one fixed, land-based interceptor site, with no land-mobile, sea-based, or space-based interceptors allowed. Limits were also placed on the location, number, and sensitivity of radars supporting missile defenses. Since the United States withdrew from the ABM treaty in 2002, the Missile Defense Agency has pursued research and development efforts into many of the formerly prohibited approaches to fielding missile defenses. The goal of MDA's efforts is to construct a layered defense—one capable of engaging enemy missiles during all phases of their flight—by combining disparate sensors and systems aimed at particular phases of flight with an overarching command, control, battle management, and communications system.

Work on midcourse-phase and terminal-phase defenses is farthest advanced. Two terminal-phase systems, both operated by the Army, are currently being fielded—the Patriot Advanced Capability-3 (PAC-3) system has more than 500 operational interceptors, and the Army activated its first Terminal High-Altitude Area Defense (THAAD) battery in May 2008. Two midcourse-phase systems—the Ground-Based Midcourse Defense system (operated by the Army) and the Aegis ballistic missile defense (Aegis BMD) system (operated by the Navy)— have also begun to be fielded. Development efforts are continuing on those and numerous other missile defense systems, as well as on a variety of sensors to detect and track threat missiles.

Boost-Phase Defenses

MDA is pursuing several programs that would use lasers or interceptors to engage a threat missile while its booster was still firing.

The Airborne Laser system consists of a highly modified Boeing 747 aircraft that contains a high-power chemical laser, several lower-power lasers to aid in pointing and focusing the high-power laser, and various sensors. Design of the Airborne Laser (in its current form) began in 1996, and the first developmental aircraft is scheduled to conduct a shoot-down test in 2009. Current plans, which are contingent on the outcome of that test, call for building a second developmental aircraft for continued testing from 2009 to 2018 and then procuring seven operational aircraft.

MDA is also developing a land-mobile interceptor system called the Kinetic Energy Interceptor (KEI). That program is currently focusing on midcourse intercepts, but the system is also being designed to intercept missiles during their boost phase. The first flight test of the system's high-acceleration booster is scheduled for 2009, and developers are aiming to have the KEI ready for operations sometime after 2015. They also envision developing a sea-based version of the KEI in the future.

MDA is in the early stages of research on other potential boost-phase intercept systems. One concept being explored is air-launched interceptors, using several different combinations of aircraft platforms and interceptors. Another effort, the Space Test Bed, is investigating the idea of space-based interceptors.

Midcourse-Phase Defenses

MDA is continuing its development efforts to expand or improve systems that are designed to engage threat missiles after the booster burns out but before the warhead reenters the atmosphere.

The Ground-Based Midcourse Defense system is intended to defend the United States against long-range missiles. It uses three-stage Ground-Based Interceptors (GBIs) located in silos at Fort Greely in Alaska and Vandenberg Air Force Base in California. The first phase of fielding the system (called the initial defensive capability) was completed in December 2005, with eight GBIs at Fort Greely and two at Vandenberg. By the end of 2007, the number of interceptors at those sites had increased to 21 and 3, respectively. MDA's planned Block 4.0 program for missile defenses in Europe would add a third interceptor site, currently slated for Poland, to the GMD system. That site would use a two-stage version of the GBI rather than the three-stage version used in the United States. (Plans for expanding the GMD system to Europe are described in more detail in Chapter 2.)

Another current midcourse-phase defense, the Aegis BMD system, is designed to use the SPY-1 radar installed on many Navy warships to track missiles and a modified version of the Navy's Standard Missile (SM) to intercept them. The most recent version of the interceptor is the SM-3 Block IA, but further upgrades are being developed. The SM-3 Block IB, with an improved kill vehicle, is slated to start entering the fleet in 2011; the SM-3 Block IIA, with a larger second stage for higher burnout velocity and further improvements to the kill vehicle, is expected to be ready for deployment in about 2015. As of the end of 2007, 10 Navy ships were capable of tracking threat missiles and launching Aegis BMD interceptors, and another 7 ships were capable of performing only the radar-tracking portion of the BMD mission. MDA's plans call for outfitting a total of 18 ships for the full Aegis BMD mission.

In addition, the Kinetic Energy Interceptor that is under development is being considered for midcourse intercepts. The KEI program is pursuing a common booster that could be used for land-mobile, land-fixed (silo-based), and sea-mobile launches for either midcourse- or boost-phase intercepts. For midcourse- phase intercepts, plans call for the KEI to be capable of carrying the Multiple Kill Vehicle, which would allow a single interceptor to launch several kill vehicles and thus increase the probability of engaging the actual warhead if decoy countermeasures were present. Variants of the Multiple Kill Vehicle, which is still being developed, could also potentially be carried by the GMD system's ground-based interceptors or by a later, post-Block IIA version of the Aegis system's SM-3 interceptor.

Terminal-Phase Defenses

The United States currently has two land-based defense systems designed to engage threat missiles after their warheads have reentered the atmosphere. MDA is also pursuing a sea-based terminal-phase missile defense.

The Patriot Advanced Capability-3 system is intended to provide terminal-phase defense against short- and medium-range missiles. The Army is responsible for the system, which is now operational. PAC-3 is eventually supposed to be supplemented by the Medium Extended Air Defense System (MEADS), a joint U.S. venture with Italy and Germany, which will use an improved version of the PAC-3 interceptor.

The other land-based system, the Terminal High-Altitude Area Defense, is a deployable terminal-phase defense that consists of an X-band tracking radar, a mobile launcher capable of carrying eight interceptors, and associated fire control and communications.[46] The Army recently activated the first THAAD unit, with 24 THAAD interceptors on three launchers, based at Fort Bliss, Texas.

A new addition to MDA's terminal-phase defense portfolio is the Sea-Based Terminal program, which is intended to use the architecture of the midcourse Aegis BMD system. As now envisioned, the Sea-Based Terminal program would first develop a near-term capability using a modified version of the SM-2 Block IV interceptor and then develop a far-term capability based on a new interceptor.

Sensors

The ability to detect and track threat missiles is critical to the success of any missile defense program. MDA's plans for a layered ballistic missile defense envision using a variety of existing or planned sensors:

- Upgraded early-warning radars—existing early- warning radars whose hardware and software have been upgraded to enhance their tracking capabilities. Those radars are located at Beale Air Force Base in California; Fylingdales, England; Thule, Greenland; and Shemya, Alaska. Other radars in Clear, Alaska, and Cape Cod, Massachusetts, will be integrated into the ballistic missile defense system once the Air Force finishes upgrading them.

- The European Midcourse Radar—an X-band radar designed for tracking missiles and discriminating between warheads and decoys. The radar, previously deployed on Kwajelein Atoll in the Pacific, is to be moved to the Czech Republic as part of MDA's plans for a European missile defense capability.

- The Sea-Based X-Band Radar—a high-power radar designed for tracking and discriminating between warheads and decoys. The radar is mounted on a movable sea platform and has participated in tests at several locations. After testing, it is to be stationed offshore at Adak, Alaska.

- The AN/TPY-2—a transportable X-band radar based on the radar of the THAAD system.[47] One AN/TPY2 has been deployed to Shariki, Japan, and MDA plans to use another as the forward-based radar for the proposed European missile defense system.

- The Space Tracking and Surveillance System (STSS)—a planned constellation of infrared satellites.[48] Two STSS demonstration satellites are slated to be launched in 2009. The size and satellite design for the operational STSS constellation (referred to as STSS Follow-On) is still being determined. The goal of the system is to track threat missiles during their entire trajectory.

- The Defense Support Program and the Space-Based Infrared System–High— constellations of Air Force surveillance satellites that are intended to provide infrared detection of missile launches.

2. OPTIONS FOR MISSILE DEFENSES IN EUROPE

The Missile Defense Agency's planned Ground-Based Midcourse Defense Block 4.0 system has two stated goals: to defend U.S. allies and deployed forces in Europe against limited threats from Iranian long-range missiles and to expand protection of the United States against those threats. Deploying that system would involve placing interceptors and radars in various European countries. MDA hopes to have the system operational by 2013.

How well would the proposed GMD Block 4.0 system achieve its stated goals? Could other current or proposed missile defense systems meet the same objectives, perhaps from existing U.S. bases or at a lower cost? To answer those questions, the Congressional Budget Office examined four options for basing missile defenses in Europe and modeled their ability to meet the Block 4.0 goals. Option 1 corresponds to the European system proposed by MDA. The other three options—which CBO designed to provide roughly the same level of European defense as the GMD Block 4.0 system against most types of threats—would use various systems that MDA has already developed or proposed. To limit the scope of this study and allow for a more direct comparison among the alternatives, only midcourse-phase defense systems were included in the analysis.

Any of those options for missile defenses in Europe would supplement other midcourse-phase defenses— specifically, the U.S.-based GMD Block 3.0 system and Aegis ballistic missile defense ships—that the Department of Defense plans to have in place at various locations around the world by about 2012. CBO also modeled the ability of those systems to defend Europe and the United States against missiles launched from Iran. This chapter describes those existing defenses as well as the components and costs of the four options for deploying missile defenses in Europe. Chapter 3 explores in detail how much defensive coverage of Europe and the United States the various alternatives would provide against different types of missile threats.

Existing Midcourse-Phase Defenses

To help meet its Block 3.0 goal (expanding defense of the United States to include limited Iranian long-range threats), MDA is continuing to add capability to the GMD system that has been operating since the end of 2005. The GMD Block 3.0 system, which is scheduled to be in place by 2012, will include 44 interceptors launched from silos: 40 at Fort Greely in Alaska and 4 at Vandenberg Air Force Base in California.[49] It will also include several radar installations and a command, control, battle management, and communications system to link the various components (see Figure 2.1).

The GMD system uses three-stage, solid-fuel Ground-Based Interceptors. Each GBI consists of an Orbital Boost Vehicle booster and an Exoatmospheric Kill Vehicle (EKV) that is capable of engaging a single target. MDA is also developing the Multiple Kill Vehicle (MKV), which would be able to engage multiple targets as a way to counter decoys deployed by an enemy missile. Designers envision that the GBI will eventually carry the MKV. However, in this analysis, CBO modeled only the EKV version of the ground-based interceptor. The MKV would presumably be heavier than the EKV, which would reduce the burnout velocity of the interceptor and thus its range.

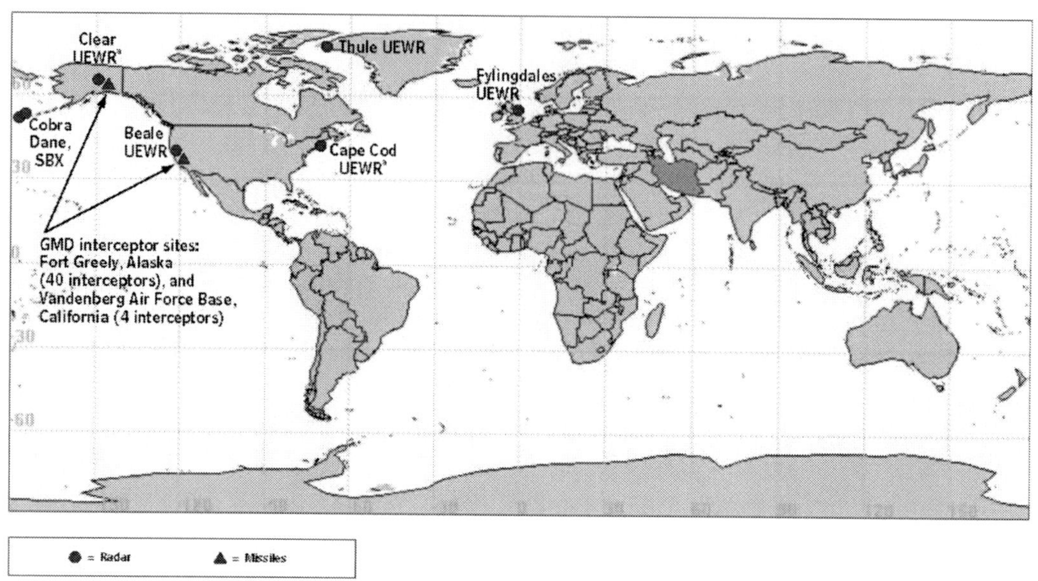

Source: Congressional Budget Office.

Notes: Iran is shown in dark gray.

    GMD = Ground-Based Midcourse Defense; UEWR = upgraded early-warning radar; SBX = Sea-Based X-Band Radar.

a. The Clear and Cape Cod UEWRs will be added to the Block 3.0 system after the Air Force finishes upgrading them.

Figure 2.1. Components of the GMD Block 3.0 System and Their Locations.

A variety of sensors can or will provide tracking for the GMD system, including upgraded early-warning radars (UEWRs) in Fylingdales, England; Thule, Greenland; Beale, California; Clear, Alaska; and Cape Cod, Massachusetts.[50] UEWRs have a very long range (about 5,000 kilometers). However, they operate in the ultrahigh frequency (UHF) range with wavelengths of about 70 centimeters (cm), which limits their spatial resolution and thus their ability to see fine detail to distinguish actual targets from decoys. The longest range radar available to the GMD system is the Cobra Dane radar located in Shemya, Alaska, which operates in the L-band at a shorter wavelength (about 20 cm), allowing better spatial resolution. The highest resolution is provided by the Sea-Based X-Band Radar (SBX), a mobile long-range radar that operates at wavelengths of about 3 cm and that will be based at Adak, Alaska. (The modeled performance characteristics of those and other sensors included in CBO's analysis are shown in Appendix B.)

In addition to the GMD system, Navy ships equipped with the Aegis ballistic missile defense system could be available to respond to Iranian missile launches. The Missile Defense Agency envisions equipping 18 ships with the Aegis BMD capability, including having a total inventory of 52 Block IB interceptors available by 2014. However, 18 ships would probably not be enough to maintain a large Aegis BMD presence in Europe over extended periods. Thus, this system would most likely be a "crisis response" defense—to be used for a limited time during periods of heightened tensions—rather than a standing defense. (The form that such a defense might take and the defensive capability it could provide are described in Chapter 3.)

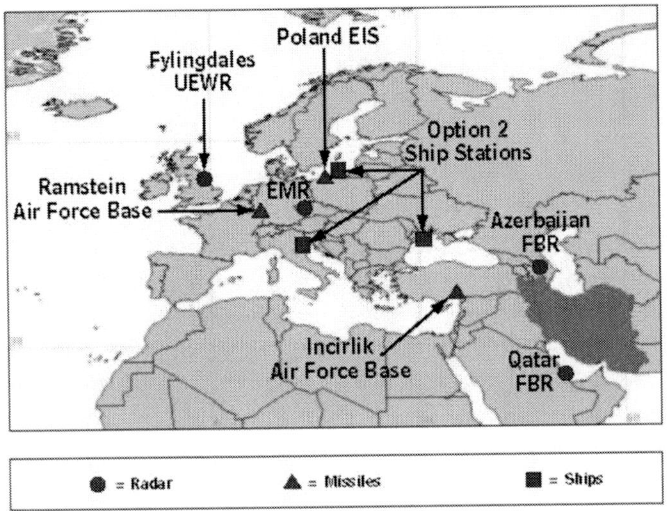

Source: Congressional Budget Office.

Notes: Iran is shown in dark gray.

UEWR = upgraded early-warning radar; EIS = European Interceptor Site; EMR = European Midcourse Radar; FBR = forward-based radar.

Figure 2.2. Components of the Options for European Missile Defenses and Their Locations.

Four Alternatives for Missile Defenses in Europe

To supplement those existing defenses, CBO examined four possible options for deploying missile defenses in Europe, with components located at various places in Europe and the Middle East (see Figure 2.2). MDA's plan to base missile defense facilities in Europe (Option 1 in this analysis) has entailed lengthy negotiations with host nations. To potentially simplify such negotiations, the other options that CBO developed would locate interceptors and radars either at sea or on existing U.S. bases in Europe and the Middle East (a forward-based radar, or FBR, is assumed to be located in the Caucasus region). At a Congressional hearing in April 2008, the director of MDA indicated that European nations might be more open to hosting interceptors that were mobile instead of deployed in fixed silos.[51] Thus, the land-based options that CBO developed (Options 3 and 4) would use mobile interceptors instead of the fixed ones that MDA plans to deploy.

Option 1 : MDA's Planned European System

The first option corresponds to the GMD Block 4.0 European capability proposed by MDA. It comprises interceptors in Poland, an X-band radar in the Czech Republic, and a forward-based radar at a location to be determined. In line with MDA's plans, that system is assumed to be fully deployed by 2013.

The interceptors in Option 1 would be located at Redzikowo air base in northern Poland, where 10 silos, each holding one interceptor, would be built. The interceptors would be two-stage versions of the GBI, with the third stage of the booster removed to increase acceleration (see Box 2.1). Those interceptors would initially carry the EKV, although they could be adapted to carry the antidecoy MKV once it was developed.

MDA's GMD Block 4.0 system would also include an X-band radar—called the European Midcourse Radar (EMR)—to be located in Brdy, Czech Republic. In July 2008, the U.S. Secretary of State and the Czech Foreign Minister signed an agreement for the Czech Republic to host the EMR; as of December 2008, however, the agreement had been approved by the upper house of the Czech parliament but not yet by the lower house. The EMR is an existing X-band radar that would be moved to Europe from Kwajalein Atoll in the Pacific, where it has been used to support missile testing. For this analysis, CBO modeled the range of the EMR using technical descriptions of the Kwajalein radar available in unclassified sources.[52] However, some recent studies have concluded that the radar's effective range may be considerably less than modeled by CBO.[53]

MDA's plans also call for deploying a forward-based radar, although the location and description of the radar have not yet been specified. For this analysis, CBO assumed that the radar would resemble an AN/TPY-2 transportable X-band radar with a range of 1,000 km. Press reports suggest that MDA has considered a location in the Caucasus region for the FBR; in this study, CBO assumed that the radar would be located in Azerbaijan. (That location was used in all four of the options.) The antenna of the AN/TPY-2 has a field of regard of 120 degrees in azimuth, with electronic steering available to move the radar beam quickly within that field. However, a mechanical steering kit is being developed to allow physical movement of the antenna, so that a single radar antenna can be extended to a full 360-degree field of regard in azimuth. CBO assumed that mechanical steering kits would be used for all of the AN/TPY-2 radars in this study.

2.1. TWO-STAGE AND THREE-STAGE GROUND-BASED INTERCEPTORS

The Missile Defense Agency (MDA) is planning to field a two-stage version of its current ground-based interceptor in Europe rather than the three-stage version used at the U.S.-based launch sites of the Ground-Based Midcourse Defense system. According to MDA, the two-stage interceptor will be very similar to the original version, with the same overall dimensions (16.6 meters long and 1.3 meters in diameter). However, the third and final stage of the interceptor's booster will be removed, and modifications will be made to the avionics module and the guidance and control software. MDA has budgeted a total of about $120 million to develop the two-stage version and integrate it into the command-andcontrol architecture of the overall missile defense system.

Those design modifications are necessary because European interceptors will be located closer to the potential launch sites of threat missiles than U.S.- based interceptors are, and they will need to be able to reach the intercept points sooner. Removing the third stage reduces the overall mass of the booster by about 1,000 kilograms. Because the first two stages will not have to lift that extra mass, the interceptor will accelerate more quickly. However, since the interceptor will no longer have the thrust provided by the third stage, its final burnout velocity—and thus its maximum range—will be lower than for the three- stage version (see the figure, below).

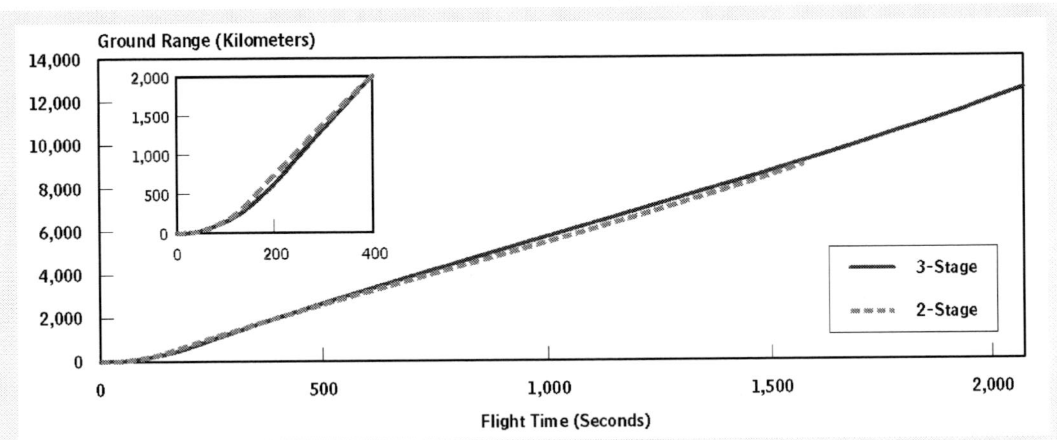

Source: Congressional Budget Office.

Note: The trajectories shown are for an interceptor's full burn time at a sample elevation angle. The inset shows detail for the earliest portion of the flight.

Figure 2.3. Ground Range Versus Flight Time for Two- and Three-Stage Versions of the Ground-Based Interceptor.

The siting of a forward-based radar is critical to successful missile defense in Europe. The earlier the trajectory of a threat missile can be determined, the more time will be available for interceptors to fly to distant intercept points, expanding the area that can be defended. CBO chose Azerbaijan as the notional location for a forward-based radar because it is near Iran and would allow early tracking of the midcourse phase of missiles launched from both northern and southern Iran toward northern Europe and the continental United States. Trajectories of intercontinental ballistic missiles heading for Alaska or Hawaii would be out of range of the radar as modeled, however, as would missiles launched from southern Iran toward southern Europe. (Proposals have been made to use Russian radars in the GMD Block 4.0 system; for more details, see Box 2.2.)

Option 2 : A Ship-Based European Missile Defense

The second alternative envisions using an upgraded version of the current ship-based Aegis BMD system to provide a standing missile defense (rather than merely a crisis-response defense) in Europe. The ships would be permanently stationed at three locations in waters around Europe. They would each carry 10 of the planned SM-3 Block IIA improved interceptors. Given MDA's schedule for deploying those interceptors, this option would be available sometime after 2015. MDA also intends that by that time, the Aegis BMD system will be able to use remote radars (those other than the ships' onboard SPY-1 radars). Remote radars would provide initial tracking of a threat missile to determine, just before an interceptor is launched, what initial trajectory the interceptor should take (referred to as launch on remote). Those radars will also provide data for in-flight tracking updates to the interceptor (referred to as engage on remote). The Aegis BMD system in this option is assumed to have that capability and to be supported by two forward-based radars and the existing UEWR in Fylingdales, as well as the ships' SPY-1 radars.

In designing this option, CBO assumed that the three ship stations would be located in the northwest Black Sea near the coast of Romania, in the northern Adriatic Sea off the coast of

Italy, and in the Baltic Sea just north of Poland (see Figure 2.2). CBO selected those locations to minimize the number of stations that would be necessary to provide roughly the same defensive coverage of Europe as the other options. CBO's cost estimate for Option 2 (described later in this chapter) is based on the assumption that this system would be used as a standing defense, requiring continuous operations and enough ships to maintain the three stations indefinitely. However, other than the two forward-based radars, this option could also represent a future crisis-response capability if no dedicated missile defenses were fielded in Europe.[54]

Treaty constraints could make it difficult to keep a U.S. missile defense ship in the Black Sea indefinitely. The Montreux Convention, which has been in force since 1936, establishes Turkish control over the flow of ships between the Mediterranean and the Black Sea. Under the convention, warships of non-Black Sea nations are not supposed to remain in the Black Sea for more than 21 days at a time.[55] Thus, if Option 2 was implemented, the ship assumed to be on station in the Black Sea might be able to stay at that location only part of the time and might need to spend the rest of the time in other, nearby locations. CBO modeled the effect of different ship locations on the defensive capability of Option 2 (as discussed in Chapter 3). Alternatively, similar defensive capability could be achieved without triggering the constraints of the Montreux Convention by replacing the Black Sea ship station in this option with a ground-based site for SM-3 Block IIA interceptors in the Black Sea region.

2.2. USING RUSSIAN RADARS FOR BALLISTIC MISSILE DEFENSE IN EUROPE

To make the proposed European missile defense system a more cooperative effort, proposals have reportedly been made to integrate Russian radars into the system. Two radars in particular have been mentioned:

- A very high frequency (VHF)-band radar in Gabala, Azerbaijan—built by the former Soviet Union and now operated by Russia—that is based on the Daryal radar design; and
- An ultrahigh frequency (UHF)-band radar in Armavir, in the Krasnodar region of Russia, that is based on the Voronezh-DM radar design.

Those radars would have both advantages and disadvantages for European missile defense. On the plus side, they are located closer to Iran than the upgraded early-warning radar in Fylingdales, England, or the proposed European Midcourse Radar in the Czech Republic. Thus, they could begin tracking missiles launched from Iran earlier in the missiles' trajectories. On the minus side, according to unclassified descriptions, both of the Russian radars operate at longer wavelengths—and therefore have lower spatial resolution—than the U.S. radars that have been proposed for use in the European defense system. Moreover, the Russian radars have a fixed field of regard that is optimized for detecting missiles headed toward Russia as the missiles clear the horizon. According to unclassified reports, the radars' azimuthal coverage (about 110 to 220 degrees for the Gabala radar and about 120 to 300 degrees for the Armavir radar) and their range of elevation angles (from just above the horizon to about 50 degrees for both radars) are appropriate for that original purpose. But those parameters are not ideally suited for tracking missiles launched from Iran toward Europe or the United States. Such missiles would tend to fly through and out of the Russian radars' field of regard very early in their trajectories (see the figure, below).

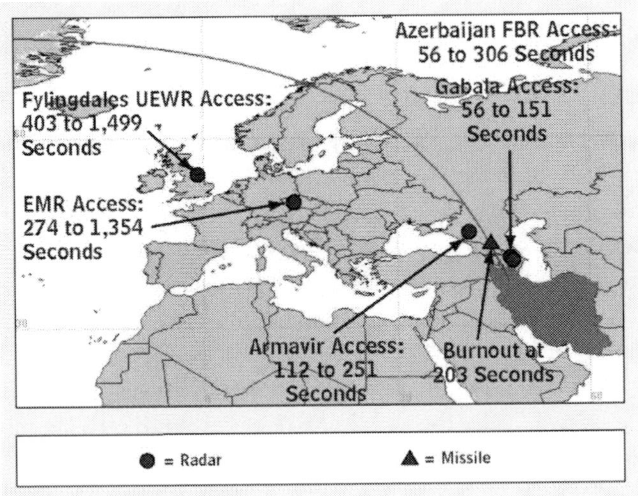

Source: Congressional Budget Office.
Notes: Trajectory and radar access are shown for a solid-fuel ICBM launched from northwestern Iran toward Los Angeles.

ICBM = intercontinental ballistic missile; UEWR = upgraded early-warning radar; EMR = European Midcourse Radar; FBR = forward-based radar.

Figure 2.4. Radar Access Times for a Sample ICBM Trajectory.

The ships used in Option 2 would be dedicated to the missile defense mission full time. Because the Navy's Aegis BMD ships are multipurpose vessels that fulfill a variety of other missions, CBO assumed that maintaining three ship stations indefinitely would not be possible with the existing or planned fleet. Thus, CBO's cost estimate for this option includes funds to procure nine ships (three for each station) that would be dedicated to missile defense. Because those ships would not be serving other missions (besides self-defense), they would not need to be as capable as the destroyers or cruisers that now perform the Aegis BMD mission. For costing purposes, CBO assumed that the new ships would be littoral combat ships (like the recently commissioned LCS 1) with a specially developed Aegis BMD module. Research and development funds to create that module are included in the option's estimated costs.

For tracking, this system would use two forward-based AN/TPY-2 radars: one in Azerbaijan (as in Option 1) and one in Qatar. The SM-3 Block IIA is not as fast as the ground-based interceptor used in Option 1, so early launch of the interceptor would be more critical. Putting a forward-based radar in Qatar would allow for early tracking of missiles launched from southern Iran.

CBO did not include the European Midcourse Radar in Options 2, 3, and 4, because each of those alternatives would use two forward-based AN/TPY-2 radars. The combined field of regard of the Fylingdales radar and the two forward-based radars would provide enough tracking coverage that adding the EMR would not change the areas that could be defended, according to CBO's modeling. However, CBO's model does not quantitatively estimate the probability of successfully intercepting and destroying the threat warhead. With its high spatial resolution, the EMR is intended to better discriminate between warheads and decoys, potentially improving the probability of successfully engaging a threat missile that deploys decoys. If that capability was desired, the EMR could be added to Options 2, 3, and 4 at an additional cost.

Option 3 : SM-3 Interceptors at U.S. Bases in Europe

The third alternative would use the same type of interceptor as Option 2, the SM-3 Block IIA, but based on land rather than at sea. The interceptor launch sites would be located at two U.S. bases—Ramstein Air Force Base in Germany and Incirlik Air Force Base in Turkey—with 10 interceptors at each site. Given the development schedule for the SM-3, this option could be available around 2015 (the same time as Option 2 and two years later than MDA's planned European capability).

The interceptor sites would be supported by new forward-based AN/TPY-2 radars in Azerbaijan and Qatar as well as by the existing Fylingdales UEWR. As in Option 2, the EMR was not assumed to be part of this alternative; if its extra tracking and discrimination were required, the EMR could be added to this missile defense system (at an additional cost) without significantly changing the system's defense coverage as modeled by CBO.

MDA is not currently pursuing the idea of basing SM-3 interceptors on land (although it is considering the concept as a risk-reduction alternative in the joint U.S.- Israeli Arrow interceptor program).[56] For this option, CBO assumed that the Vertical Launch System used to launch interceptors on Aegis BMD ships would also be used with the land-based version. However, in place of the SPY-1 radar that sends tracking updates during interceptor flights in the Aegis BMD system, CBO assumed that this option would employ a conventional antenna, similar to the In-Flight Interceptor Communications System (IFICS) used in the GMD system. CBO's cost estimate for Option 3 includes research and development funding to develop and field the land-based version of the SM-3, including an analog to the IFICS.

Option 4.Kinetic Energy Interceptors at U.S. Bases in Europe

The final alternative in this analysis would be very similar to Option 3 except that it would use the Kinetic Energy Interceptor instead of the SM-3 Block IIA. The KEIs would be launched from truck-based mobile launchers at Ramstein and Incirlik Air Force Bases. CBO assumed that there would be two missiles per launcher and that each launch site would have 10 interceptors and 5 launchers. CBO also assumed that the KEI would carry the Multiple Kill Vehicle to engage multiple targets in case a threat missile was carrying decoys. Based on the current development schedules of the KEI and MKV, this option would probably not be available before 2018, making it the latest of the alternatives that CBO examined.

Estimated Costs of the Options

To estimate the total costs of the four missile defense systems described above, CBO divided the costs into four categories:

- Research and development (R&D)—the engineering activities needed to design and develop interceptor boosters, kill vehicles, and other supporting components and infrastructure;
- Production—the manufacturing of interceptors and associated equipment (and, in the case of Option 2, the purchasing of ships);
- Construction—the activities required to build the physical infrastructure that supports a given missile defense system; and
- Operations—the routine efforts to operate and main- tain the system over a nominal 20-year lifetime.[57]

Estimates of costs for systems that are defined only conceptually or that depend on the development of new technologies involve more uncertainty than do estimates for well-defined programs that are based on proven technologies. To account for the potential effects of such uncertainty, CBO estimated a range of costs for the four missile defense options. In each case, the low estimate represents what a system might cost if few technical difficulties arose in making it fully operational. The high estimate takes into account the risk of cost growth by factoring in the extent to which costs have typically grown for similar systems in the past.[58]

Overall, CBO estimates that the planned GMD Block 4.0 system in Europe (Option 1) would cost a total of $9 billion to $13 billion (in 2009 dollars) over 20 years. A system using land-based SM-3 Block IIA interceptors at U.S. bases in Germany and Turkey (Option 3) would cost about the same amount, and a system of Kinetic Energy Interceptors at those bases (Option 4) would cost slightly more: between $10 billion and $14 billion. A permanent ship-based European missile defense (Option 2) would be more expensive—between $18 billion and $22 billion over 20 years—in part because of the costs of building new ships (see Table 2.1).

Research and Development Costs

In CBO's estimates, R&D costs include only those activities and associated costs that would be incurred specifically for missile defenses in Europe. No R&D costs have been included for systems that MDA is developing for general use. For example, development costs for the SM-3 Block IIA interceptor and the KEI have not been included because their development is not specific to European defenses. But the costs associated with developing a two-stage version of the three-stage ground-based interceptor have been included because that version is being developed specifically for deployment in Europe. No R&D costs have been included for systems that have already been developed, such as the AN/TPY-2 and EMR radars.

For the GMD Block 4.0 system in Option 1, CBO estimates that developing the two-stage version of the GBI and performing required software upgrades would cost about $400 million, based on information provided by MDA. For Option 2, CBO estimates that about $200 million would be needed to develop a missile defense module for the littoral combat ship (LCS), consistent with past module-development costs for the LCS. For Option 3, CBO estimates that a total of $400 million would be needed—about $300 million to develop the land-based SM-3 missile defense capability, consistent with an MDA estimate for the Arrow risk-reduction concept, and $100 million to develop an in-flight interceptor communications system. All of those estimates include a factor of 40 percent to account for the costs of integrating the components into the existing infrastructure. For Option 4, no Europe-specific R&D would be necessary because the system would rely on components that already exist or that MDA is developing for general use.

To account for cost risk, CBO increased each of those low estimates by a factor of 48 percent to produce the high estimates shown in Table 2.1. The 48 percent factor is consistent with past cost growth for comparable systems.

Production and Construction Costs

Manufacturing interceptors, radars, ships, and other equipment for the four options would cost a total of about $2 billion to $10 billion, depending on the option, CBO estimates. Building the necessary physical infrastructure at the interceptor launch sites and radar sites would cost another $0.3 billion to $1.1 billion (not including possible cost growth).

Interceptors

When designing the options for this analysis, CBO assumed that 10 interceptors would be deployed at each launch site. Because the number of launch sites varies among the options, however, the total number of deployed interceptors also varies. In addition to deployed interceptors, CBO included spare interceptors in each option's inventory, with the number of spares equaling 20 percent of the number deployed. Thus, Option 1 includes a total of 22 interceptors: 10 installed in silos in Poland, 2 spares, and 10 for testing (assuming one test every two years over the 20-year lifetime of the system). Costs for test interceptors were included in Option 1 because the two-stage GBI is specific to the European system; no test interceptors were included in the other options because both the SM-3 Block IIA and the KEI are being developed for general use, and testing stock will presumably be part of their overall programs. Option 2 includes a total of 72 interceptors: 10 each for six ships (assuming that, consistent with current practice, missiles can be transferred between ships in port but not on station) and 12 spares. Options 3 and 4 each include a total of 24 interceptors: 10 apiece at the launch sites in Germany and Turkey plus 4 spares.

To calculate total production costs for each option's interceptors, CBO used a two-step approach. It estimated the costs of producing the first unit of each component of an interceptor and of assembling those components into the first interceptor off the production line. It then estimated costs for further purchases of the same type of interceptor by using learning-curve methods, which account for the fact that later units of something tend to have lower per- unit production costs than earlier units.

An interceptor consists of several parts: the booster, the booster's avionics (electronic communications and navigation systems), the kill vehicle, and, for mobile interceptors, the launch canister. CBO used various methods to estimate the costs of purchasing the first units of those components:

- Booster costs were estimated with a model developed by the technical consulting firm Technomics; the model uses a cost-estimating relationship based on the total impulse (thrust multiplied by burn time) of each stage of a booster and other technical parameters to calculate the cost of the first production model of the booster.
- Costs for the booster's avionics and the kill vehicle were estimated with the Unmanned Spacecraft Cost Model developed by Tecolote Research. That model uses

cost-estimating relationships based on the mass of various types of components. As inputs to the model, CBO estimated the mass of the different components using information from MDA and other unclassified sources.

- Canister costs were based on estimates from MDA.

Table 2.1. Cost Estimates for the European Missile Defense Options

(Billions of 2009 dollars)	Option 1		Option 2		Option 3		Option 4	
	Low	High	Low	High	Low	High	Low	High
Research and Development[a]								
Interceptors	0.3	0.4	0.2	0.2	0.4	0.5	0	0
Radars	0	0	0	0	0	0	0	0
System integration	0.1	0.2	0.1	0.1	0.1	0.2	0	0
Subtotal	**0.4**	**0.5**	**0.2**	**0.3**	**0.5**	**0.7**	**0**	**0**
Production								
Interceptors	1.2	1.2	2.1	2.8	0.7	1.0	1.9	2.5
Radars	0.3	0.3	0.3	0.3	0.3	0.3	0.3	0.3
Ships	0	0	5.9	5.9	0	0	0	0
Ground equipment	0.6	0.8	0	0	0.2	0.3	0.2	0.3
Communication sets	0.4	0.4	1.0	1.2	0.5	0.6	0.5	0.6
Other	0.3	0.4	0.2	0.2	0.3	0.4	0.3	0.4
Subtotal	**2.8**	**3.2**	**9.5**	**10.4**	**2.1**	**2.6**	**3.2**	**4.1**
Site Construction	1.1	1.4	0.3	0.3	0.5	0.7	0.5	0.7
Operations (Over 20 years)								
Routine operations	4.6	6.8	3.2	4.7	5.9	8.8	5.9	8.8
Ship operations	0	0	5.1	6.2	0	0	0	0
Operational testing	0.4	0.8	0	0	0	0	0	0
Subtotal	**5.0**	**7.6**	**8.3**	**10.9**	**5.9**	**8.8**	**5.9**	**8.8**
Total	**9.2**	**12.8**	**18.3**	**21.9**	**9.0**	**12.8**	**9.6**	**13.6**

Source: Congressional Budget Office.

Notes: Option 1 = silo-based GBI; Option 2 = sea-based SM-3 Block IIA; Option 3 = land-based SM-3 Block IIA; Option 4 = land-based KEI.

The low estimates assume that few technical difficulties arise in making a system fully operational; the high estimates account for the extent to which costs have typically grown for similar systems in the past.

GBI = Ground-Based Interceptor; SM = Standard Missile; KEI = Kinetic Energy Interceptor.

a. The estimates do not include development costs for components that the Missile Defense Agency (MDA) already plans to develop for applications not specific to European defense. For Option 4, no Europe-specific R&D would be necessary because the system would rely on components that already exist or that MDA is developing for general use.

Integrating and assembling the components would add 12 percent to the total cost of an interceptor, CBO estimated, and government systems engineering and project management would add another 30 percent. Those percentages are consistent with Tecolote's cost-estimating relationship for such work. On the basis of those calculations, CBO estimated that the first two-stage GBI off the production line would cost about $66 million, the first SM-3 Block IIA interceptor would cost about $37 million, and the first KEI would cost about $94 million.

As with previous estimates, CBO accounted for cost risk by applying factors to those low estimates that reflect historical cost growth for comparable systems. The high estimates assume that production costs for the boosters, avionics, and canisters could grow by about 38 percent and that production costs for the kill vehicle could rise by about 19 percent. However, CBO assumed that no cost risk would be associated with the two-stage GBI because that interceptor is a very close variant of the three-stage GBI that is currently deployed.

Costs for the remaining interceptors that would be purchased under each option were estimated by analyzing trends in actual costs for the ground-based interceptors that MDA recently purchased. CBO's analysis suggests that doubling the number of interceptors being purchased reduces the average cost per interceptor by about 5 percent. Buying the 22 interceptors envisioned in Option 1 would result in an average per-unit cost of slightly over $55 million, CBO estimates, meaning that total interceptor production costs under Option 1 would amount to about $1.2 billion (with no significant risk of cost growth). CBO assumed that other interceptors would show a similar trend of cost declining as quantity increased, so producing 72 SM-3 Block IIA interceptors for Option 2 would cost between $2.1 billion and $2.8 billion, and producing 24 of the same interceptors for Option 3 would cost between $0.7 billion and $1.0 billion. Producing 24 Kinetic Energy Interceptors for Option 4 would cost between $1.9 billion and $2.5 billion.

Radars and Other Equipment

CBO's estimates of production costs for radars were based on information from MDA. Those costs total roughly $300 million for each of the options, with the European Midcourse Radar and AN/TPY-2 radar both estimated to cost about $150 million apiece. Option 3 also includes about $100 million to pay for an in-flight interceptor communications system that would transmit tracking updates from the available radars to interceptors in flight.

Cost estimates for Option 1 for ground equipment, communications equipment to link the facilities of the European defense system, site security, and construction of the facilities were based on information provided by MDA. CBO adapted those estimates as necessary for Options 2, 3, and 4.

Ships

CBO assumed that nine new ships would have to be procured under Option 2 so that three ship stations could be maintained indefinitely as a standing defense. Rather than purchasing more of the current multimission Aegis warships, CBO assumed that the Navy would use dedicated missile defense ships modeled on the littoral combat ship. A missile defense LCS would have a total unit cost of about $650 million, CBO estimates: $560 million for the ship itself (based on an earlier CBO estimate of average LCS costs) and the remainder for the missile defense module, including a SPY-1 radar and Vertical Launch System cells.

CBO assumed that production costs for the ships would not grow significantly beyond the margins already included in that $650 million estimate. Total costs would be about $5.9 billion.

The Navy could, however, choose to use upgraded versions of its existing and planned Aegis-capable surface combatants to provide missile defense for Europe. In that case the Navy would forgo performing the missions those ships now perform, but a substantial portion of the $5.9 billion in funding for constructing new dedicated missile defense ships would be unnecessary.

Operations Costs

According to the Missile Defense Agency, each of the locations of the proposed European defense system— interceptor site, EMR site, and FBR site—will cost about $70 million to operate in 2013, the year they are scheduled to become operational. All told, operations costs for the system will total about $230 million per year, MDA estimates. CBO assumed that operations costs would continue at that level throughout the nominal 20-year lifetime of the system. Thus, CBO estimates total costs of routine operations for Option 1 at about $4.6 billion over that period, not counting possible cost growth. For the other land-based systems, Options 3 and 4, CBO used the same $70 million per-site estimate of annual operations costs for each of the four locations (two interceptor sites and two FBR sites). As a result, estimated operations costs for those options total about $5.9 billion over 20 years. Likewise, Option 2 would require about $3.2 billion to operate its two FBR sites over 20 years. In addition, the nine missile defense ships would each cost about $30 million per year to operate, CBO estimates, for total ship operations costs of about $5.1 billion (without cost growth). For that estimate, CBO used actual average operating costs for Navy frigates as a proxy for the littoral combat ship.

To account for the possible growth of operations costs, CBO increased those low estimates by 50 percent for radar and ground-based interceptor sites and by 20 percent for ships.

CBO assumed that only Option 1 would conduct additional interceptor tests beyond those already planned under current or projected MDA schedules. In general, operational tests of missile defenses have three components: target missiles that are launched to simulate enemy missiles, interceptors that are fired at those targets, and analysis of the data from the test. CBO assumed that MDA would conduct one test every two years, for a total of 10 operational tests over the 20-year period. The costs of the 10 interceptors used in those tests are included in the production costs for Option 1. The remaining costs for those tests would total about $40 million per test, CBO estimated on the basis of information from MDA—about $20 million for the target missiles and their launch and another $20 million for the data analysis. Thus, 10 operational tests over 20 years would cost $0.4 billion. For the high estimate, CBO assumed that the costs of the targets and data analysis could increase twofold, to about $0.8 billion in all.

3. DEFENSIVE CAPABILITIES OF ALTERNATIVE MIDCOURSE-PHASE MISSILE DEFENSES

To compare the defensive capabilities of the various missile defense systems described in Chapter 2, the Congressional Budget Office modeled the ability of those systems to intercept missiles launched from Iran. The analysis covered both near-term threats (the shorter-range Shahab-3, Shahab-3A, and Ashura missiles that Iran has tested or claims to have developed) and potential future threats from Iran (including liquid-fuel intermediate- range ballistic missiles and both liquid- and solid-fuel intercontinental ballistic missiles). The primary measure of defensive capability that CBO computed is the area defended against a given type of missile, which is presented in maps comparing those areas. To make the options easier to compare, CBO also computed two summary measures: the number of European NATO capitals and the fraction of the U.S. population that a given system would defend.

The area threatened by a missile—and the ability of missile defenses to engage threats—depends strongly on the locations of the launch sites for both the threat missile and the interceptor. CBO considered three launch sites in Iran: one each in the northwestern, northeastern, and southeastern "corners" of the country. Those locations do not correspond to any specific known Iranian missile sites; rather, they are intended to explore the effect of geography on defensive capability by choosing extreme points from the range of potential launch sites. In each case, CBO chose a launch site that is at least 200 kilometers from the Iranian border or coastline in all directions, on the assumption that missile stations would be placed away from borders to avoid direct attack. Given their shorter range and the emphasis on European defense in this study, near-term threat missiles were assumed to be launched only from the northwestern site. For the potential future threats, all three Iranian launch sites were included in CBO's modeling. For an area to be considered defended against a given missile, it must be defended against launches from *all* of the sites that are capable of reaching it with that missile.

In this analysis, CBO assumed that the various missile defense systems would be able to achieve their intended level of operational effectiveness. However, a number of technical analyses have questioned the efficacy of the planned systems, particularly if an adversary uses countermeasures. CBO did not explicitly model the systems' effectiveness in the presence of countermeasures, but that issue is discussed in Box 3.1.

The analytic results shown in this chapter depend on the assumptions that CBO made about the performance of the threat missiles and the defensive systems and about the locations of the components of those systems. Because many of the systems in this analysis are under development or are proxies for systems that could potentially be developed, their actual performance parameters are still uncertain. Different sets of assumptions would lead to different results. (For a discussion of the sensitivity of CBO's analysis to selected performance assumptions, see Appendix B.)

The U.S.-Based GMD Block 3.0 System

Before considering the capability of dedicated missile defenses in Europe, it is useful to look at the capability that would be available if no dedicated European defenses were fielded.

The Missile Defense Agency plans to have the Ground-Based Midcourse Defense Block 3.0 system—comprising three-stage Ground-Based Interceptors in Alaska and California and tracking radars at various locations—operational by about 2012.[59] Thus, the capability of any dedicated European defenses that were fielded after that time would supplement the defensive capability provided by the Block 3.0 system.

The GMD Block 3.0 system is intended to defend the United States against limited long-range threats from Iran. Because its interceptor sites are far from Europe, the system will not provide any defense of Europe against Iran's near-term or potential future threats. However, according to CBO's modeling, the Block 3.0 system will be able to defend almost all of the United States (including Hawaii) and much of Canada against liquid- or solid- fuel ICBMs launched from Iran (see Figure 3.1). The exception is that Alaska will be defended against solid- fuel ICBMs but not liquid-fuel ICBMs.

3.1. CAPABILITIES AGAINST COUNTERMEASURES

Along with developing missiles, some nations have worked to develop countermeasures that could hinder missile defense systems. Common countermeasures include decoy warheads that are deployed to confuse interceptors; jammers, chaff, or flares that are designed to disrupt sensors trying to track a threat warhead; and maneuverable warheads that can change their trajectory during flight.

Each of the options that the Congressional Budget Office (CBO) modeled for this analysis consists of existing or planned systems that use techniques intended to mitigate the effects of countermeasures. (Those techniques are summarized in the table at right.) CBO's model does not estimate the probability of a successful intercept, and thus it does not quantify the relative value of the various approaches to deal with countermeasures.

One type of countermeasure commonly discussed in the missile defense literature is the deployment of decoys. Potential ways of handling decoys include deploying sensors that can distinguish the actual warhead from surrounding decoys (usually referred to as discrimination) and deploying multiple kill vehicles on a single interceptor with the aim of engaging all of the objects that could be warheads. In an ideal case, those two techniques would be combined to increase the chance of successfully engaging the warhead. As modeled, none of the options in this study would use both techniques; however, all of them could potentially do so.

For these options, the optimum way to use radar to discriminate between warheads and decoys is to have continuous tracking with high-resolution X-band radar from the time that the decoys and warheads are deployed (shortly after the booster burns out) until the intercept. Continuous tracking is also critical to engaging warheads that can maneuver during the midcourse phase of flight. Option 1, with both the European Midcourse Radar (EMR) and a forward-based radar (FBR), would have the most X-band radar coverage over the engagement portion of a threat missile's trajectory. It would also be capable of tracking missiles from burnout to intercept for many (though not all) trajectories. However, constraints on steering both the FBR and the EMR could preclude full tracking for multiple, widely separated missiles launched at about the same time (see Box 3.2 on page 30). Continuous tracking for multiple missiles and for all trajectories would require additional radars beyond those included in Option 1.

Options 2, 3, and 4 are assumed to include two FBRs but not the EMR, so high-resolution tracking would be available only for the early portion of a threat missile's trajectory. Tracking later in the trajectory would come from the lower-resolution Fylingdales or SPY-1 radars. Adding the EMR to those options (at an extra cost of about $600 million to procure and install the radar and about $70 million per year to operate it) would improve the discrimination capability to match that of Option 1, with little change to the area that could be defended.

As modeled, only Option 4 is assumed to incorporate the planned Multiple Kill Vehicle (MKV), which is intended to allow a single interceptor to engage multiple objects. Future plans call for deploying the MKV on Ground-Based Interceptors, so that kill vehicles could be added to Option 1 at some point. However, the extra mass of the MKV would reduce the area that could be defended under Option 1. During development of the Standard Missile-3 (SM-3) Block IIA interceptor, the Missile Defense

Agency considered the possibility of having it carry the MKV (perhaps a variant of the one modeled here), but the agency recently decided to stick with a unitary warhead for that version of the interceptor. However, a possible follow-on version of the interceptor, sometimes referred to as the SM-3 Block IIB, might carry the MKV. How that would affect the area defended would depend on the mass of the MKV and the modifications made to the interceptor.

Table 3.1 Summary of Techniques Used to Mitigate the Effect of Countermeasures

Technique	Desired Effect	Option 1	Option 2	Option 3	Option 4
High-Resolution X-Band Radar	Discriminate between warhead and decoys	Yes (FBR and EMR)	Partial (FBR only, as modeled)	Partial (FBR only, as modeled)	Partial(FBR only, as modeled)
Multiple Kill Vehicle	Engage multiple targets to reduce the effect of decoys	Not as modeled	Not as modeled	Not as modeled	Yes
Radar Wavelength Diversity	Reduce susceptibility to chaff and jammers	Yes (X-band and UHF)	Yes (X-band, UHF, and S-band)	Yes Yes (X-band and UHF)	Yes Yes (X-band and UHF)
Two-Color Infrared Sensor on Kill Vehicle	Reduce susceptibility to infrared stealth, improve kill vehicle's discrimination between warhead and decoys	Yes	Yes	Yes	Yes

Source: Congressional Budget Office.

Note: FBR = forward-based radar; EMR = European Midcourse Radar; UHF = ultrahigh frequency.

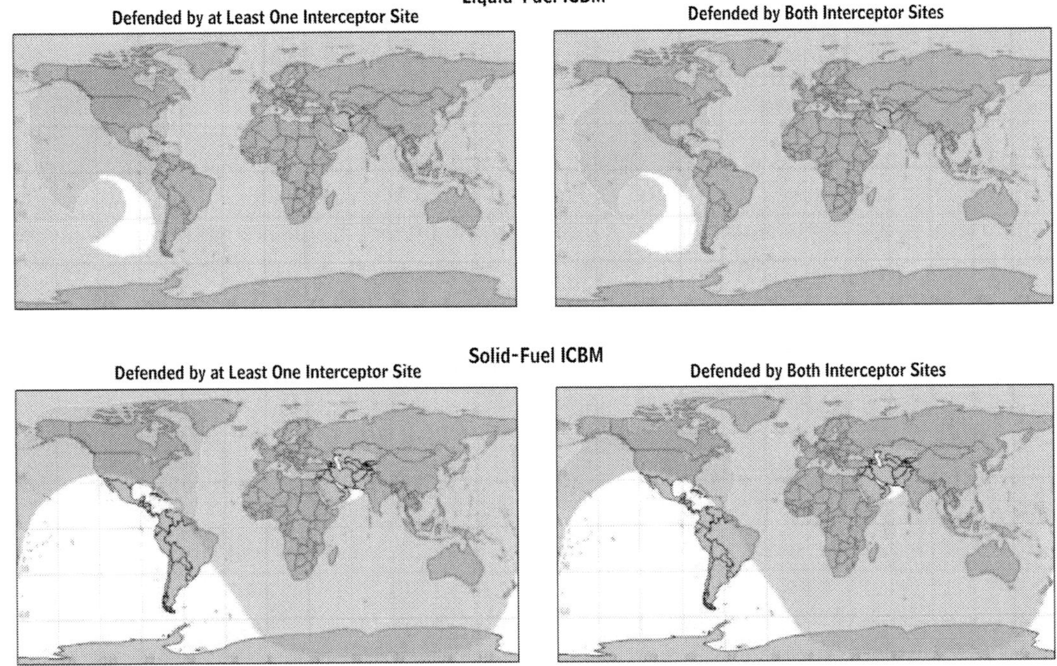

Source: Congressional Budget Office.

Notes: Blue shading indicates the area defended against a given missile threat. Red shading indicates undefended areas within range of that threat.

Interceptor sites for the Block 3.0 system are located at Fort Greely in Alaska and Vandenberg Air Force Base in California.

GMD = Ground-Based Midcourse Defense; ICBM = intercontinental ballistic missile.

Figure 3.1. Areas Defended by the GMD Block 3.0 System Against ICBMs from Iran.

Most of the Block 3.0 system's defense is redundant—in other words, each of the system's interceptor launch sites is capable of defending almost the entire continental United States (see the right-hand panels of Figure 3.1). Intercept timelines would not allow an interceptor to be launched from the second site if the initial interceptor from the first site was unsuccessful (a practice known as shoot-look-shoot; see Box 3.2). Thus, the full potential value of having redundant interceptor sites would not be realized. But the redundancy provides some protection against the temporary loss of one site—for example, because of natural disasters or equipment failure.

To intercept U.S.-bound missiles from Iran, the GMD Block 3.0 system will rely on tracking from radars in Fylingdales, England, and Thule, Greenland. However, it will not be capable of defending those radar sites against Iranian missiles, which makes the system vulnerable to attacks in which multiple missiles first target the radars and then target the United States. That vulnerability could be removed by using local defenses to protect the radars—say, Aegis ballistic missile defense ships or terminal-phase systems such as the Terminal High-Altitude Area Defense or Medium Extended Air Defense System.

A Potential Crisis-Response Defense

Another system that would be available in the absence of dedicated European missile defenses is Aegis BMD ships equipped with Standard Missile-3 Block IB interceptors. Those interceptors are scheduled to start being deployed in about 2011. At that point in the Aegis BMD development plan, the missile defense system would have to use onboard SPY-1 radars to track threats. Because Aegis ships can communicate with each other, the BMD system could use SPY-1 radars on a network of ships to provide tracking throughout the engagement with a threat missile. However, although the system could use other radars (such as an upgraded early-warning radar) to provide initial tracking of the threat missile, it would not be able to use those radars to provide tracking updates after the interceptor was launched. Thus, the number of ships required to provide defense over a broad area would depend mainly on the field of regard of the SPY-1 radar rather than on the performance of the interceptor. (The Aegis BMD system in Option 2, by contrast, would use Block IIA interceptors, which are more advanced, and external radars throughout the engagement; it would not be available until around 2015.)

CBO modeled the defensive capability provided by Aegis BMD ships with SM-3 Block IB interceptors operating around Europe. For its modeling, CBO assumed that seven ships would be operating in different locations: two in the Black Sea, one in the Adriatic Sea, one in the Aegean Sea, one in the western Mediterranean, one off the coast of Poland, and one in the English Channel (see Figure 3.2). With SPY-1 radars, that distribution of ships would provide radar access over a large fraction of Europe at engagement altitudes, although there would be gaps in the radar access in some locations. Those gaps correspond to regions where late tracking updates would not be available to interceptors. Intercepts that occurred in those regions might have less-up-to-date tracking information than intercepts in other areas and thus might have a lower probability of success. However, for any given trajectory of a threat missile, an interceptor generally has a range of possible intercept locations, which means that the gaps in radar access could be avoided in many cases. Consequently, those gaps might have little impact on the overall area defended.

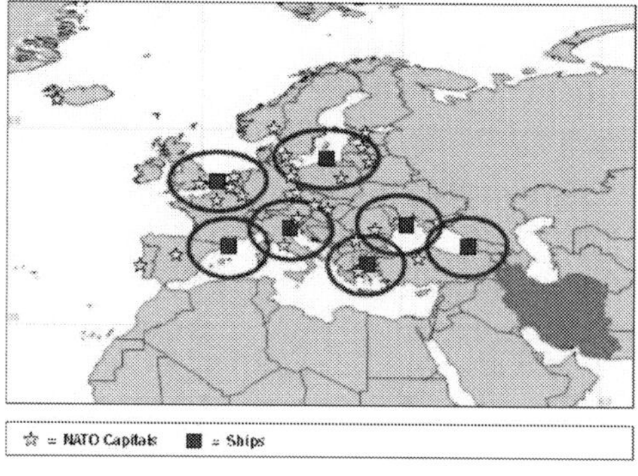

Source: Congressional Budget Office.

Notes: Dark blue outlines indicate the footprint of Aegis ships' SPY-1 radars at an altitude of 400 kilometers for the seven ship locations that CBO modeled. Iran is shown in dark gray.

BMD = ballistic missile defense; NATO = North Atlantic Treaty Organization.

Figure 3.2. Radar Footprint for Aegis BMD Ships.

To provide continuous missile defense for an extended period, additional ships would have to be available to rotate periodically to the seven locations. (A typical multiplier for Navy operations calls for having three to four ships for each long-term station.) Currently, MDA plans to outfit a total of 18 Aegis BMD ships, most of which will be based in the Pacific, where transit times to Europe are longer than for Atlantic-based ships. Because not enough ships are likely to be available to maintain that capability indefinitely, it would probably be used only during periods of heightened tension.

Against near-term threats from Iran, most of the defensive coverage provided by this crisis-response system would come from the ships in the Black Sea. That coverage would extend into threatened regions adjacent to the Black Sea, including parts of Turkey (see Figure 3.3). In the case of IRBMs, some of the trajectories that a missile could fly would be beyond the range of SPY-1 radars on the nearest ships. If that happened, the IRBM's track could not be determined until it had flown within radar range of one of the ships farther from Iran, reducing the time available for intercept and resulting in scattered areas of defensive coverage. ICBMs on trajectories with shortened burn times would fly at a lower altitude than IRBMs and could be visible to the SPY-1 radars sooner, so the area defended against ICBMs would have fewer gaps. However, that defense would not extend to all of Europe. In addition, this crisis-response system with Aegis SM-3 Block IB interceptors located around Europe would not provide any additional defense of the United States against Iranian ICBMs.

CBO's Four Options for Deploying Standing Missile Defenses in Europe

CBO also analyzed the extent to which Europe and the United States could be defended by the four options described in Chapter 2: MDA's proposed European capability (Option 1), SM-3 Block IIA interceptors deployed on Aegis BMD ships at three stations (Option 2) or on land at U.S. Air Force bases in Germany and Turkey (Option 3), or Kinetic Energy Interceptors located at those bases (Option 4). According to CBO's modeling, Option 4 would provide nearly complete coverage of the parts of Europe within range of near-term Iranian threats, and Options 2 and 3 would provide coverage of most, but not all, of those areas. Option 1 would offer the least defense of areas within range of near-term Iranian threats. All of the alternatives would provide substantial coverage of Europe against IRBMs and solid-fuel ICBMs launched from Iran. With its interceptors located farther northwest than the others, however, Option 1 would leave parts of Greece, Turkey, and other areas of southeastern Europe undefended against those missiles (unless other resources were added to MDA's proposed system). Against the more challenging liquid-fuel ICBMs, all of the options would leave large parts of Europe undefended.

In addition to their coverage of Europe, some of the alternatives could offer another layer of defense to protect the United States from potential Iranian ICBMs. (That defense would be in addition to the coverage offered by the U.S.-based GMD Block 3.0 system.) Option 1 would provide the most extensive coverage of the United States against ICBMs, defending all of the continental United States. Option 4 would offer substantial defense of the United States but would still leave large areas undefended. Options 2 and 3 would cover little or none of the United States unless interceptor sites were added on U.S. soil.

3.2. Attacks with Multiple Missiles and Shoot-Look-Shoot Defense

The estimates of defensive capability presented in this study are based on the assumption that a missile defense system will be dealing with a single threat missile at a time. However, an adversary could try to overwhelm missile defenses by launching multiple missiles. In recent years, both North Korea and Iran have conducted missile tests in a salvo configuration, with several missiles launched at roughly the same time.

Launching multiple missiles almost simultaneously on divergent trajectories could reduce the ability of the modeled options to provide tracking. Both the European Midcourse Radar and the forward-based radar would be capable of tracking missiles over a wide range of azimuth angles, through a combination of electronically steering the radar beam within the instantaneous field of view and mechanically steering the antenna to move that field of view[*] Although steering electronically between multiple targets is essentially instantaneous, steering the antenna mechanically is relatively slow. Thus, if targets were far enough apart to be outside the same instantaneous field of view, the radar's ability to mechanically steer quickly enough to maintain tracking could limit the ability of a defense system to engage multiple missiles at the same time.

The total number of threat missiles (whether fired singly or in a salvo) that the options in this study could handle would depend on the guidelines for launching interceptors—that is, the firing doctrine. To increase the likelihood of successfully destroying a given missile, more than one interceptor could be fired at it. The director of the Missile Defense Agency was recently quoted as saying that "salvo launching [of interceptors] makes sense for.. .systems where you don't have a lot of battlespace and you want to get off two shots to make sure of your intercept.... [It does not] make as much sense for the long-range system... normally you would fire, determine if you are successful, and if you are not, you fire again."[†] The latter approach is known as shoot-look-shoot.

The Congressional Budget Office (CBO) analyzed the possibility of using the shoot-look-shoot approach with the missile defense options in this study. For threat missiles launched at European targets, the extent to which the options would be capable of shoot-look-shoot defense varies considerably depending on the type of missile and its launch location. For example, Options 1, 2, and 4 would provide shoot-look-shoot defense for large parts of Europe against intermediate-range ballistic missiles (IRBMs) launched from all three modeled locations in Iran. Option 3 would offer shoot-look-shoot defense for about half of Europe against IRBMs launched from northeastern and southeastern Iran, but for only a small portion of southern Europe against IRBMs launched from northwestern Iran. In the case of liquid-fuel intercontinental ballistic missiles (ICBMs), shoot-look-shoot defense would not be available in any of the options for substantial parts of Europe against ICBMs launched from northwestern Iran; Options 3 and 4 would provide no shoot-lookshoot defense anywhere in Europe against those threats.

---

[*] The Congressional Budget Office assumed that both radars would be able to operate over the full 360-degree range of azimuth (the direction of the trajectory relative to north).

[†] Thomas Duffy, "MDA Reconsidering Ground-Based Midcourse Salvo Tests," *Inside Missile Defense* (April 9, 2008).

In the absence of other supporting defenses, operators would presumably launch two interceptors against any threat missile determined to be headed for European targets where shoot-look-shoot was not possible. They might opt for a single interceptor if shoot-look-shoot was considered feasible. CBO's cost estimates for the four options assume an inventory of 10 interceptors at each launch site, so each site would be able to handle between 5 and 10 threat missiles targeted at Europe. (Conclusions about the maximum number of targets that could be engaged do not take into account any possible constraints that the sensors might place on the number of targets engaged at the same time or any limits that the interceptor launch systems might impose on how closely in time interceptor launches can occur.)

If the options in this study were supported by more forward-based defenses—particularly a future boost-phase defense system—shoot-look-shoot between the options and those supporting defenses could allow for a more economical use of midcourse interceptors. In some cases, midcourse interceptors would engage only targets that the forward-based defenses failed to destroy. Similarly, if the options were supported by terminal-phase systems (such as the Terminal High-Altitude Area Defense) in specific locations, threat missiles headed for those locations might be engaged with a single midcourse interceptor, and the local terminal-phase system would serve as backup if the intercept failed. In that case, the options would perhaps use a single interceptor per engagement and thus each interceptor site could handle up to 10 threat missiles launched at European targets.

For ICBMs launched at the United States, none of the options by themselves would be capable of shootlook-shoot defense against missiles launched from all of the modeled locations in Iran—although Options 1 and 2 would provide some shoot-look-shoot defense for portions of the United States against ICBMs launched from northeastern or southeastern Iran. However, all four of the options, to the extent they could defend regions of the United States, would be capable of shoot-look-shoot in those regions if the second interceptor came from one of the Ground- Based Midcourse Defense system sites in Alaska or California. Thus, for threat missiles that were determined to be heading toward the United States, it is possible that operators of the midcourse defenses in Europe might elect to fire a single interceptor at each missile, allowing the maximum of 10 threat missiles to be engaged per European interceptor site.

Ability to Defend Europe

The areas within range of near-term Iranian missiles extend to central Turkey and the Caucasus in the case of the Shahab-3 and Shahab-3A, and beyond the Black Sea into southeastern Europe in the case of the Ashura (see Figure 3.4). Option 1, with a single interceptor site in Poland, would provide the least defensive coverage of those regions (none at all for areas within range of the Shahab-3). That conclusion from CBO's model is consistent with the results of modeling by MDA. (The agency has indicated that other resources would be required to defend those regions.) The other three options include interceptor sites in the Black Sea or eastern Mediterranean regions and thus would be able to defend more of the areas within range of those near-term threats. Given the high acceleration of Kinetic Energy Interceptors, Option 4 would provide the most extensive defensive coverage against those missiles.[60]

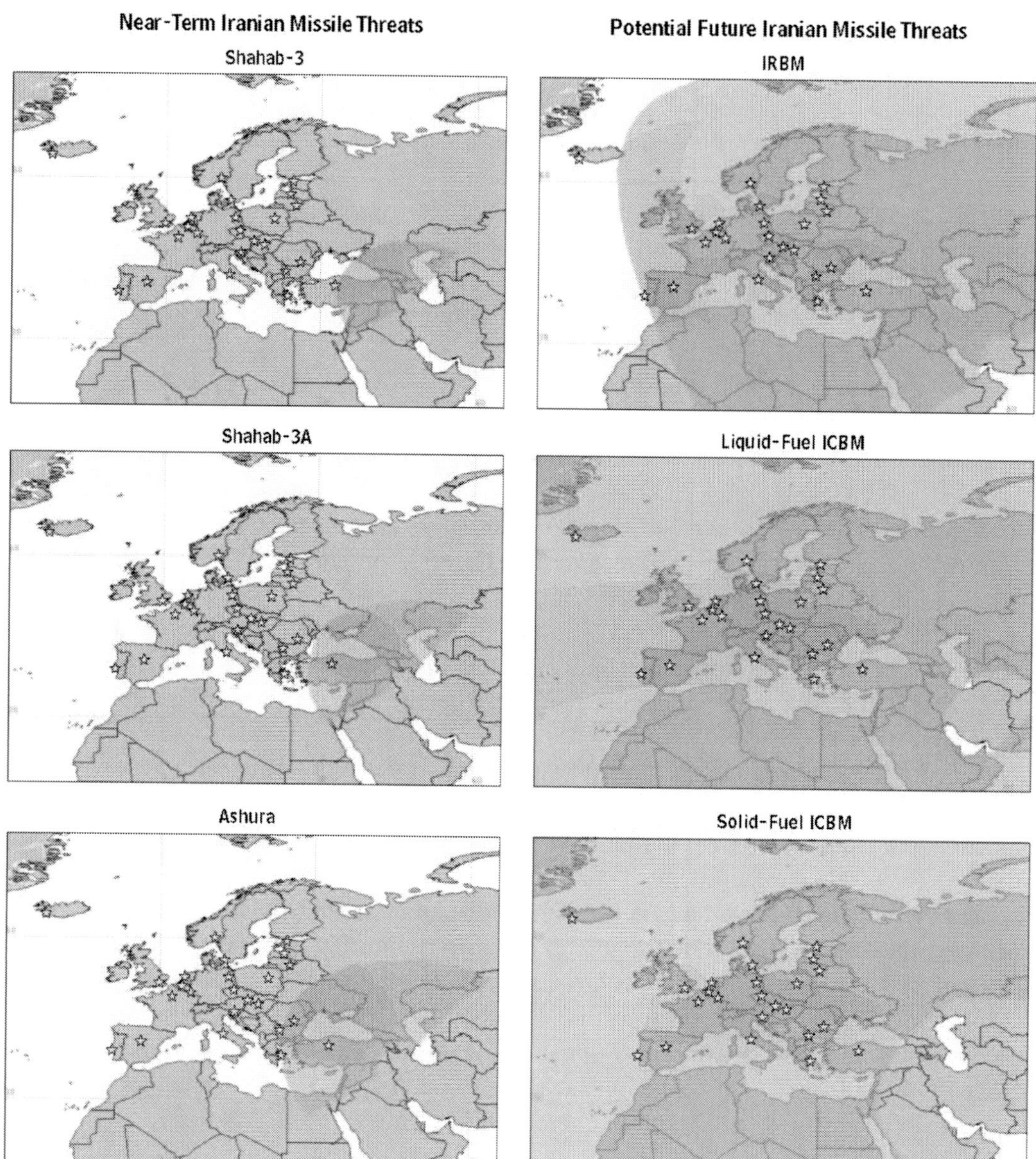

Source: Congressional Budget Office.

Notes: Blue shading indicates the area defended against a given missile threat by Aegis ships using SM-3 Block IB interceptors deployed in the seven locations shown in Figure 3.2. Red shading indicates undefended areas within range of a given threat. Yellow stars show the locations of NATO capitals.

BMD = ballistic missile defense; SM = Standard Missile; IRBM = intermediate-range ballistic missile; ICBM = intercontinental ballistic missile; NATO = North Atlantic Treaty Organization.

Figure 3.3. Areas Defended by Aegis BMD Ships Using SM-3 Block IB Interceptors.

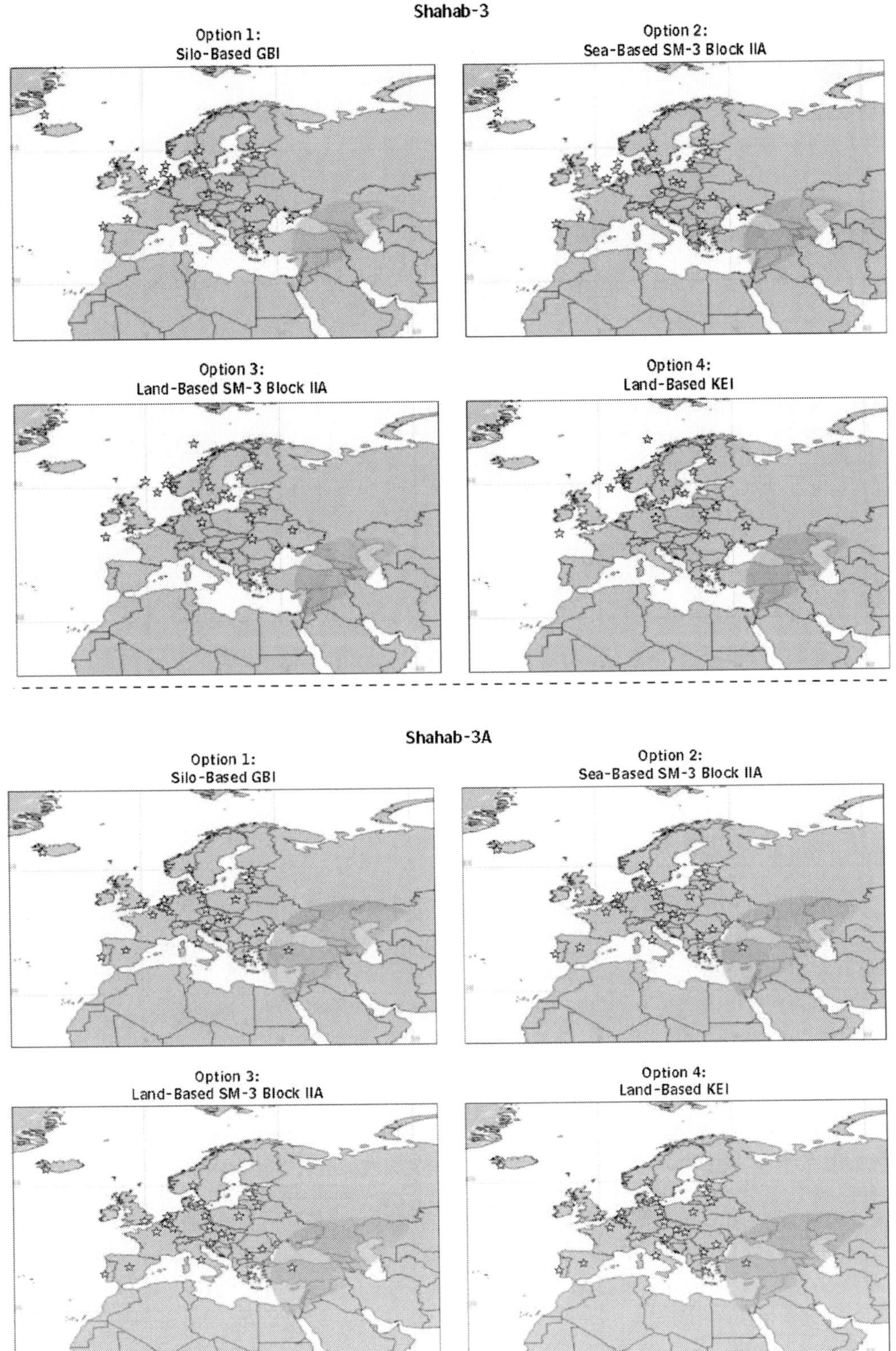

Figure Continued

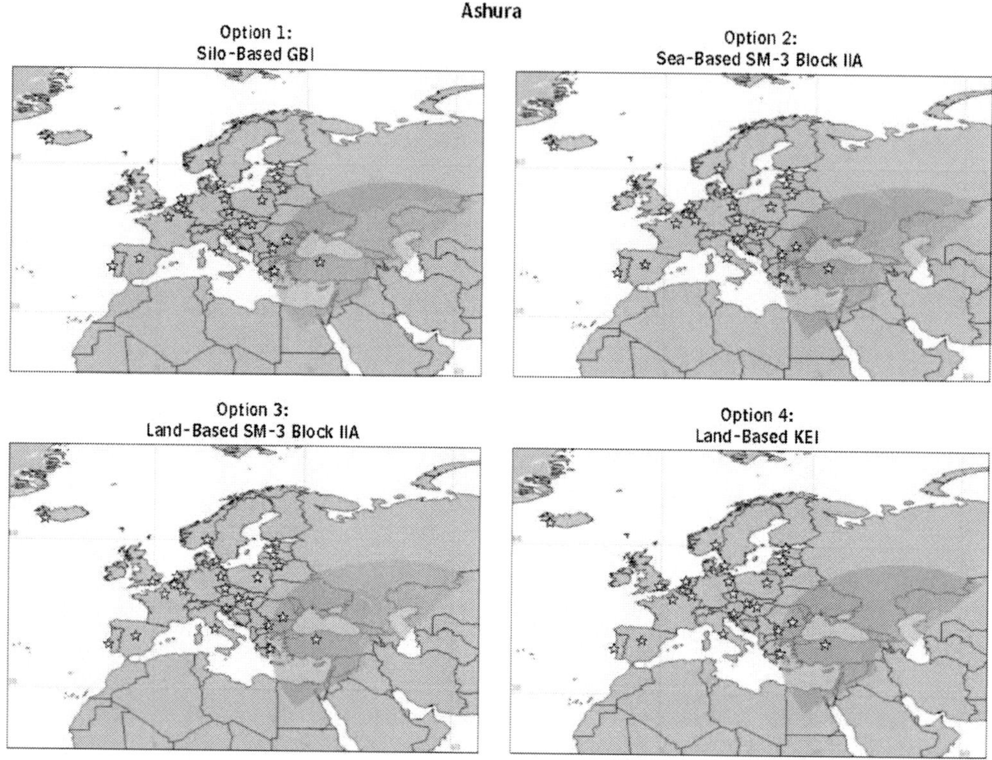

Source: Congressional Budget Office.

Notes: Blue shading indicates the area defended against a given missile threat. Red shading indicates undefended areas within range of that threat. Yellow stars show the locations of NATO capitals.

GBI = Ground-Based Interceptor; SM = Standard Missile; KEI = Kinetic Energy Interceptor; NATO = North Atlantic Treaty Organization.

Figure 3.4. Areas Defended by the Missile Defense Options Against Near-Term Threats from Iran.

The potential future Iranian IRBM that CBO modeled would be capable of reaching all of continental Europe, the United Kingdom, and Ireland. All four options would have substantial capability to defend Europe against that IRBM threat, although only Option 4 would completely cover the threatened portions of NATO countries (see Figure 3.5).

As with the near-term threats, Options 2, 3, and 4 would offer more extensive coverage of southeastern Europe against IRBMs than MDA's proposed system would because those options would have interceptor sites closer to that region. Option 1 would need additional resources to defend that area. As an example of how the defensive capability of MDA's proposed system might change if more resources were available, CBO modeled the extra coverage provided by adding a single station for Aegis BMD ships with SM-3 Block IIA interceptors in the northwestern Black Sea (see the area outlined in blue in the Option 1 panel in Figure 3.5). Other possibilities for expanding coverage exist, such as using THAAD or MEADS batteries to provide area defense in selected locations. CBO's cost estimate for Option 1 (described in Chapter 2) does not include additional resources to expand coverage of southeastern Europe. If land-based SM-3 Block IIA interceptors were available, adding a second interceptor site would cost a total of about $2.1 billion, CBO estimates: $700 million to procure the equipment and $1.4 billion to operate the site over 20 years. If a sea-based Aegis

BMD system was used, the incremental cost of a second interceptor site would depend on whether the Navy employed existing ships and how the ships were operated.[61]

Against solid-fuel ICBMs, each option would provide much the same coverage of Europe as it would against IRBMs. Liquid-fuel ICBMs, however, present a more challenging threat because they have a longer burn time and fly at lower altitudes to European targets than IRBMs or solid-fuel ICBMs. All of the options would leave substantial portions of Europe undefended against liquid- fuel ICBMs (see Figure 3.6). Some potential adversaries might view attacking Europe with an ICBM—which would be capable of a much longer range—as an in efficient use of missile technology and development resources, especially if an IRBM was available. Nevertheless, the prospect presents a challenge to European missile defenses as modeled in this study.

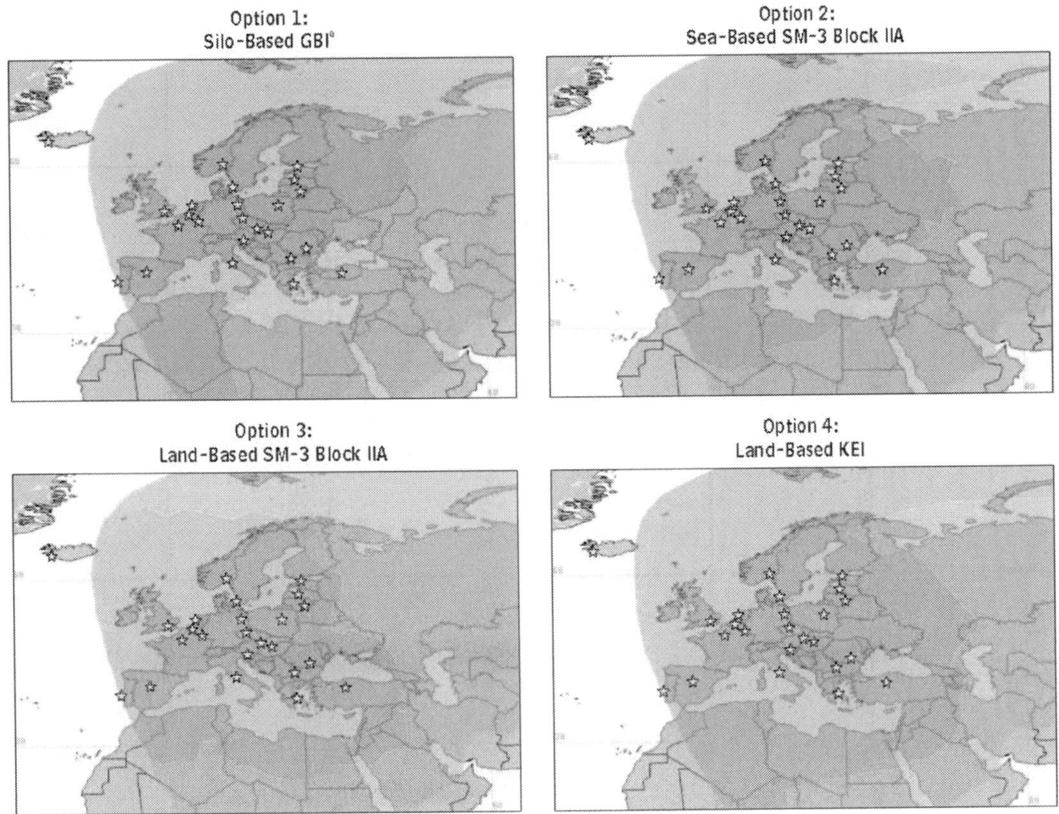

Source: Congressional Budget Office.

Notes: Blue shading indicates the area defended against a given missile threat. Red shading indicates undefended areas within range of that threat. Yellow stars show the locations of NATO capitals.

IRBM = intermediate-range ballistic missile; GBI = Ground-Based Interceptor; SM = Standard Missile; KEI = Kinetic Energy Interceptor; NATO = North Atlantic Treaty Organization.

a. The area outlined in blue indicates additional coverage that would be provided if a site for ship-based SM-3 Block IIA interceptors was added in the northwestern Black Sea.

Figure 3.5. Areas Defended by the Missile Defense Options Against IRBMs from Iran.

Given that challenge, planners might choose to add more interceptor sites to improve their ability to defend Europe against liquid-fuel ICBMs. For example, adding one interceptor site in Poland and another in Romania to Option 3—in addition to the sites in Germany and Turkey—would significantly expand the area defended (see the area outlined in blue in the Option 3 panel in Figure 3.6). Even so, a few parts of Europe (such as the southern halves of Italy and the Iberian Peninsula) would remain vulnerable. CBO estimates that adding land-based SM-3 Block IIA interceptor sites to Option 3 would cost a total of about $2.1 billion per site: $700 million for the equipment and $1.4 billion for operations over 20 years.

Option 2's defensive coverage is based on the assumption of maintaining three ship stations, including one in the northwestern Black Sea. As noted in Chapter 2, treaty constraints could make it difficult to keep a missile defense ship stationed in the Black Sea indefinitely, in which case the ship would have to spend part of the time at other, nearby locations. CBO analyzed how Option 2's coverage would change if the ship station in the Black Sea was replaced with one in the eastern Mediterranean or the Aegean Sea. Against near-term threats, a BMD ship stationed in the eastern Mediterranean would provide less defensive coverage of southern Russia and the Caucasus region, but slightly more coverage of Turkey and the Middle East, than a ship stationed in the Black Sea. A ship stationed in the Aegean would provide far less coverage of Turkey against near-term threats than one in the Black Sea. Against a potential IRBM, both alternative ship locations would offer overall defensive capability similar to that of a Black Sea location, although with less coverage of the Black Sea and eastern Ukraine. In addition, a ship stationed in the Aegean would defend only half as much of Turkey against IRBMs as a ship in the Black Sea or eastern Mediterranean. In the case of solid- fuel ICBMs, moving ship stations would have little effect on Option 2's defensive coverage. The largest change would involve defensive capability against liquid-fuel ICBMs: Both alternative ship locations would lessen coverage of southeastern Europe (including Ukraine, Romania, and Bulgaria) against those missiles.

None of the options, as modeled, would be able to defend all of the capital cities of European NATO countries against all of the types of missiles in this analysis that could potentially reach them. Only one NATO capital (Ankara, Turkey) is within range of the Shahab-3A missile, and only three (Ankara; Athens, Greece; and Bucharest, Romania) are within range of the Ashura. Options 2, 3, and 4 would be capable of defending those cities against those threats, but Option 1's defensive coverage would not extend to Ankara (see Figure 3.7). Likewise, Options 2, 3, and 4 could defend all of the European NATO capitals within range of potential Iranian IRBMs or solid-fuel ICBMs, whereas Option 1 would not defend Ankara or Athens. Against potential Iranian liquid-fuel ICBMs, however, all of the options would leave a significant fraction of threatened capitals undefended.

The various analyses above apply to threat missiles flying minimum-energy trajectories (flight paths that would give them the maximum range for a given total amount of fuel), with the range reduced to hit the desired target by reducing the amount of fuel burned. In some cases, however, missiles on lofted or depressed trajectories could present a more challenging threat to defenses—especially IRBMs or ICBMs aimed at Europe (see Appendix A).[62]

To explore that possibility, CBO modeled how the options' ability to defend Europe would change if faced with IRBMs flying depressed trajectories. With such trajectories, the area that could be defended would be reduced along the edge nearest the launch site of the threat missile. For example, in the case of an IRBM launched from northwestern Iran, the southeastern edge of the area of defensive coverage would move northward by at least 500 kilometers. The actual extent of the reduction in coverage would depend on the design of the threat missiles. When missiles fly depressed trajectories, they remain in the atmosphere longer, subjecting them to greater structural stresses than missiles on minimum-energy trajectories. Thus, trajectories that are substantially depressed may not be physically possible.

Ability to Defend the United States

The only missiles in this analysis that could reach the United States from Iran are ICBMs. The four options for European missile defenses would, to varying degrees, defend the United States against the potential ICBM threats modeled by CBO (see Figure 3.8 on page 41). Because the GMD Block 3.0 system is assumed to be in place by the time the options become operational, the options' defensive coverage of the United States would be in addition to the nearly complete defense of the United States available from the Block 3.0 system.

Of the modeled options, MDA's proposed European system would provide the most extensive defense of the United States, covering the entire continental United States against liquid-fuel ICBMs and covering all of the threatened portion of the continental United States plus part of Alaska against solid-fuel ICBMs. (That coverage would be reduced if the system used a forward-based radar located in Israel instead of the Caucasus; see Box 3.3 on page 44.) Option 4, with its Kinetic Energy Interceptors, would also provide substantial added coverage of the United States, particularly against solid-fuel ICBMs. The systems using SM-3 Block IIA interceptors (Options 2 and 3) offer the least additional defense of the United States: almost none against solid-fuel ICBMs and coverage of only parts of the northeastern (and, in the case of Option 2, central) United States against liquid- fuel ICBMs.

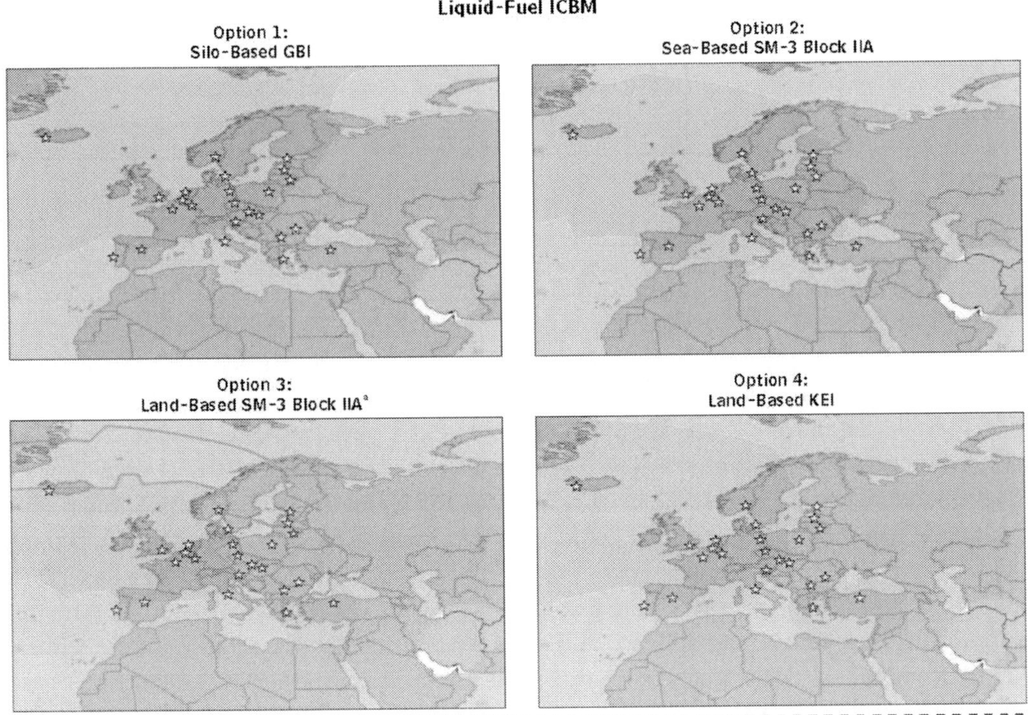

Figure Continued

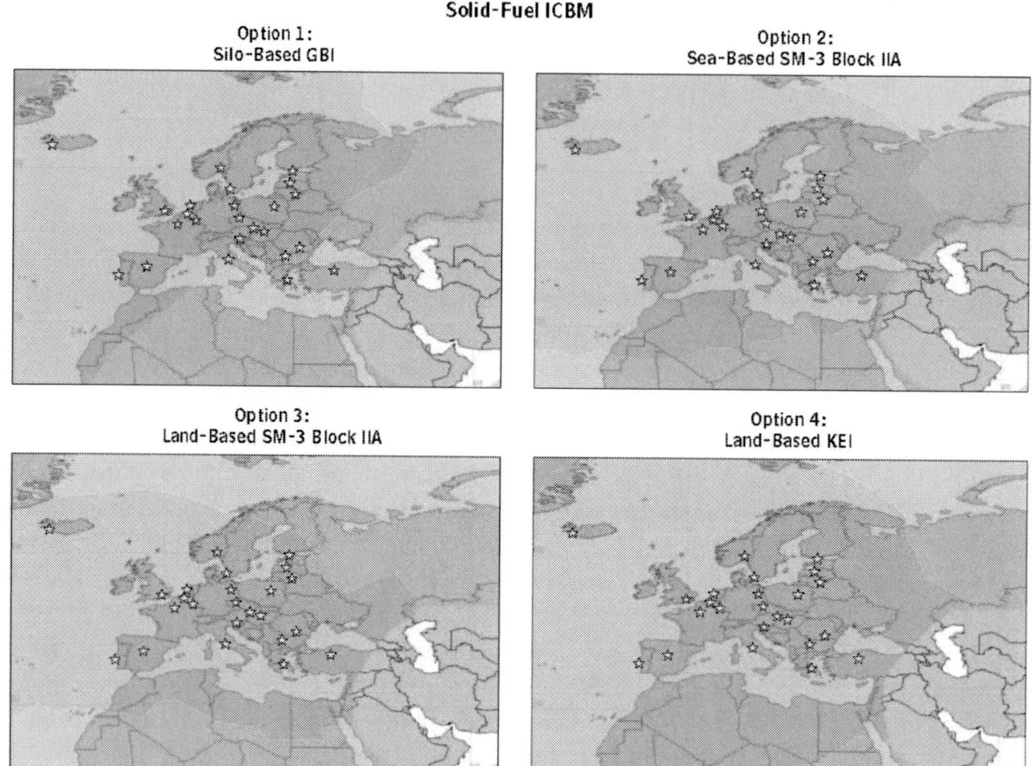

Source: Congressional Budget Office.

Notes: Blue shading indicates the area defended against a given missile threat. Red shading indicates undefended areas within range of that threat. Yellow stars show the locations of NATO capitals.

ICBM = intercontinental ballistic missile; GBI = Ground-Based Interceptor; SM = Standard Missile; KEI = Kinetic Energy Interceptor; NATO = North Atlantic Treaty Organization.

a. The areas outlined in blue indicate additional coverage that would be provided if sites for land-based SM-3 Block IIA interceptors were added in Poland and Romania.

Figure 3.6. Areas of Europe and the Middle East That the Options Would Defend Against ICBMs from Iran.

U.S. defense could be expanded under Options 2 and 3 by adding an interceptor site in the United States. For example, with an extra launch site for SM-3 Block IIA interceptors in Cape Cod, Massachusetts—supported by UEWRs in Cape Cod, Thule, and Fylingdales—Option 3 could defend the eastern half of the threatened portion of the United States (see Figure 3.8 on page 41). The expansion of coverage would be similar under Option 2 with a sea-based interceptor site near Cape Cod. If additional coverage of the western United States was required, a second interceptor site could be added in the northwestern part of the country. For that site, however, the engagement geometry and sensor coverage against Iranian threats would be essentially the same as for the existing GMD sites in the western United States, and the proximity of the interceptor sites would preclude shootlook-shoot defense, so the value of adding that redundant SM-3 defense on the West Coast would be questionable. Such a site might be able to defend parts of the United States against attack by sea-based missiles off the West Coast that would be out of range of the GMD sites, but analyzing such a threat is beyond the scope of this study. As with a supplemental site in Europe, adding a land- based SM-3 Block IIA site in the United States would cost about $700 million for procurement and about $1.4 billion for operations over 20 years, CBO estimates.

As a summary measure, CBO analyzed the level of redundancy of the U.S. defense against Iranian ICBMs in terms of the number of interceptor sites providing defense as a function of the percentage of the U.S. population defended. Nearly all of the U.S. population potentially within range of an Iranian liquid-fuel ICBM will be covered by at least one of the GMD Block 3.0 system's two interceptor sites, and 97 percent will be covered by both sites (see Figure 3.9 on page 43). Option 1 would supplement the coverage of those two sites with its interceptor site in Poland, with the result that more than 95 percent of the threatened U.S. population would be defended by three interceptor sites. Likewise, Option 4's additional coverage would mean that about 75 percent or more of the threatened U.S. population would be defended by three interceptor sites.[63] Such redundant defense is desirable as a hedge against attacks with multiple missiles, natural disasters, or technical problems that could disable an interceptor site. Further, the additional U.S. coverage provided by all of the options, when combined with that of the GMD Block 3.0 system, would allow for the use of shoot-look-shoot defense (see Box 3.2 on page 30), which could improve the efficiency with which interceptors were used to engage threats.[64] (Shootlook-shoot defense is not possible between the two Block 3.0 sites alone.)

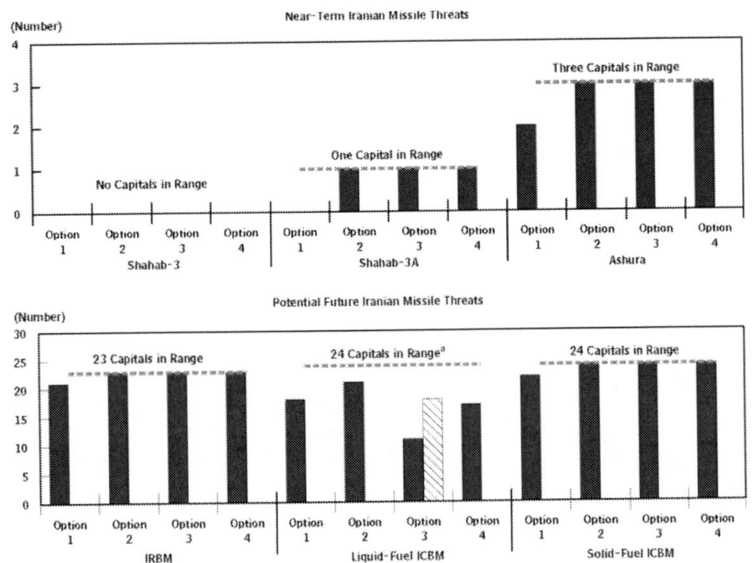

Source: Congressional Budget Office.

Notes: Option 1 = silo-based GBI; Option 2 = sea-based SM-3 Block IIA; Option 3 = land-based SM-3 Block IIA; Option 4 = land-based KEI.

NATO = North Atlantic Treaty Organization; IRBM = intermediate-range ballistic missile; ICBM = intercontinental ballistic missile; GBI = Ground-Based Interceptor; SM = Standard Missile; KEI = Kinetic Energy Interceptor.

a. The striped column for Option 3 against liquid-fuel ICBMs indicates additional coverage that would be provided if interceptor launch sites were added in Poland and Romania.

Figure 3.7. Number of European NATO Capitals That the Options Would Defend Against Various Missile Threats.

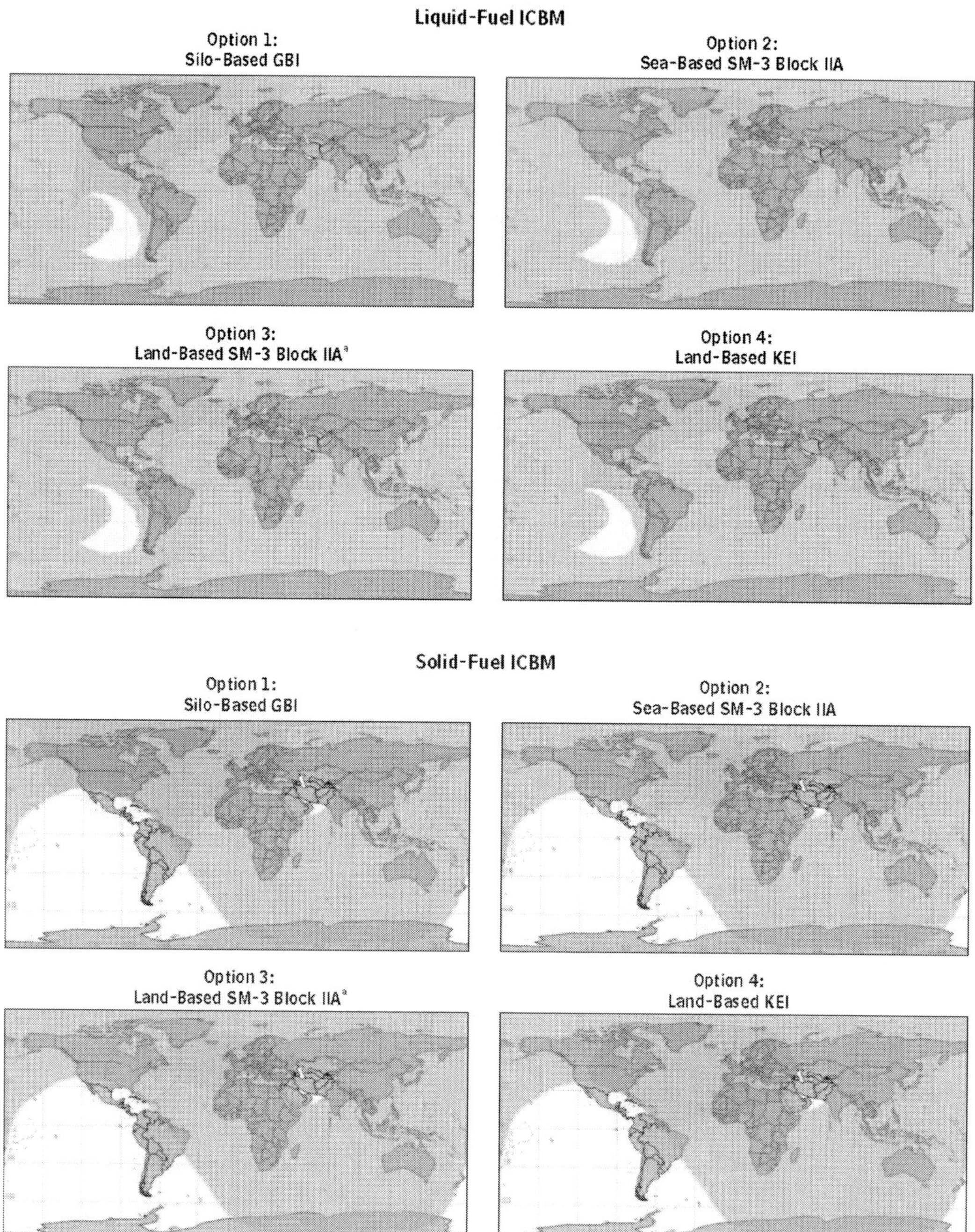

Notes: Blue shading indicates the area defended against a given missile threat. Red shading indicates undefended areas within range of that threat.

ICBM = intercontinental ballistic missile; GBI = Ground-Based Interceptor; SM = Standard Missile; KEI = Kinetic Energy Interceptor.

b. The area outlined in blue indicates additional coverage that would be provided if a site for land-based SM-3 Block IIA interceptors was added in the Cape Cod, Massachusetts, region.

Figure 3.8. Total Area That the Options Would Defend Against ICBMs from Iran.

Ability to Intercept Russian ICBMs

The question of whether MDA's proposed European system could be used to intercept Russian ICBMs has been the subject of some debate. Russian officials, expressing doubt about the imminence of the missile threat from Iran, have argued that the Block 4.0 system is actually intended to defend against Russian missiles. However, given the large number of missiles that Russia possesses compared with the number of interceptors in the planned system, it is clear that the European capability—as proposed—could be easily overwhelmed by missiles launched from Russia.

The question of whether the Block 4.0 system could be used to intercept a single Russian missile has also been debated in the press. MDA has presented analysis that the system would not be able to intercept an ICBM launched from a base in western Russia, but some critics of MDA's plans have published studies indicating that it would be possible to engage Russian ICBMs with interceptors in Poland.[65]

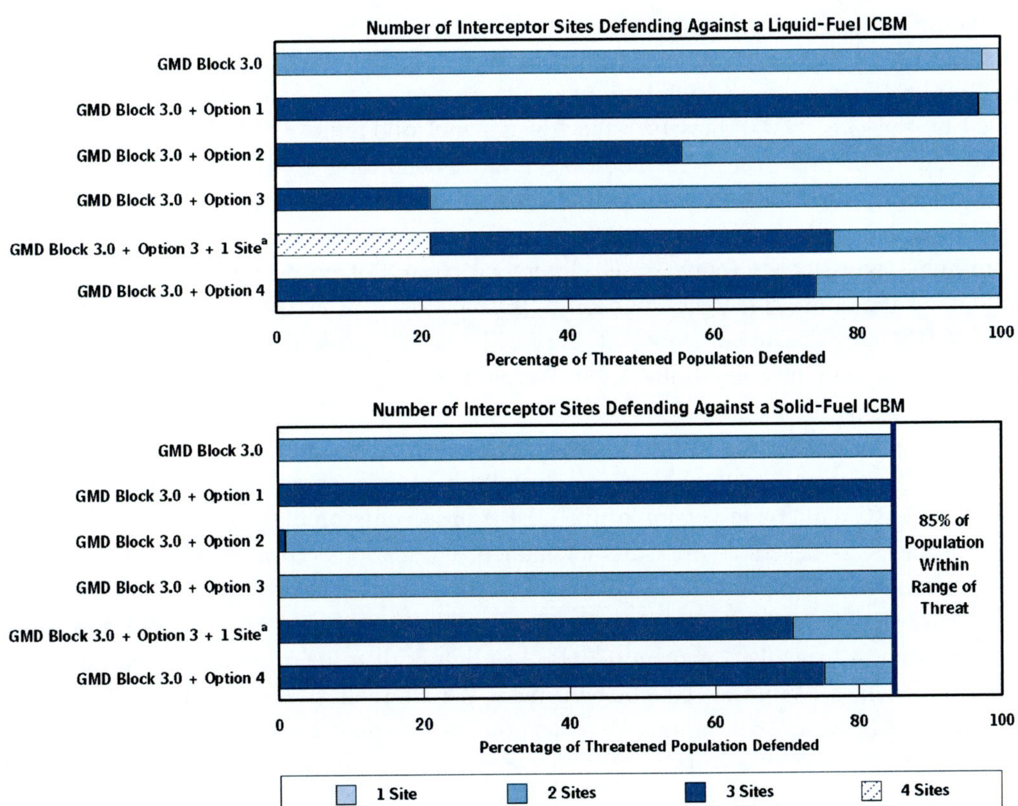

Source: Congressional Budget Office.

Notes: Option 1 = silo-based GBI; Option 2 = sea-based SM-3 Block IIA; Option 3 = land-based SM-3 Block IIA; Option 4 = land-based KEI.

GMD = Ground-Based Midcourse Defense; ICBM = intercontinental ballistic missile; GBI = Ground-Based Interceptor; SM = Standard Missile; KEI = Kinetic Energy Interceptor.

a. Indicates additional coverage that would be provided if a site for land-based SM-3 Block IIA interceptors was added in the Cape Cod, Massachusetts, region.

Figure 3.9. Level of Redundant Defense of the United States Provided by the Missile Defense Options.

CBO has analyzed the defensive capability that the European Block 4.0 system would provide against a Russian ICBM—specifically, an SS-25 (the same missile that CBO used as a proxy for a potential Iranian solid- fuel ICBM). In its modeling, CBO assumed that the ICBM would be launched from the Yoshkar-Ola base east of Moscow. Missiles launched from that base toward t he United States would fly trajectories that passed over Scandinavia, presenting advantageous engagement geometry for interceptors based in Poland. ICBMs launched from Russian bases farther east, such as Novosibirsk, would fly more directly over the North Pole and thus would be more challenging for interceptors in Poland to engage.

Before looking at the defense added by the European system, it is useful to consider the capability of the U.S.- based GMD Block 3.0 system against Russian missiles. Using existing radars, that system would provide complete coverage of the United States against the modeled Russian ICBM (see the upper panel of Figure 3.10 on page 46). Most of the radar tracking of such a missile would come from the Fylingdales and Thule UEWRs. However, those radars themselves could not be defended against a Russian ICBM by interceptors launched from the United States.

Adding the European Midcourse Radar in the Czech Republic, even without deploying interceptors in Poland, would slightly expand the area of northeastern Canada that could be defended by the U.S. GMD sites (see the lower panel of Figure 3.10). The main potential benefit of the EMR, however, is the addition of an X-band radar to the tracking system. The short wavelength—and thus the high spatial resolution—of X-band radar could improve the fidelity of tracking and enhance the ability to distinguish an actual warhead from decoys.

Deploying two-stage Ground-Based Interceptors in Poland, supported by the EMR, would defend the entire threatened portion of Europe, as well as eastern Canada, against a Russian ICBM (see the upper panel of Figure 3.11). That additional defensive coverage would not extend into the United States, but it would come very close to the United States, so changes in the modeling assumptions could alter those results.

To explore the sensitivity of the results, CBO constructed alternate assumptions for the two-stage GBI using information available in public sources about the components of the interceptor.[66] CBO's alternate version of the GBI is based only on the technical parameters of the rocket stages as described for satellite launch applications, with no additional weight added to account for expanded avionics and communications capabilities that might be needed to use the rocket for an interceptor. The total mass of the alternate version is about 20,850 kilograms— roughly 3 percent (or 600 kg) lighter than the original version that CBO used in its modeling. With the reduction in mass, the alternate two-stage GBI has a higher velocity at burnout, which substantially expands the area it can defend (see the lower panel of Figure 3.11). In the case of a Russian ICBM launched from Yoshkar-Ola, that coverage area includes roughly half of the United States.

3.3. Placing a Forward-Based Radar in Israel

Recently, the United States deployed an AN/TPY-2 radar to Israel to support Israeli missile defense efforts there. According to press reports, some U.S. officials have proposed connecting that radar to the Missile Defense Agency's planned Block 4.0

European system.[‡] To evaluate the effect of such a radar placement, the Congressional Budget Office (CBO) modeled how the defensive capability of Option 1 would change if the Block 4.0 system used a forward- based radar (FBR) near Tel Aviv, Israel, rather than one in Azerbaijan (the location that CBO assumed for Option 1 in this analysis). The rest of the Block 4.0 system would remain the same: two-stage Ground-Based Interceptors in Poland supported by the European Midcourse Radar (EMR) in the Czech Republic.[§]

CBO's modeling indicates that replacing an FBR in Azerbaijan with one in Israel would reduce the portion of eastern Europe that could be defended against intermediate-range ballistic missiles and liquid- or solid-fuel intercontinental ballistic missiles (ICBMs) launched from Iran (see the figure at right). The reason is that many likely trajectories of Iranian missiles bound for eastern Europe would be outside the field of regard of the Israeli radar, which would be located more than 1,500 kilometers (km) southwest of an FBR in Azerbaijan and more than 1,000 km from the Iranian border. Such missiles could only be tracked once they came within range of the EMR, which would reduce the time available for intercepting them and thus reduce the area defended. Moreover, the EMR would generally not be able to observe those missiles at the time of burnout, which could lessen the system's ability to discriminate between actual warheads and any decoys that might be deployed.

ICBMs headed for the western United States from Iran would also fly outside the field of regard of an FBR in Israel. Consequently, Option 1's Poland- based interceptors would provide less defensive coverage of the United States with an FBR in Israel than with one in Azerbaijan.

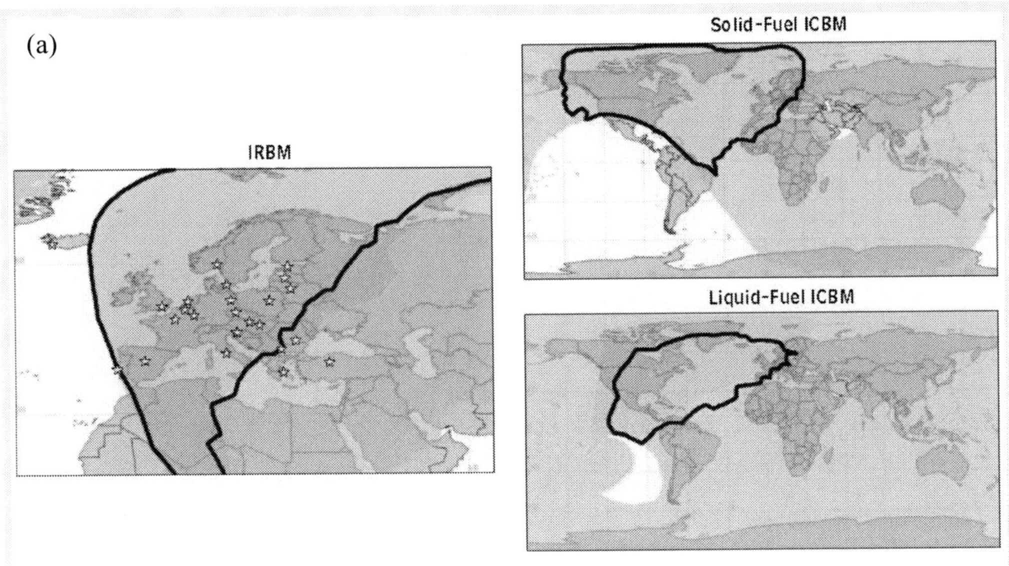

Figure 3.10 Continued on next page.

[‡] See, for example, Dave Ahearn, "U.S. Lawmakers Urge Putting Radar in Israel, to Be Tied in with European Missile Defense," *Defense Daily* (May 13, 2008).

[§] Including an FBR in Israel along with the one in Azerbaijan (rather than replacing the FBR in Azerbaijan) would increase the defensive capability of the proposed Block 4.0 system by adding any new areas defended (as shown in the figure here) to those defended with the original, single FBR.

(b)

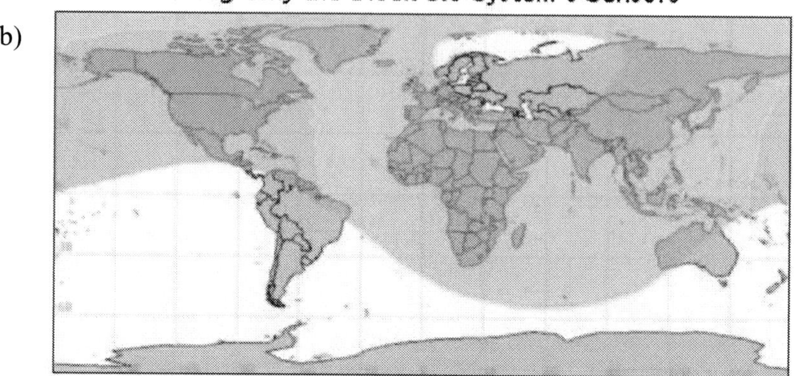

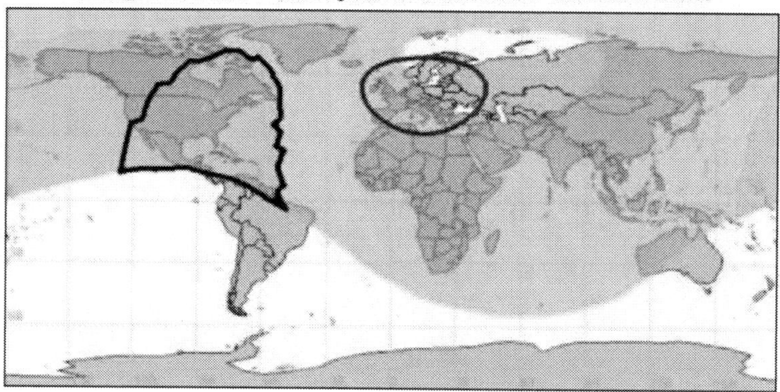

(a) Source: Congressional Budget Office.

    Notes: Blue shading indicates the area defended against a given missile threat with an FBR in Azerbaijan. Black outline indicates the area defended with an FBR near Tel Aviv, Israel. Red shading indicates undefended areas within range of a given threat. Yellow stars show the locations of NATO capitals.

    FBR = forward-based radar; IRBM = intermediate-range ballistic missile; ICBM = intercontinental ballistic missile; NATO = North Atlantic Treaty Organization.

Option 1's Defensive Coverage with Different FBR Locations.

(b) Source: Congressional Budget Office.

    Notes: Blue shading indicates the area defended by GMD Block 3.0 interceptors launched from Fort Greely, Alaska, against an SS-25 missile launched from the Yoshkar-Ola base in Russia. Red shading indicates undefended areas within range of the Russian missile.

    GMD = Ground-Based Midcourse Defense; ICBM = intercontinental ballistic missile; EMR = European Midcourse Radar.

    a. Dark blue outline shows the EMR's footprint at an engagement altitude of 400 kilometers. Black outline indicates the portion of the defended area for which the EMR could be used to track the incoming missile.

Figure 3.10. Areas Defended by the GMD Block 3.0 System Against a Solid-Fuel ICBM from Russia.

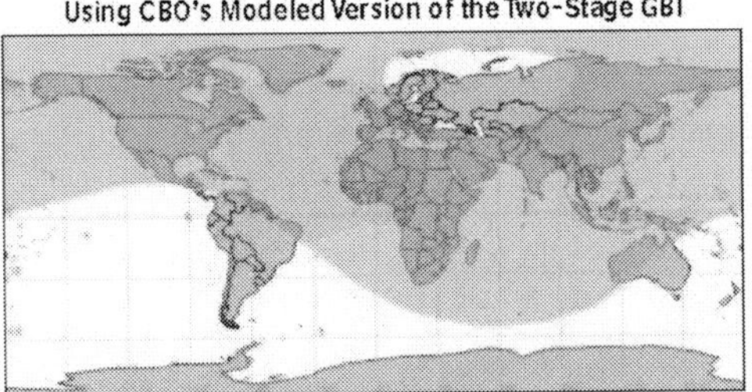

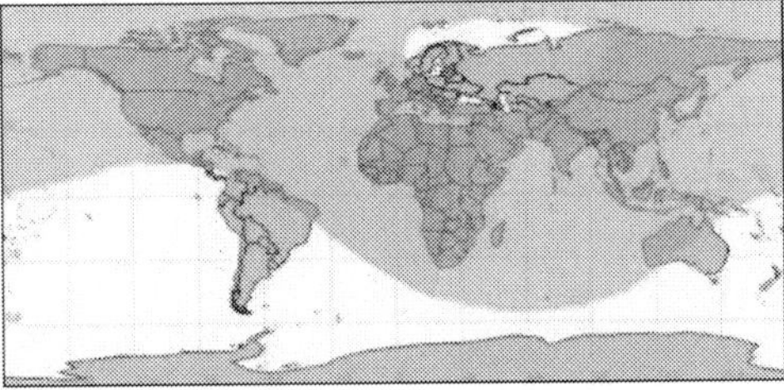

Source: Congressional Budget Office.

Notes: Blue shading indicates the area defended by the Missile Defense Agency's proposed European system (Option 1, silo-based GBI) against an SS-25 missile launched from the Yoshkar-Ola base in Russia. Red shading indicates undefended areas within range of the Russian missile.

ICBM = intercontinental ballistic missile; GBI = Ground- Based Interceptor.

Figure 3.11. Areas Defended by Option 1 Against a Solid-Fuel ICBM from Russia.

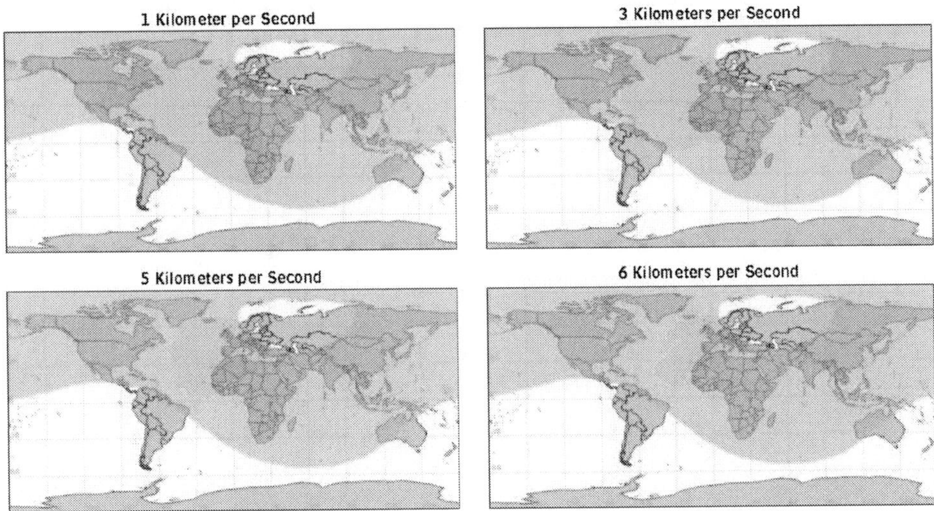

Source: Congressional Budget Office.

Notes: Blue shading indicates the area defended by the Missile Defense Agency's proposed European system (Option 1, silo-based GBI) against an SS-25 solid-fuel missile launched from the Yoshkar-Ola base in Russia. Each panel is based on a different assumption about the minimum relative velocity between the interceptor and the threat missile required for a successful intercept. In its modeling for this study, CBO used a value of 3 kilometers per second.

ICBM = intercontinental ballistic missile; GBI = Ground-Based Interceptor.

Figure 3.12. Sensitivity of Option 1's Defensive Coverage Against a Russian ICBM to Various Assumptions About Minimum Relative Velocity.

Interceptors in Poland would not be able to defend Israel against the missiles that Iran claims to have now or could develop in the future. Moving the FBR to Israel would not change that situation, because the interceptor launch site in Poland is about 2,500 km from Israel, whereas missiles from Iran would need to travel as little as about 1,000 km to reach Israel. However, Options 2, 3, and 4 in this analysis, which would include interceptors in locations closer to Iran, could defend Israel against some of those threats.

Defensive coverage also depends on other parameters of CBO's modeling. For midcourse-phase intercepts, CBO assumed that the ballistic trajectory of a threat missile would have to be determined before an interceptor was launched. If interceptors were launched before the threat missile's booster burned out, the potential area of defensive coverage could be much larger—but the probability of a successful intercept could be substantially lower because of the greater uncertainty in the projection of the threat missile's trajectory. In the particular case of ICBMs launched from western Russia and interceptors based in Poland, the size of the defended area is very sensitive to the relative velocity required for a successful intercept.[67] In that case, the trajectories of the ICBMs would pass close to the interceptor site, but the timing is such that the missiles would have gone beyond the interceptor site by the time of engagement. Thus, the interceptor would be approaching the threat missile from the rear at a fairly low relative velocity.

In its modeling, CBO required a minimum relative velocity of 3 kilometers per second for a successful intercept. However, lower or higher values could also be valid—in particular, low relative velocities might suffice if the kill vehicle hit the ideal aim point with sufficient accuracy or if the threat missile contained a salvage-fused warhead, which is designed to detonate if struck by an antimissile weapon. Conversely, higher relative velocities might be necessary to ensure complete destruction of the warhead if submunitions were used.

To explore how sensitive the area of defensive coverage is to the required relative velocity, CBO modeled intercepts of Russian ICBMs at various minimum relative velocities: 1 km/sec, 3 km/sec, 5 km/sec, and 6 km/sec. At a low required relative velocity (1 km/sec), interceptors in Poland would be capable of defending much of the United States as well as Europe against Russian ICBMs (see Figure 3.2). A higher requirement for relative velocity would shrink the area of defensive coverage to Europe and parts of the eastern Atlantic Ocean.[68] (For further discussion of relative velocity and the sensitivity of CBO's analysis to various assumptions, see Appendix B.)

APPENDIX A. BALLISTIC MISSILE BASICS

Ballistic missiles, in the simplest sense, have two main parts: a rocket and a weapon payload. The rocket provides a brief burst of power (a "boost" that typically lasts for a few minutes) and guidance in order to place the payload on a specific trajectory. The payload then coasts on that "ballistic"—unpowered and free-flying—trajectory to its target. The maximum range over which the rocket (or booster) can deliver the payload depends on the amount of force (thrust) it can provide, how long it provides that thrust (the burn time), and the mass of the payload. Small changes in payload mass can produce large changes in range, so great effort goes into reducing the mass of the payload. Because the body of the rocket that encases the fuel also acts as a sort of payload, boosters are often split into stages. The dead weight of the structure for each stage can be jettisoned when that stage has finished firing, reducing the total mass that the booster has to lift and thereby increasing the range.

Solid versus Liquid Fuel

Rockets provide thrust by burning propellant, which can be liquid, solid, or a mixture of the two (referred to as hybrid). Within those broad categories, many different varieties of propellant exist. Propellant typically has two components—fuel and oxidizer—which react to form a hot gas. The gas is expanded through a nozzle at the end of the rocket, pushing the rocket forward. The thrust that an engine generates depends on the amount of hot exhaust gas produced per unit of time and the velocity of the gas as it exits the rocket. Exhaust velocity is usually stated in terms of the specific impulse parameter (I_{sp}), which has units of seconds and equals the exhaust velocity divided by the gravitational acceleration at sea level (g). The specific impulse of a given rocket stage depends primarily on the type of fuel used, although the physical design of the engine and operational conditions also play a role.

Solid and liquid fuels offer different advantages to missile designers. Liquid fuels are generally capable of higher I_{sp} than solid fuels. However, liquid propellants can be difficult to work with. For example, they can be extremely toxic and in some cases require cryogenic temperatures. Those properties make liquid fuels less than ideal for road-mobile missile systems (although some do exist, including Iran's Shahab-3 and Shahab-3A).

Solid fuels are generally more stable and easier to work with, a distinct advantage for road-mobile and ship-based systems. In addition, solid-fuel missiles can usually be launched on shorter notice than liquid-fuel missiles, which require time to load fuel into the missile. Faster launches increase responsiveness (which commanders desire in military systems) and reduce the time available for enemy surveillance to become aware of an imminent launch.

The biggest disadvantages of solid fuels relate to the nature of their combustion. Once a solid-fuel engine has begun to fire, it will continue to burn along the entire exposed surface of the fuel until all of the fuel is expended. The thrust from a solid-fuel engine can be made to vary over the course of the burn by customizing the shape in which the fuel is cast when the engine is constructed. However, that thrust profile cannot be adjusted while the engine is firing or be stopped and restarted, whereas liquid-fuel engines allow for more precise control. Also, because combustion occurs along an extended surface, the entire casing of a solid-fuel engine must be sturdy enough to withstand high pressures, which increases the structural "dead weight" that the rocket has to carry. For a given range, solid-fuel missiles generally have shorter burn times than liquid-fuel missiles, so missile defense systems have less time available to engage a solid-fuel missile in the boost phase (while its booster is still firing). However, the shorter burn time means that solid-fuel missiles enter the ballistic portion of flight earlier, so defense systems that target missiles during that midcourse phase may have more time to engage them.

Range

The maximum range that a particular missile can attain depends on the velocity of the payload at the end of the boost phase, referred to as the burn-out velocity (V_{bo}). A reasonable estimate of V_{bo} can be made with just a few operational parameters: the mass of the payload, the total mass of each of the stages, the mass of the propellant in each stage, and the I_{sp} for each stage. The actual V_{bo} will also be determined by the aerodynamic properties of the missile and the specific trajectory flown.

For a given flight of a ballistic missile, range depends on the trajectory on which the booster places the payload. Ballistic missiles are usually launched from a vertical position. After a short period of vertical thrust, the booster is generally made to tilt (pitch over) slightly from the vertical. After that pitch-over maneuver, the thrust is usually realigned with the body of the missile. Because the thrust is no longer aligned with the (vertical) gravitational force, the missile will begin to turn toward the horizontal, a phenomenon referred to as a gravity turn. Missiles generally use a gravity turn to steer themselves onto a trajectory that has the desired angle with respect to the horizontal (known as the flight-path or elevation angle), after which the thrust is redirected to stop the gravity turn. There is an optimal flight-path angle that will maximize the range of the missile; that trajectory is referred to as a minimum-energy trajectory because it allows the maximum range for a given amount of fuel.

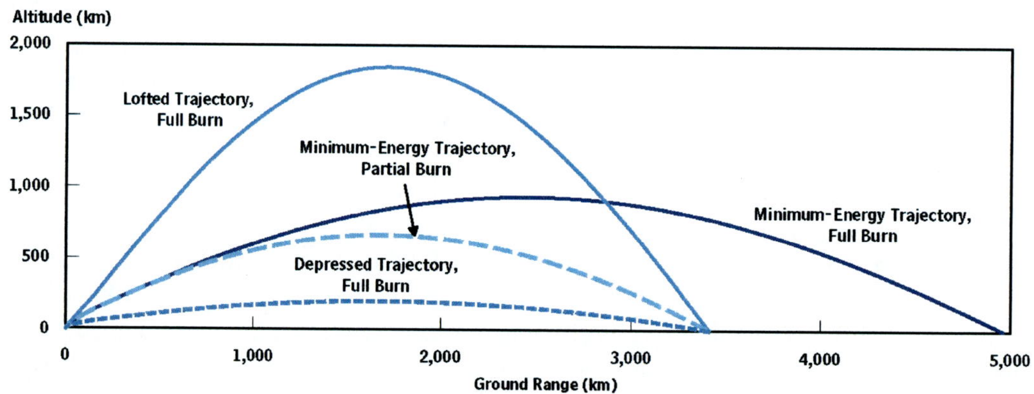

Source: Congressional Budget Office.

Note: IRBM = intermediate-range ballistic missile; km = kilometers.

Figure A-1. Altitude versus Ground Range for Various IRBM Trajectories.

Of course, missiles need to be able to hit targets that are closer than their maximum range. Several ways exist to reduce the range from the maximum. One approach is to follow the same flight profile as a minimum-energy trajectory but terminate the thrust early. That is straightforward for liquid-fuel missiles but more complicated for solid-fuel missiles because they generally burn until all of their fuel is spent. However, a solid-fuel missile can reduce forward thrust by venting its exhaust gases out the sides of the missile or by executing a maneuver (called a generalized energy management, or GEM, maneuver) to waste some of the fuel—the missile equivalent of driving around in circles. Besides terminating thrust, range can also be reduced by using a different flight profile (see Figure A-1), at either a higher elevation angle (lofted trajectory) or a lower elevation angle (depressed trajectory). Generally, missiles have limits on what trajectories they can fly because of their minimum burn time and other design constraints, so there is a minimum range over which a given missile can be used to strike.

In some cases, lofted or depressed trajectories may be more challenging for missile defenses than minimum-energy trajectories. A lofted trajectory, which resembles a lob shot in tennis, may allow a missile to fly above the range of sensors or interceptors, thereby evading or delaying detection or engagement. However, at higher altitude, the missile may clear the horizon and thus become visible to a given sensor earlier than with a minimum-energy trajectory; the missile is also in the air longer, potentially affording more time for engagement. Lofted trajectories can be more challenging to defenses that target missiles in the terminal phase of their flight, because the payload travels closer to vertical and is in the atmosphere for a shorter time after reentry.

Depressed trajectories, by contrast, require more fuel than minimum-energy trajectories. But, like a baseball pitcher's fastball, a missile on a depressed trajectory travels a more direct line to the target and reaches the target faster, which can reduce the amount of time available for intercept. Also, at lower altitude, the missile may be able to remain below the horizon of a given sensor longer and thus delay or evade detection.

A wide range of possibilities exist for combining thrust termination with various angles of lofted or depressed trajectories, so an exhaustive analysis of the capabilities of a missile defense system would require extensive resources. For this chapter, the Congressional Budget Office assumed that enemy missiles would be flying minimum-energy trajectories, with thrust termination used to reduce the range from the maximum.

APPENDIX B. ANALYTIC METHODS AND SENSITIVITY OF THE RESULTS TO CHANGES IN ASSUMPTIONS

To estimate the defensive capability of a given missile defense system, the Congressional Budget Office (CBO) began by simulating the possible trajectories that threat missiles with minimum-energy flight profiles (see Appendix A) could take from each of the three hypothetical launch sites in Iran. The area threatened by a particular missile—that is, the region between the missile's minimum and maximum ranges—was split into a grid by varying azimuth angles and booster burn times (and thus range) over small intervals throughout the full range. For shorter-range missiles, CBO considered only the set of azimuth angles that threatened Europe, consistent with the scope of this study. For intercontinental ballistic missiles (ICBMs), CBO considered the full 360-degree range in azimuth.

For the next step—modeling the ability of a given interceptor at a given location to defend against threats— CBO first created a fan of possible interceptor trajectories by varying the initial azimuth and elevation angles by small intervals over the full range. Then, for each threat trajectory in the grid, CBO determined which combinations of initial azimuth and elevation angles for the interceptor would produce a trajectory that intersected with the chosen threat trajectory. Any trajectory that came within 100 kilometers (km) of the threat trajectory at the closest point of approach was considered to have intersected the threat and thus to be a potential intercept trajectory[69]. In general, multiple combinations of azimuth and elevation angles yielded potential intercept trajectories for each threat trajectory.

Criteria for a Successful Intercept

For a potential intercept trajectory to be considered as a successful intercept, it had to meet certain criteria in terms of the geometry and the timeline of the intercept. All of the interceptors that CBO modeled are designed to conduct exoatmospheric intercepts (that is, to intercept missiles outside the atmosphere). Thus, in its modeling, CBO included a requirement that the altitude of the threat missile at the intercept point be at least 100 km in all cases. In addition, the Standard Missile-3 (SM-3) Block IB interceptor requires tracking updates from the SPY-1 radar during an engagement, so the intercept must occur inside the radar's field of regard. To meet that requirement, CBO limited the altitude of the threat missile to no more than 650 km at the point of intercept for engagements with SM-3 Block IB interceptors.

All of the interceptors that CBO considered in this study use hit-to-kill technology, destroying a threat warhead through the kinetic energy of the collision. A minimum kinetic energy is required to ensure destruction of the warhead, which translates to a minimum allowable relative velocity between the interceptor and the threat warhead. Little information about the requirements for a kinetic kill is available in unclassified literature. One detailed study estimated that a direct hit from a kill vehicle weighing 40 kilograms (kg) would require a relative velocity of about 1.5 km per second (sec) to ensure destruction.[70] Greater kinetic energy expands the volume of the region damaged by the collision, which can help correct for an impact that is slightly off from the ideal hit point. The same study found that for an impact that is offset by 20 centimeters (cm), the required velocity for a 40 kg kill vehicle is estimated at 2.5 km/sec, whereas an offset of 30 cm necessitates 3.0 km/sec. If the warhead contains submunitions, a relative velocity of 6 km/sec or more may be needed to ensure a high probability of complete destruction. For this analysis, CBO assumed that a relative velocity of at least 3.0 km/sec would be necessary to destroy a threat warhead.

The most limiting requirement on potential intercept trajectories is the timeline available for intercept. The interceptor's flight time (from launch to the closest point of approach to its target) must be sufficiently less than the flight time of the threat missile to allow for detecting the launch, tracking the threat missile, and deciding on the optimum intercept trajectory.

After the launch of a threat missile, the defense system must become aware of the launch, nominally through infrared satellites—known as overhead nonimaging infrared (ONIR) satellites. After being cued by that detection, tracking radars will begin to measure the trajectory of the threat missile as soon as the missile enters their field of regard. For the midcourse-phase intercepts modeled in this study, CBO required that the ballistic trajectory of the threat missile (its trajectory after its booster has burned out) be determined before an interceptor is launched. To allow for that determination, CBO required a lead time of 30 seconds after burnout for the ONIR satellites to detect that burnout has occurred, followed by 5 seconds of access from a tracking radar and then 30 seconds for deciding on the defensive strategy and launching the interceptor. In some cases, if a radar is near the launch site of the threat missile, the missile may be within the radar's field of regard at burnout, and the 5 seconds of access may occur directly after the alert of burnout from the ONIR satellites. In other cases, the threat missile may fly farther along its trajectory before it enters the field of regard of the tracking radar, requiring more lead time for an engagement.

In all, the available lead time—equivalent to the flight time of the threat missile to the closest point of approach minus the flight time of the interceptor to the same point—must be equal to or greater than the sum of the following elements:

- The threat missile's burn time,
- Thirty seconds for an ONIR satellite to determine that the missile has burned out,
- Any delay before the missile enters the field of regard of a tracking radar (the delay may be zero with optimal radar placement),
- Five seconds of access by the tracking radar to determine the missile's ballistic trajectory, and
- Thirty seconds for decisionmaking and the interceptor launch process.

Sensitivity to Modeled Performance Parameters

In its modeling, CBO used performance parameters from unclassified sources for the interceptors and threat missiles. In some cases, those parameters could differ to some degree from the actual performance of the missiles. In particular, two types of interceptors—the SM-3 Block IIA and the Kinetic Energy Interceptor (KEI)—are still in the development stages, and the performance of the actual production versions could differ from the ones modeled in this study. To explore the sensitivity of the model's results to variations in performance, CBO constructed alternate models for the interceptors with different performance parameters. It also examined the effects of altering the assumed ranges of various tracking radars.

Burnout Velocity

An important parameter of an interceptor is its velocity when its booster burns out, which largely determines the interceptor's range. For its sensitivity analysis, CBO varied the burnout velocity of the SM-3 Block IIA and the KEI by 10 percent from the values modeled in the rest of the study. For the SM-3, burnout velocity was decreased by 10 percent from the nominal value; for the KEI, it was both increased and decreased by 10 percent.[71]Such changes in burnout velocity could result if the total mass of the interceptor (including the kill vehicle) or the specific impulse of the rocket motors differed from the assumed values.

In the case of both interceptors, defensive coverage of Europe does not change substantially with those differences in burnout velocity. The largest change involves the SM-3's defensive capability against an Iranian intermediate-range ballistic missile: Some portions of eastern Europe that would be defended with the higher assumed velocity would not be defended with the lower velocity (as an example, see Figure B-1, which shows how coverage would change for Option 3). Defensive coverage of the United States against potential ICBMs is much more affected by changes in burnout velocity, especially for the KEI (see Figure B-2).

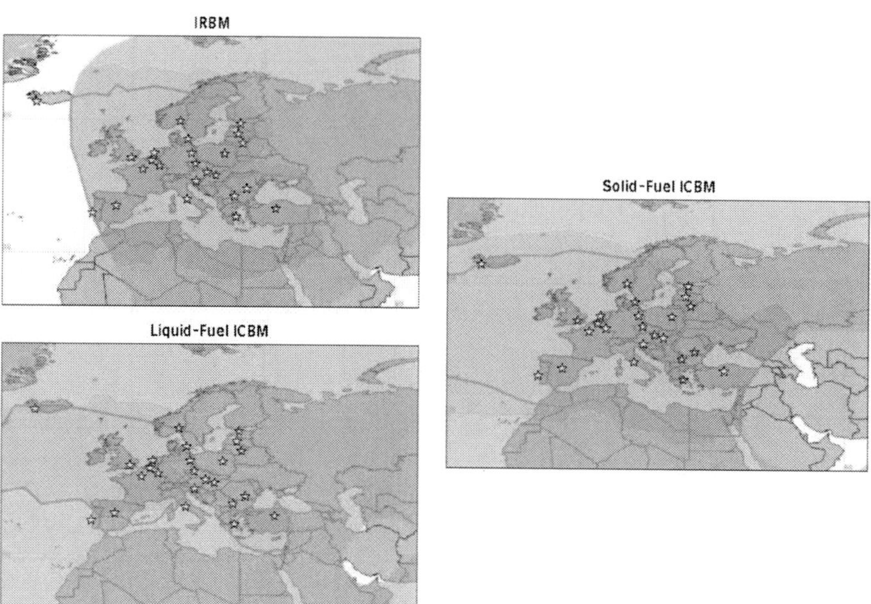

Source: Congressional Budget Office.

Notes: Option 3 places land-based SM-3 Block IIA interceptors at two existing U.S. bases in Europe. Blue shading indicates the area defended against a given missile threat. Blue outlines show the area defended if Option 3's SM-3 Block IIA interceptors had a burnout velocity 10 percent lower than the nominal value. Red shading indicates undefended areas within range of a given threat. Yellow stars show the locations of NATO capitals.

IRBM = intermediate-range ballistic missile; ICBM = intercontinental ballistic missile; SM = Standard Missile; NATO = North Atlantic Treaty Organization.

Figure B.1. Sensitivity of Option 3's Defensive Coverage to Various Assumptions About the Burnout Velocity of the Interceptor.

Radar Range

Another possible source of variation in performance is the effective range of the tracking radars. Recent studies have concluded that the range at which the European Midcourse Radar (EMR) could track reentry vehicles and discriminate between them and decoys would be much shorter than the ranges assumed by the Missile Defense Agency or used in this study.[72] In CBO's model, the only requirement for radar coverage is that the ballistic trajectory of a threat missile spend 5 seconds in the field of regard of a tracking radar to determine the trajectory. In most cases, that initial tracking is provided by the forward-based radar (FBR). In the few cases in which the initial tracking is provided by the EMR, the time at which access begins is limited primarily by the horizon, so a reduction in range would generally not change the defended area. The main impact of a reduction in the EMR's range would be to decrease the area over which the radar could provide updated trajectories after an interceptor was launched and could discriminate decoys, potentially reducing the probability of a successful intercept for trajectories not within range of the EMR. CBO did not quantitatively model the probability of a successful intercept. Thus, the analysis is not sensitive to the impact of a shorter range for the EMR.

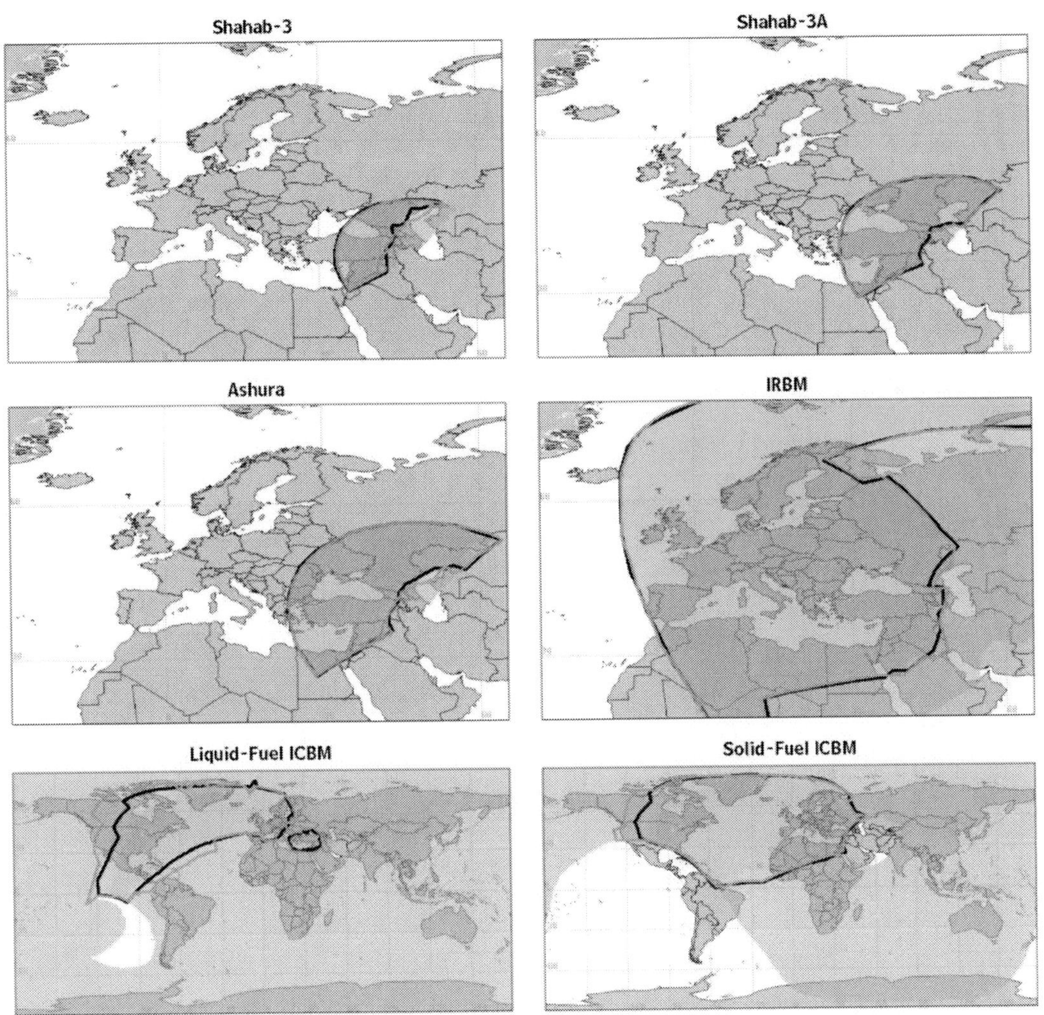

Source: Congressional Budget Office.

Notes: Option 4 places land-based KEIs at two existing U.S. bases in Europe.

Blue shading indicates the area defended against a given missile threat if Option 4's KEIs had a burnout velocity 10 percent lower than the nominal value of 3 kilometers per second. Black outlines show the area defended if the KEIs had the nominal burnout velocity, and blue outlines show the area defended if the KEIs had a burnout velocity 10 percent higher than the nominal value. Red shading indicates undefended areas within range of a given threat.

IRBM = intermediate-range ballistic missile; ICBM = intercontinental ballistic missile; KEI = Kinetic Energy Interceptor.

Figure B.2. Sensitivity of Option 4's Defensive Coverage to Various Assumptions About the Burnout Velocity of the Interceptor.

Changes in the range of the FBR, however, could affect the modeled results. CBO assumed that the AN/TPY-2 (the radar system used for the FBR) would have a range of 1,000 km (see Table B-1). Future upgrades have been proposed to increase the range of that radar through the use of an adjunct sensor. CBO estimated that increasing the range to 2,000 km would allow the FBR at the modeled location in Azerbaijan to observe many of the more easterly ICBM trajectories heading from Iran to the United States that are currently out of range. Such a change would expand the defensive coverage of Option 1, for example, west to include Alaska and portions of Russia.[73] Extending the range of an FBR in Azerbaijan beyond 2,000 km, however, would not increase its defensive capability against Iranian missile threats.

Table B.1. Performance Characteristics Assumed for the Radars Used in the Missile Defense Options

Radar	Band	Wavelength (cm)	Range (km)	Elevation Angle (Degrees)		Azimuth Angle (Degrees)	
				Minimum	Maximum	Minimum	Maximum
Fyling-dales	UHF	67	4,820	3	85	0	360
Thule	UHF	67	5,555	3	85	297	177
Clear	UHF	67	4,910	3	85	170	110
Cape Cod	UHF	67	5,555	3	85	347	227
Cobra Dane	L	23	48,000	1	80	259	19
EMR	X	3	5,000	1	90	0	360
SBX	X	3	5,000	2	90	0	360
SPY-1	S	9	650	1	90	0	360
FBR	X	3	1,000	1	90	0	360

Source: Congressional Budget Office based on information from the Missile Defense Agency; *Jane's Strategic Weapons Systems* (Coulsdon, Surrey, United Kingdom: Jane's Information Group, 2008); David Vallado, *Fundamentals of Astrodynamics and Applications*, 2nd ed. (El Segundo, Calif.: Microcosm Press, 2001); J.F. Crawford and others, "Ground-Based Radar-Prototype Antenna" (paper presented at the National Conference on Antennas and Propagation, York, United Kingdom, March 30–April 1, 1999); Dean Wilkening, "Airborne Boost-Phase Ballistic Missile Defense," Science and Global Security, vol. 12 (2004), pp. 1–67; Larry Chasteen, *National Missile Defense and Early Warning Radars: Background and Issues*, CRS Report for Congress RL30654 (Congressional Research Service, August 2000).

Note: cm = centimeters; km = kilometers; UHF = ultrahigh frequency; EMR = European Midcourse Radar; SBX = Sea-Based X-Band Radar; FBR = forward-based radar.

End Notes

[1] Missile Defense Agency, *Fiscal Year 2009 Budget Estimates: Overview*, 08-MDA-3 199 (January 23, 2008), p. 6.

[2] Public Law 106-3 8, 113 Stat. 205.

[3] Missile Defense Agency, "MDA Mission," www.mda.mil/ mdalink/html/aboutus.html, accessed on April 18, 2008. The flight of a ballistic missile is generally separated into three phases. The boost phase lasts from launch until the missile's rocket engines have finished firing. After that, the missile enters the midcourse phase, when the payload (which may or may not have separated from the rocket booster) follows a ballistic trajectory outside the atmosphere. The terminal phase begins with the payload reentering the atmosphere and lasts until impact.

[4] Missile Defense Agency, *Fiscal Year 2009 Budget Estimates*.

[5] That total does not include approximately $200 million in development funding related to the European system that is included in the budget for Block 3.0. Part of that $200 million is intended to adapt MDA's current three-stage ground-based interceptor to the two-stage version that would be used in Europe.

[6] Missile Defense Agency, *Proposed U.S. Missile Defense Assets in Europe*, 07-MDA-2650 (June 15, 2007), p. 1, www.mda.mil/ mdalink/pdf/euroassets.pdf.

[7] According to MDA's classification scheme, short-range ballistic missiles are those with a maximum range of 600 kilometers, medium-range ballistic missiles have a range of 600 to 1,300 kilometers, intermediate-range

ballistic missiles have a range of 1,300 to 5,500 kilometers, and intercontinental ballistic missiles have a range of more than 5,500 kilometers.

8 "U.S. BMD [Ballistic Missile Defense] Plans Gain NATO's Endorsement but Not Russia's," *WMD Insights* (June 2008), pp. 26–35, www.wmdinsights.com/PDF/ WMDInsights_Jun08Issue.pdf.

9 North Atlantic Treaty Organization, *Bucharest Summit Declaration* (April 3, 2008), www.nato.int/docu/pr/2008/p08-049e.html.

10 See, for example, "Moscow Rejects U.S. Written Proposals on Missile Defense, Downplays New Iranian Missile Test," *WMD Insights* (February 2008), pp. 38–44, www.wmdinsights.com/PDF/WMDInsights_Feb08Issue.pdf.

11 The White House, Office of the Press Secretary, *U.S.–Russia Strategic Framework Declaration* (April 6, 2008), www.cfr.org/publication/16193/usrussia_strategic_framework_ declaration.html.

12 For a summary of public opinion in Europe, see "Special Report: The European Ballistic Missile Defense Dispute," *WMD Insights* (April 2007), pp. 1–15, www.wmdinsights.com/PDF/ WMDInsights_Apr07Issue.pdf.

13 John Liang, "U.S. Official: A PAC-3 Battery in Poland Would Mean Moving an Existing Unit," *Inside Missile Defense* (August 27, 2008).

14 All of the options would also use the existing early-warning radar at Fylingdales, England, which was recently upgraded to improve its tracking capability for missile defense.

15 MDA has not designated a specific location for the FBR, but some press reports indicate that it has been considering the Caucasus region as a possible location. See, for example, Nathan Hodge, "Caucasus Considered as Base for U.S. Missile Sensor," *Jane's Defence News* (July 27, 2006).

16 The distinction between categories of costs is made only for the purposes of this study. Historically, funding for MDA, including funding for production and operations, has all come under the budget category of research, development, test, and evaluation. Recently, however, MDA's budget justification materials have designated some funds under the category of military construction.

17 For most components, the cost-risk factors that CBO used were developed by the RAND Corporation and were based on unpublished updates to Jeanne M. Jarvaise, Jeffrey A. Drezner, and Daniel M. Norton, *The Defense System Cost Performance Database: Cost Growth Analysis Using Selected Acquisition Reports*, MR-625-OSD (Santa Monica, Calif.: RAND, 1996).

18 As the name implies, the Multiple Kill Vehicle would carry several kill vehicles (the section that separates from the interceptor booster and maneuvers to intercept the target) and thus would allow a single interceptor to engage more than one target— enhancing the probability of engaging the actual warhead in the presence of decoys.

19 National Intelligence Council, *Foreign Missile Developments and the Ballistic Missile Threat to the United States Through 2015*, unclassified summary of a National Intelligence Estimate (September 1999), www.dni.gov/nic/special_missilethreat1999.html.

20 See, for example, Lisbeth Gronlund and others, *Technical Realities: An Analysis of the 2004 Deployment of a U.S. National Missile Defense System* (Cambridge, Mass.: Union of Concerned Scientists, May 2004); and Richard L. Garwin, "Holes in the Missile Shield," *Scientific American* (November 1, 2004), p. 70.

21 Congressional Budget Office, *Alternatives for Boost-Phase Missile Defense* (July 2004).

22 National Air and Space Intelligence Center, *Ballistic and Cruise Missile Threat*, NASIC-1031-0985-06 (March 2006), pp. 9 and 17.

23 National Intelligence Council, *Iran: Nuclear Intentions and Capabilities*, National Intelligence Estimate (November 2007).

24 General Eugene Habiger, quoted in Joseph Cirincione, *The Declining Ballistic Missile Threat, 2005*, Policy Outlook (Washington, D.C.: Carnegie Endowment for International Peace, February 2005), p. 9.

25 National Intelligence Council, *Foreign Missile Developments and the Ballistic Missile Threat to the United States Through 2015*, unclassified summary of a National Intelligence Estimate (December 2001), p. 15.

26 Public Law 106-38; 113 Stat. 205.

27 Missile Defense Agency, *Fiscal Year 2009 Budget Estimates Overview*, 08-MDA-3199 (January 2008).

28 Dinshaw Mistry, "European Missile Defense: Assessing Iran's ICBM Capabilities," *Arms Control Today* (October 2007).

29 Technical descriptions, ranges, and even names of Iranian missiles vary considerably among different unclassified sources. Thus, the descriptions of specific missiles in this chapter may differ from descriptions elsewhere that are based on other sources.

30 National Air and Space Intelligence Center, *Ballistic and Cruise Missile Threat*, NASIC-1031-0985-06 (March 2006), p. 10.

31 Ibid.

32 Lt. Gen. Henry Obering as quoted in David Bond, ed., "Washington Outlook," *Aviation Week and Space Technology* (December 3, 2007).

33 See, for example, Peter Crail, "Iran Lauds Development of Solid- Fuel Missile," *Arms Control Today* (January/February 2008).

[34] Nazili Fatahi and Alan Cowell, "Iran Claims Success in Tests Firing Long-Range Missiles," *New York Times*, November 13, 2008.

[35] CSS-5 is a NATO designation; China refers to the missile as the DF-21. China was widely reported to have used that missile when it shot down an aging Chinese weather satellite in January 2007.

[36] Daniel A. Pinkston, *The North Korean Ballistic Missile Program* (Carlisle, Pa.: Army War College, Strategic Studies Institute, February 2008).

[37] Fred Barnes, "The Commander," *The Weekly Standard* (June 2, 2003).

[38] John Holum, senior advisor for arms control and international security at the State Department, in a March 2000 speech, as quoted in Bradley Graham, *Hit to Kill* (New York: Perseus Books Group, 2001), p. 164.

[39] The original agreement limited each party to two interceptor sites, but a 1974 protocol changed that to a single site.

[40] For a detailed account of the debate within the Clinton Administration about missile defenses, see Graham, *Hit to Kill*.

[41] Department of State, *ABM Treaty Fact Sheet* (December 13, 2001), http://2001-2009.state.gov/t/ac/rls/fs/2001/6848.htm (accessed June 25, 2008).

[42] Richard Weitz, "Special Report: The European Ballistic Missile Defense Dispute," *WMD Insights* (April 2007), p. 2; and Steve Gutterman, "Medvedev: Russia to Deploy Missiles near Poland," *Washington Post*, November 5, 2008.

[43] For example, with the solid-fuel ICBM that CBO included in this analysis, if the thrust is terminated just 5 seconds short of the full 203-second burn time, the location of final impact changes by more than 2,000 km from that of a full-burn trajectory.

[44] The amount of maneuverability that the kill vehicle has, usually quantified as the total change in velocity (delta-V) of which it is capable, varies by the phase of flight. Boost-phase intercept kill vehicles may require several kilometers per second of delta-V, whereas midcourse intercept kill vehicles, which operate during the more predictable ballistic portion of the trajectory, can have considerably less. However, a relatively high delta-V could be required for midcourse intercepts if the threat warhead was capable of maneuvering during the midcourse phase.

[45] Hit-to-kill interceptors rely on the kinetic energy of the collision with a target to destroy the target. Since kinetic energy is proportional to the square of the relative velocity between the colliding bodies, there is some minimum value of relative velocity that will ensure that the collision is sufficiently violent to destroy the target. For this study, CBO assumed a minimum relative velocity of 3 km per second; the rationale for that value is discussed in Appendix B.

[46] The THAAD interceptor is capable of engagements both inside the atmosphere (endoatmospheric) and outside the atmosphere (exoatmospheric) and thus could be considered both a terminal- phase and a late midcourse-phase defense system.

[47] The AN/TPY-2 was formerly known as the Forward-Based X- Band Transportable radar.

[48] STSS was originally referred to as the Space-Based Infrared System–Low.

[49] Vandenberg also has a fifth silo that is designated for testing purposes.

[50] The Clear and Cape Cod UEWRs are supposed to be incorporated into the missile defense system after the Air Force finishes upgrading them.

[51] Dave Ahern, "Allied Nations Interested in Buying THAAD Ballistic Missile Defense Systems," *Defense Daily* (April 22, 2008).

[52] J.F. Crawford and others, "Ground Based Radar—Prototype (GBR-P) Antenna," *IEE National Conference on Antennas and Propagation: 30 March–1 April 1999*, Conference Publication No. 461 (London: Institution of Electrical Engineers, 1999), p. 249; and "Ground-Based Midcourse Defense (GMD) Segment, *Jane's Strategic Weapons Systems* (Coulsdon, Surrey, United Kingdom: Jane's Information Group, 2007).

[53] George N. Lewis and Theodore A. Postol, "The European Missile Defense Folly," *Bulletin of the Atomic Scientists*, vol. 64, no. 2 (May/June 2008), p. 32.

[54] It is also possible that the forward-based radars could be deployed in times of crisis, since the type of radar envisioned in this option (the AN/TPY-2) is transportable. However, establishing the required communications and integrating the radars into the overall command-and-control system on short notice could be difficult.

[55] For more information about the Montreux Convention, see www.ntip.navy.mil/montreux_convention.shtml.

[56] Missile Defense Agency, Systems Engineering and Integration, "U.S. and Israel Upper Tier Ballistic Missile Defense Element Options for Defense of Israel" (briefing provided to the Congressional Budget Office, May 5, 2008).

[57] The distinction between those categories of costs is made only for the purposes of this study. Historically, funding for MDA, including for production and operations, has all come under the budget category of research, development, test, and evaluation, although recently some funds have come under the budget category of military construction.

[58] Those cost-risk factors, developed by the RAND Corporation, are based on unpublished updates to Jeanne M. Jarvaise, Jeffrey A. Drezner, and Daniel M. Norton, *The Defense System Cost Perfor- mance Database: Cost Growth Analysis Using Selected Acquisition Reports,* MR-625-OSD (Santa Monica, Calif.: RAND, 1996).

[59] For more details about the components of the Block 3.0 system and the other missile defense systems described here, see Chapter 2.

[60] As described in Chapter 2, CBO assumed in its modeling that near-term threat missiles would be launched from northwestern Iran to maximize their reach into Europe. In some cases, however, the same missiles launched from other parts of Iran might be able to reach portions of Europe and could be more difficult for some of the options to defend against.

[61] Those possibilities for expanding Option 1's coverage of southeastern Europe do not use additional two-stage Ground-Based Interceptors because those interceptors accelerate too slowly to be useful closer to the launch sites of Iranian missiles.

[62] Lofted or depressed trajectories would not be a problem with ICBMs aimed at the United States from Iran because those missiles would have to travel trajectories close to minimum energy to be able to reach the United States.

[63] All of that additional coverage would come from the KEI site in Germany; the site in Turkey would not provide any coverage of the United States.

[64] CBO has not modeled the possibility of shoot-look-shoot between an SM-3 Block IIA site in the eastern United States and the GMD sites on the West Coast.

[65] See, for example, George N. Lewis and Theodore A. Postol, "European Missile Defense: The Technological Basis of Russian Concerns," *Arms Control Today* (October 2007), www.armscontrol.org/act/2007_10/LewisPostol.

[66] Steven J. Isakowitz and others, *International Reference Guide to Space Launch Systems,* 4th ed. (Reston, Va.: American Institute of Aeronautics and Astronautics, 2004).

[67] Relative velocity is the velocity of one object (the interceptor) as seen by another object (the threat missile). It depends on the speed of each of the missiles and the directions they are flying. Like cars driving on a two-way highway, objects heading in opposite directions have higher relative velocity, and objects heading in the same direction have lower relative velocity.

[68] The analysis of defense against missiles launched from Iran is less sensitive to the cutoff for minimum relative velocity because of the locations of the launch sites for threat missiles and interceptors in that case.

[69] The value of 100 km was chosen to be consistent with the size of the intervals used for elevation and azimuth angles. In general, it would be possible to determine a "firing solution" (the actual choice of angles that a real intercept attempt might make) with a smaller separation by choosing angular values lying between the intervals that CBO selected. The intent of CBO's approach was to determine, with a reasonable amount of computation, the range of values for elevation and azimuth angles within which it would be possible to obtain a firing solution.

[70] Richard M. Lloyd, *Physics of Direct Hit and Near Miss Warhead Technology,* vol. 194 of Paul Zarchan, ed., *Progress in Astronautics and Aeronautics* (Reston, Va.: American Institute of Aeronautics and Astronautics, 2001).

[71] Because the Block IIA is an upgrade of an existing missile with well-known performance characteristics, its burnout velocity is unlikely to substantially exceed the expected value.

[72] George N. Lewis and Theodore A. Postol, "The European Missile Defense Folly," *Bulletin of the Atomic Scientists,* vol. 64, no. 2 (May/June 2008), p. 32.

[73] Option 1 consists of two-stage Ground-Based Interceptors in silos and X-band radars in two locations.

In: Options for Deploying Missile Defenses in Europe
Editor: Melissa V. Jordan pp.153-166

ISBN: 978-1-60741-889-4
© 2010 Nova Science Publishers, Inc.

Chapter 7

PROPOSED U.S. MISSILE DEFENSE ASSETS IN EUROPE[*]

Department of State and Department of Defense

INTRODUCTION

Some of the world's most dangerous and unpredictable regimes either have already acquired, or are attempting to acquire, weapons of mass destruction. These regimes are also developing and/or acquiring ballistic missiles of increasing ranges, payloads, lethality, and sophistication as a means of delivery. In the future, these regimes could use these asymmetric weapons to pursue their objectives through force, coercion, and/or intimidation as they have done in the past.

Today's ballistic missile threat from potentially hostile states is fundamentally different from Cold War era threats and risks. In response, the United States is fielding limited and purely defensive capabilities. In our comprehensive strategy to combat weapons of mass destruction, missile defense is just one element of a multi-faceted approach, which includes diplomacy, export controls, threat reduction assistance, nonproliferation regimes, and counter-proliferation programs. At the same time, missile defense is our ultimate insurance policy if these other elements of our strategy fail. History has taught us that, despite our best efforts, the free world will be challenged by military surprises as well as failures in diplomacy, intelligence, and deterrence. Given this reality, missile defenses have become highly desirable because they both reinforce deterrence and hedge against its failure.

Because of the expanding ballistic missile threat, it is essential that we develop and deploy missile defenses capable of protecting not only the United States and our deployed forces, but also our friends and allies. Trans-atlantic security is indivisible. We have learned from experience that decoupling our defenses from Europe is very much against the interests of the United States and our European allies. If Europe is not secure, the United States is not

---

[*] This is an edited, reformatted and augmented version of a U. S. Department of State and U. S. Department of Defense publication dated June 2007.

secure. To ensure our common security, we need defenses stationed and operational in Europe **before** a threat fully emerges. For this reason, negotiations are currently underway to locate up to ten silo-based long-range missile defense interceptors in Poland and a midcourse tracking and discrimination radar in the Czech Republic. These defensive interceptors contain no explosives, and destroy attacking reentry vehicles by kinetic energy, that is, a body-on-body collision outside of the atmosphere between the kinetic kill interceptor and the reentry vehicle.

THE THREAT IS REAL AND GROWING

The pace of ballistic missile proliferation, and the threat this creates, is rapidly increasing. Consider these trends:

- In 1972, only nine states possessed ballistic missiles
- In 1990, as the Cold War was drawing to a close, 16 states possessed ballistic missiles of varying ranges
- By the end of 2006, the number increased to 25 states

The number of states that currently possess medium-, intermediate-, and/or intercontinental-range ballistic missiles (missiles that can reach our friends and allies, and in some cases the United States itself) *has increased from five to nine*. Clearly, the international security environment is more complex and less predictable since the fall of the Berlin Wall in 1989 and the collapse of the Soviet Union in 1991.

Of particular concern are the ballistic missile development and testing programs underway in North Korea and Iran, and their related proliferation activities.

Great Prophet II Starts With Launches From Jalnabad

- Missiles launched as part of exercise during early hours of November 2, 2006
- Iranian TV showed:
  - Scud-class SRBMs, Shahab MRBM.
  - Multiple launch of six rockets and/or missiles
- Reported by Iranian government as "dozens" of launches with claims of cluster warheads

On January 11, 2007, Lieutenant General Michael Maples, Director of the U.S. Defense Intelligence Agency, testified to the U.S. Senate that "North Korea has an ambitious ballistic missile development program and has exported missiles and missile technology to other countries, including Iran." General Maples also pointed out that North Korea continues to develop and test the Taepo Dong 2 intercontinental ballistic missile and nuclear weapons, as evidenced by their well-publicized series of missile launches on July 4, 2006, and their nuclear test in October 2006.

On November 2, 2006, during the "Great Prophet II" exercise, Iran launched numerous short-range rockets as well as short- and medium-range ballistic missiles. Among the missiles launched was the Shahab-3, which has a 1,300 kilometer range and is capable of reaching Turkey and Tel Aviv.

The Iranian missile development program has received considerable assistance from Russian, Chinese, and North Korean entities. The Shahab-3 is based on the North Korean No Dong missile. Iranian officials have publicly claimed that a 2,000 kilometer range variant of the Shahab-3 is under development as well as a new solid-propellant medium-range ballistic missile (MRBM). That would provide Iran the capability to strike significant parts of southeastern and central Europe, Turkey, Israel, and U.S. and allied military bases in the Persian Gulf.

Iran is also seeking to develop medium-range ballistic missiles (MRBMs) of increasing ranges, intermediate-range ballistic missiles (IRBMs), and possibly intercontinental ballistic missiles (ICBMs). The U.S. Intelligence Community assesses that with continued foreign assistance, Iran could be able to develop an ICBM capable of reaching the United States and all regions of Europe before 2015. Iran is also developing space launch vehicles – a key building block for an ICBM.

Iran SRBM, MRBM			
Missile	Propellant	Deployment Mode	Launchers
Fateh-110	Solid	Road-mobile	Fewer than 50
Scud C SRBM	Liquid	Road-mobile	Fewer than 50
Shahab-3	Liquid	Road-mobile	Fewer than 20
Shahab-3 Variant	Liquid	Road-mobile	Not yet deployed

A ballistic missile is a weapon that is launched from a fixed or mobile platform and follows a predictable arc towards its intended target. Ballistic missiles can travel anywhere from short distances (as little as 100 kilometers), to very long distances (10,000 kilometers or more). Depending on the missile design and sophistication, ballistic missiles can be armed with conventional explosives or weapons of mass destruction (nuclear, chemical, or biological payloads).

Noting the strong international consensus regarding the missile threat, NATO Secretary General Jaap de Hoop Scheffer stated after the April 19, 2007, North Atlantic Council meeting in Brussels, "there is absolutely a shared threat perception between the allies. Allies all agree that there is a threat from ballistic missiles."

BENEFITS OF BALLISTIC MISSILE DEFENSE IN EUROPE

The deployment of U.S. missile defense assets in Europe would provide:

- An improved capability to defend the United States against ballistic missile attack from the Middle East
- The capability to extend defensive coverage to Europe against longer-range ballistic missiles which would enhance the collective security of the NATO Alliance, strengthen trans-atlantic unity, reaffirm America's commitments to European security, and avoid the decoupling of European and American security interests
- An opportunity for technology sharing and cost savings that can substantially enhance development of the envisioned NATO Active Layered Theater Ballistic Missile Defense (ALTBMD) program
- An opportunity for NATO to potentially utilize the U.S. sensor infrastructure for use in a future NATO defensive system for protecting population and territory – if NATO approves such a military requirement – against ballistic missiles of all ranges and increasing sophistication
- Increased situational awareness and information sharing for Host Nations, NATO, and its Member States
- An additional option to deal with ballistic missile attacks besides offensive retaliation or military preemption
- The ability to dissuade potentially hostile states from indigenous development or foreign acquisition of ballistic missiles in the first place, by undermining their military utility and thus promoting European and U.S. nonproliferation goals
- Enhanced deterrence against attempts to coerce or intimidate European allies and friends

PROPOSED U.S. MISSILE DEFENSE ASSETS IN EUROPE

The proposal to deploy components of the U.S. Ballistic Missile Defense System (BMDS) to Europe consists of:

Ten interceptors proposed to be based in Poland. These ground-based interceptors, nearly identical to those in Alaska and California, would be housed in underground silos in an interceptor field about the size of a football field. As with the interceptors based in Alaska and California, these interceptors are designed only for defensive purposes and employ small hit-to-kill vehicles (weighing about 75 kilograms) instead of explosives to destroy their targets at collision speeds in excess of 7 km per second and at more than 200 km above the earth's surface.

The interceptors planned for Poland are nearly identical to the three-stage interceptors based in the U.S. except that they are a two-stage variant that is quicker, lighter, and better suited for the engagement ranges and timelines for Europe. The silos that house the ground-based interceptors have substantially smaller dimensions (e.g., diameter and length) than those used for offensive missiles, such as the U.S. Minuteman III ICBM. Any modification would require extensive, lengthy, and costly changes that would be clearly visible to any observer.

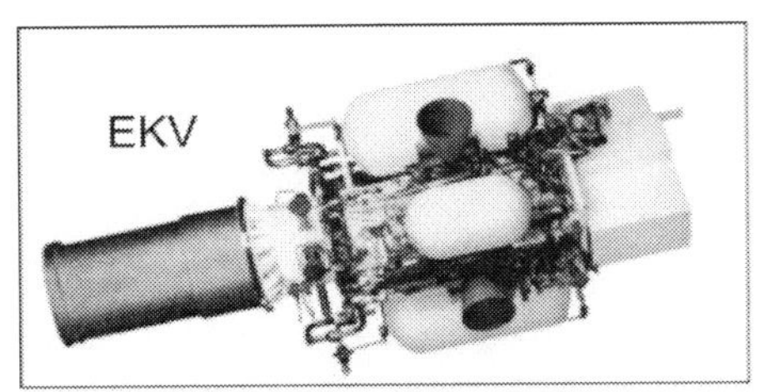

- European interceptor site
  - Up to ten silo-based long-range interceptors located in central Europe (2011-2013)

- European midcourse radar
  - Relocation of a narrow-beam, midcourse tracking radar currently used in our Paci?c test range to central Europe (2011)

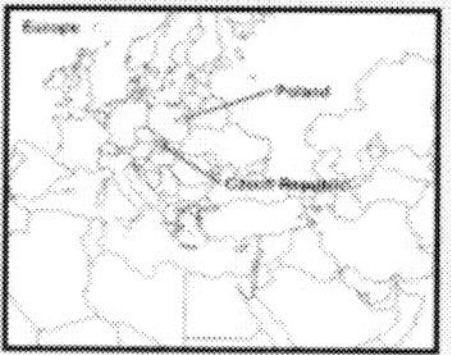

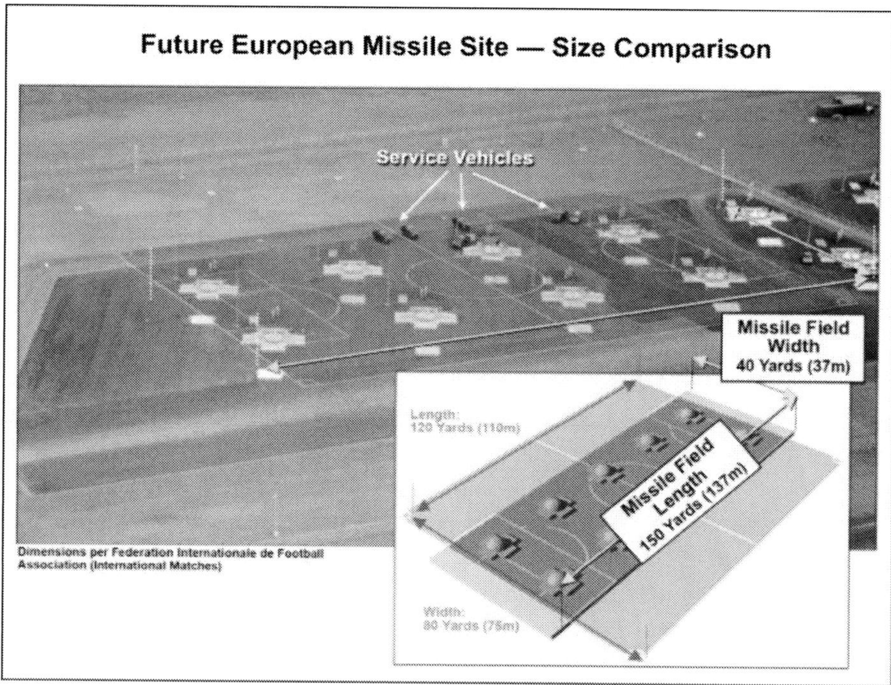

The ground-based interceptors are comprised of a booster vehicle and an exoatmospheric kill vehicle (EKV). Upon launch, the booster fl ies to a projected intercept point and releases the EKV which then uses on-board sensors (with assistance from ground-based assets) to acquire the target ballistic missile. The EKV performs fi nal discrimination and steers itself to collide with the enemy warhead, destroying it by the sheer kinetic force of impact.

A Midcourse Radar proposed for deployment to the Czech Republic. This X-band radar will be optimized to point its narrow beam at Iranian ballistic missile threats in flight. This is not a surveillance radar that scans continuously through 360 degrees, but instead uses information from early warning satellites and other transportable sea- and land-based sensors (such as mobile forward-based X-band radars placed closer to ballistic missile threat locations for earlier acquisition and precise tracking) to pinpoint or "cue" its very thin beam to fi nd and track ballistic missiles after they are launched. The emissions of this radar will not endanger people as the beam is extremely narrow (diameter of a couple of meters at a distance of 25 km) and must be elevated from ground level to acquire missiles in fl ight. X-band radars are used at most airports and do not pose a health risk. The X-band radar will not operate continuously 24 hours a day, 7 days a week.

The information obtained by this radar will be used to identify and distinguish the missile warhead from other missile parts (such as separated booster rockets) and potential countermeasures. Most importantly, it will be used to guide interceptor missiles to the projected trajectory of the ballistic missile warhead.

The radar proposed for deployment to the Czech Republic is currently located at Kwajalein Atoll in the Marshall Islands (central Pacific Ocean) where it has been used to support missile defense tests over the past decade. Upon completion of negotiations and site preparation, it will be relocated to Europe. It is important to note that this radar has successfully operated without any harmful effects to the people in the nearby family housing area or the children in the nearby school.

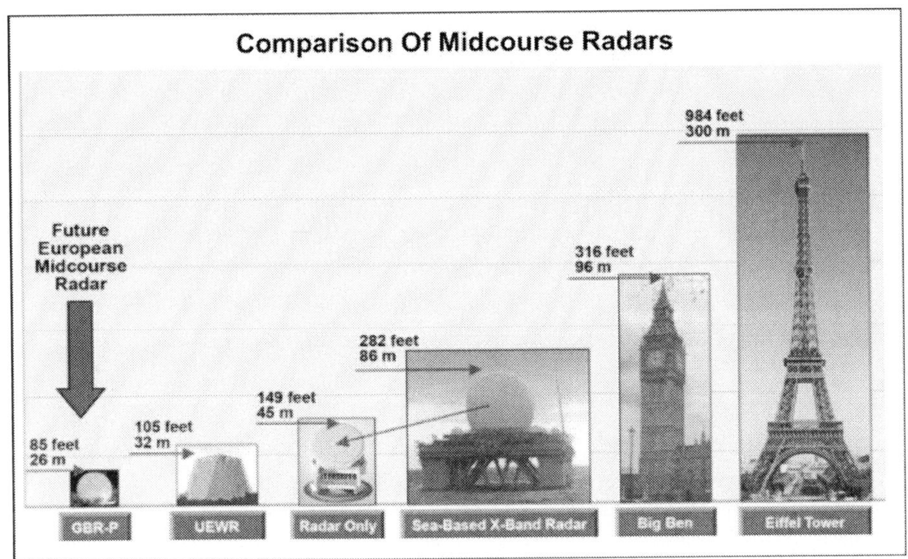

Command and control support composed of a network of computers and communications equipment. This network, part of the larger U.S. command and control system, transmits and receives data on threat missile launches, missile flight profi les, and projected target locations, that enable political and military leaders to determine when and where to launch weapons to intercept them. The system is designed to rapidly provide a wide range of information to decision makers because of the short distances in Europe and the great speed of ballistic missiles that require threat assessment and interceptor launch decisions in just minutes.

The command and control system enables approved decision makers and the operational crews to be alerted to ballistic missile launches, understand and assess the situation, make informed decisions, feed information to interceptors to find and destroy incoming ballistic missile warheads, and then evaluate mission success.

Proposed U.S. Assets in Europe Supported by the U.S. Ballistic Missile Defense System (BMDS)

The siting of ground-based interceptors in Poland and a midcourse radar in the Czech Republic is supported by other additional existing and developing assets of the global BMDS. The BMDS provides an integrated network of sensors, short- and medium-range interceptors, and command and control capabilities that can enhance the proposed U.S. European missile defense assets. The information required to assess and make interceptor launch decisions is enabled by the command and control and communications network provided by the global BMDS system, which is incorporating, assessing, and distributing crucial track information that is obtained by satellites, and/or by land-based and sea- based radars and sensors.

U.S. PATRIOT, Aegis/SM-3, and Terminal High Altitude Area Defense (THAAD) could be made available to provide augmenting coverage for short- and medium-range threats. These assets could be used to support emerging NATO and national capabilities as needed to ensure layered coverage for all European nations requiring such protection.

Transportable forward land-based radars could provide an enhancement to the capabilities of the proposed European interceptor and midcourse radar sites. This type of radar is a high-resolution, X-Band class, phased- array radar based upon the THAAD radar hardware and software design. It is designed to be air transportable, roll-on/roll-off ship transportable, and rail transportable. The value of this radar is that when deployed closerto the threat, it provides earlieracquisition and more precise tracking data that expands coverage areas and extends ranges for more sophisticated engagement strategies. This type of radar is currently deployed in Japan. While deployment has not been proposed to potential host nations closer to the threat in the Middle East, an additional X-band radar will be available to support (as needed) proposed Europe-based U.S. missile defense assets.

- Forward-based radar
  - Available to deploy to area closer to Iranian threat to provide earlier detection, cueing, and enhanced tracking information

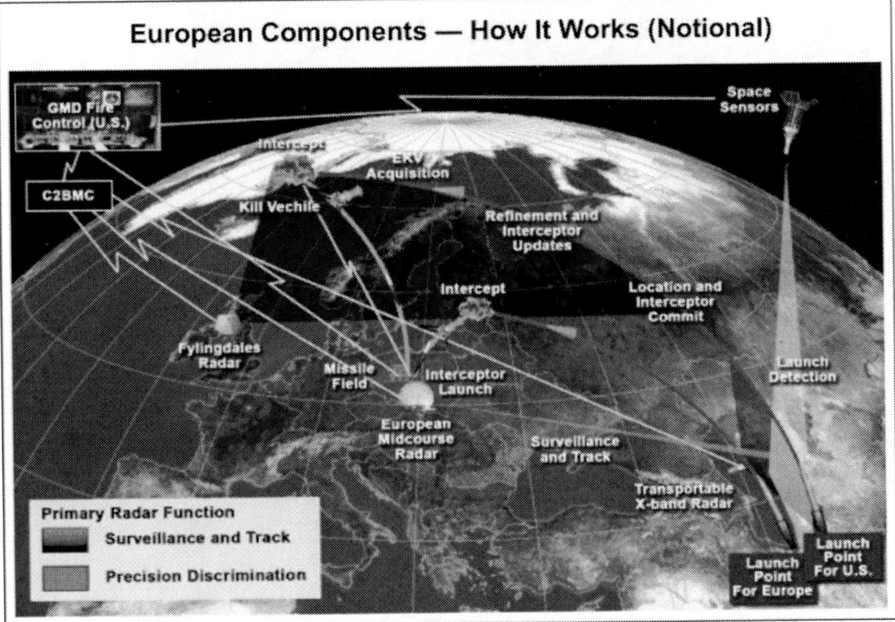

Why Poland and the Czech Republic?

- U.S. missile defense interceptors in Alaska and California do not provide protection for Europe
- Technical analysis shows that Poland and the Czech Republic are the optimal locations for fielding U.S. missile defense assets in Europe:
  - Provides defensive coverage for the majority of Europe from longer-range ballistic missiles launched from the Middle East
  - Provides redundant coverage for the U.S. against ICBMs launched from the Middle East
- Placing the interceptor field in Poland and the radar in the Czech Republic maximizes the defensive coverage of both Europe and the United States
- As the following graphic demonstrates, Poland and the Czech Republic are geographically well located on the European continent to defend against longer-range ballistic missiles

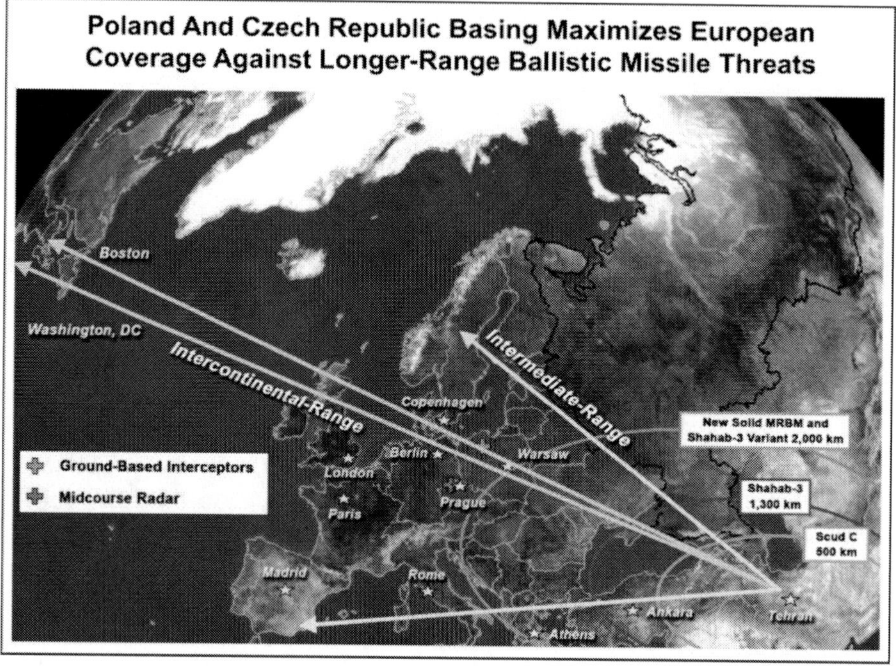

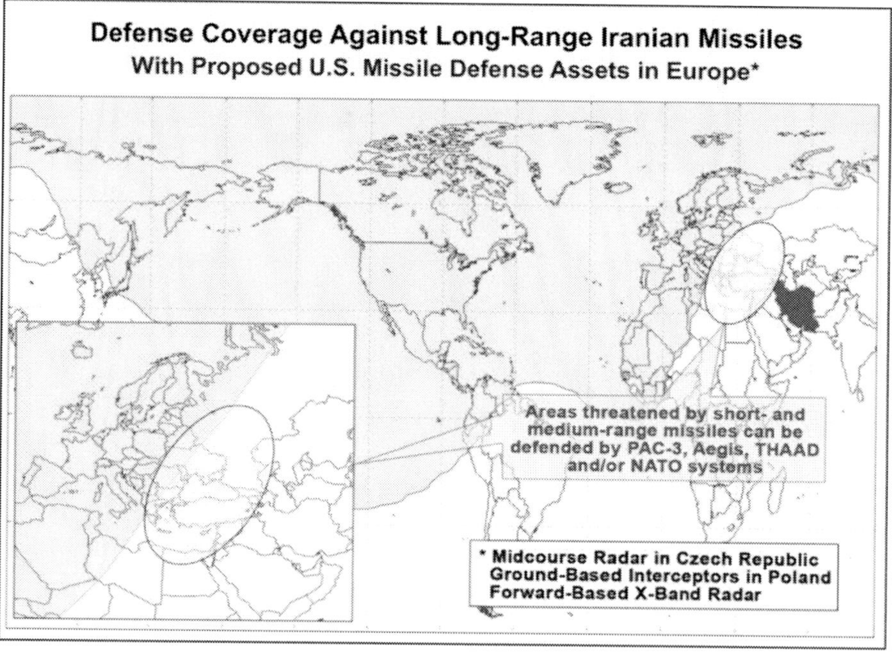

ADDRESSING CONCERNS

1. Why the Sudden Concern?

Reality and timing of Iranian threat

- Defenses take years to deploy. Work on missile defense in Europe must begin now in order to meet the growing threat from Iran
- Iran has demonstrated the capability to develop, and intent to use, ballistic missiles of increasingly longer range (they currently have short-range ballistic missiles (SRBM) and medium-range ballistic missile (MRBM) technology)
- Public announcement of space-launch vehicle test success (U.S. cannot confirm)
- In 1998, intelligence experts indicated North Korea was years away from testing multi-stage rockets; the next month, they tested this capability. We cannot afford to be surprised by waking up one morning and discovering that Iran has an ICBM capability

2. How Do We Know the System is Effective and Safe?

In 2003, ballistic missile defenses consistently demonstrated the ability to effectively intercept short-range enemy missile attacks during Operation Iraqi Freedom. Patriot PAC-2 and PAC-3 intercepted nine out of nine short-range ballistic missiles. Defenses against intermediate- and long- range attacks have not yet been needed in war. Through ground and ßight tests, and modeling and simulation, such defenses have been repeatedly and successfully tested over the past decade. Hit-to-kill technologies have been demonstrated to work, and the ballistic missile defense system has been successfully integrated. Over the last few years, the Missile Defense Agency has had 17 successes in the last 18 ßighttests in the Patriot PAC-3, the Aegis Standard Missile-3 (SM-3), THAAD, and the Ground-based Midcourse Defense (GMD) programs. Since 2001, there have been 27 out of 35 successful hit-to-kill midcourse and terminal intercepts.

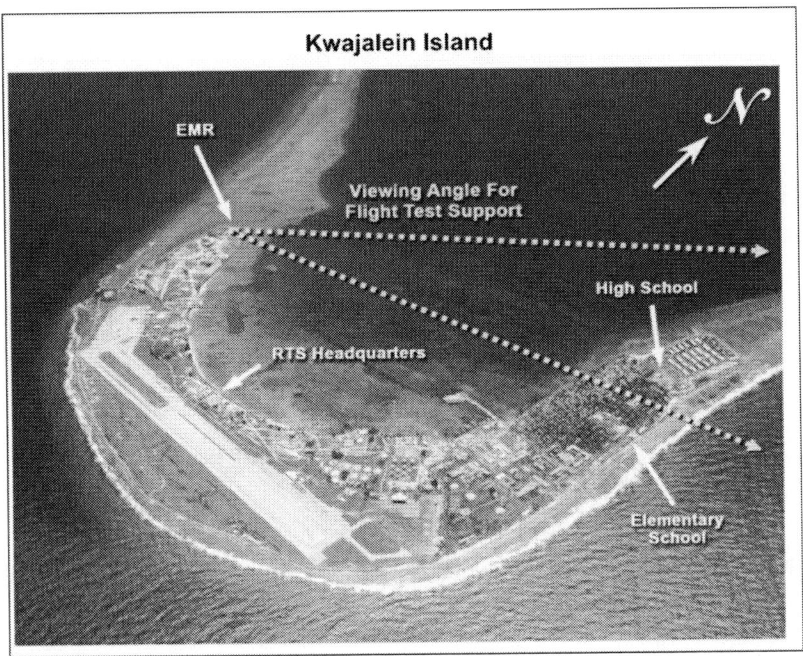

Safety is very important when fielding ballistic missile defenses. X-band radars have been operating for decades to observe weather and track aircraft and satellites. The beam from the radar is only several meters wide at 25 kilometers above the ground and is pointed into the sky and away from people on the ground. In fact, the U.S. has safely placed an X-band radar on the Kwajalein Atoll only a short distance from buildings that house workers and school children.

3. Would These Missile Defense Capabilities Threaten Russia?

No. The United States has kept, and is continuing to keep, Russia informed about U.S. missile defense policy, plans, and programs. We have used both bilateral diplomatic and Department of Defense-Ministry of Defense channels, as well as the multilateral NATO-Russia Council channel. Any prospective U.S. missile defense assets deployed in Europe would not be directed at Russia. Instead, these central European locations provide optimal defensive coverage against threats launched from the Middle East involving a limited number of intermediate- or intercontinental-range ballistic missiles launched at either Europe or the United States. U.S. missile defense deployments in Europe would not undermine Russia's strategic nuclear forces. Under the Moscow Treaty, Russia is permitted between 1,700-2,200 strategic nuclear warheads. Regardless of the location of any possible U.S. defensive assets, Russia's large strategic offensive force could overwhelm the U.S. system's limited number of deployed interceptors. Furthermore, in theoretical one-on-one engagements, U.S. interceptors in central Europe would not be capable of intercepting Russian ICBMs launched at the United States. As the graphic above demonstrates, there would not be sufficient time to detect, track, and intercept ballistic missiles launched from western Russia toward the United States. Fielding U.S. missile defense capabilities in Europe will not trigger an arms race between Russia and the United States. We have proposed transparency and confidence-building measures to Russia. Additionally, in April 2007, senior U.S. officials tabled a comprehensive proposal for bilateral missile defense cooperation with Russia.

4. Would the X-Band Radar in the Czech Republic Affect the Use of Cell Phones, Radios, Garage Door Openers, and Televisions?

No. Such personal devices operate outside the X-band frequency and would not be affected.

5. Would an Intercept of a Ballistic Missile Attack Over Europe Create Debris that Would Fall on People in Europe?

Most debris from a successful destruction of a ballistic missile attack would burn up during reentry into the Earth's atmosphere. Another way to look at this issue is to consider that any harm caused by this debris would pale in comparison to a successful nuclear attack on a European city.

INTERCEPT DEBRIS

- Intercept debris is minor compared to an intact Weapon of Mass Destruction (WMD) warhead hitting a major population center
- An intercepted warhead produces very little debris
  - Closing speed between the interceptor and warhead is more than 7 km per second
  - Intercept occurs at an altitude of more than 200 km, well outside the earth's atmosphere
  - Resulting kinetic energy vaporizes much of the reentry vehicle, warhead, and kill vehicle
- U.S. flight tests have shown that very little debris reaches the earth – pieces average no more than 21 cm long
- Probability of any casualty on the ground is very low
  - 3 in 1,000 intercepts to 1 in 2.5M intercepts depending on population density

6. Can a Ballistic Missile Defense Capability Have a Deterrent Effect?

Yes. Ballistic missile defense can work to deter the enemy because it reduces the political and military utility of offensive missiles. For example, if Allied deployed forces or civilian populations were defenseless, Iran may view its ballistic missile arsenal as an unchecked means to coerce other countries and/or even attack them. If Iran believes, however, that its ballistic missile attack might be defeated by a defensive system, it might be deterred from building up and using that arsenal to project its national power. Missile defenses are not a replacement for an offensive deterrent capability; they instead constitute an additional and critical dimension of contemporary deterrence. Also, over the longer term, missile defenses discourage the proliferation of ballistic missiles as the means of delivering weapons of mass destruction by undermining the military utility of these ballistic missiles.

7. Will the U.S. Missile Defense Assets in Europe Provide Coverage to All Countries in Europe?

- U.S. missile defense systems in Europe would have the capability to extend coverage to all European NATO Allies at risk from long-range ballistic missile attack from the Middle East. Additionally, there are several countries (e.g., Greece and Turkey) that are not at risk of a long- range missile attack from Iran due to their proximity to the threat. Rather, they are vulnerable to short- and medium-range attack, for which Iran has demonstrated capabilities

- The U.S. European assets could, in the future, be offered by the United States, Poland, and the Czech Republic as a contribution to a NATO capability to defend against long-range threats, if NATO approves a military requirement to acquire a missile defense capability to protect population and territory against ballistic missiles of all ranges

- The future NATO ALTBMD capability or any NATO Member State's missile defense system could complement the U.S. European missile defense deployments by providing coverage against shorter range threats

- Current NATO Air Command and Control System (ACCS) architecture and the U.S. BMDS C2BMC systems have been designed to be compatible, easing their integration

INDEX

E

F

G

H

Q

R

S

T

U